DEMOCRACY
WITHOUT BORDERS

This book carves out a new area of democratization studies by analysing the transnational dimension and the role of non-state actors across three geographical regions. While most studies of democratization are at state level, *Democracy without Borders* looks at non-state, and sub-state and transnational actors in democratization in three regions: Eastern Europe, Africa and Latin America.

Based on theoretically-grounded, empirical research, the book stresses the importance of understanding democratization as the construction of citizenship as well as processes of institution-building. The volume as a whole points to the importance of examining the relationships between external and transnational actors and the domestic context of societies in transition.

Democracy without Borders provides a welcome new perspective on the subject of democratization which remains a central concern in political science as well as in the social sciences in general. It is an important, alternative contribution to the debate which will be of great interest to those interested in democratization from the perspective of international relations, area studies and political science; those concerned with the role of the EU in world affairs; and non-state actors.

Jean Grugel is lecturer in Politics at the University of Sheffield. She is the co-editor of *Regionalism across the North/South Divide*, also published by Routledge (1998).

ROUTLEDGE/ECPR STUDIES IN EUROPEAN POLITICAL SCIENCE

ecpr

Edited by Hans Keman, *Vrije University, The Netherlands* and Jan W. Van Deth, *University of Mannheim, Germany, on behalf of the European Consortium for Political Research.*

The Routledge/ECPR Studies in European Political Science series is published in association with the European Consortium for Political Research – the leading organization concerned with the growth and development of political science in Europe. The series presents high-quality edited volumes on topics at the leading edge of current interest in political science and related fields, with contributions from European scholars and others who have presented work at ECPR workshops or research groups.

Also available from Routledge in association with the ECPR:
SEX EQUALITY POLICY IN WESTERN EUROPE, *Edited by Frances Gardiner*; DEMOCRACY AND GREEN POLITICAL THOUGHT, *Edited by Brian Doherty and Marius de Geus*; THE NEW POLITICS OF UNEMPLOYMENT, *Edited by Hugh Compston*; CITIZENSHIP, DEMO-CRACY AND JUSTICE IN THE NEW EUROPE, *Edited by Percy B. Lehning and Albert Weale*; PRIVATE GROUPS AND PUBLIC LIFE, *Edited by Jan W. Van Deth*; THE POLITICAL CONTEXT OF COLLECTIVE ACTION, *Edited by Ricca Edmondson*; THEORIES OF SECESSION, *Edited by Percy Lehning*; REGIONALISM ACROSS THE NORTH/SOUTH DIVIDE, *Edited by Jean Grugel and Wil Hout*.

DEMOCRACY WITHOUT BORDERS

Transnationalization and conditionality
in new democracies

Edited by Jean Grugel

Routledge
Taylor & Francis Group

LONDON AND NEW YORK

First published 1999 by Routledge

2 Park Square, Milton Park, Abingdon, Oxon OX14 4RN
711 Third Avenue, New York, NY 10017, USA

*Routledge is an imprint of the Taylor & Francis Group,
an informa business*

First issued in paperback 2016

Transferred to Digital Printing 2007

Typeset in Garamond by Curran Publishing Services

British Library Cataloguing in Publication Data
A catalogue record for this book is available from
the British Library

Library of Congress Cataloguing in Publication Data

Democracy without borders: transnationalisation and
conditionality in new democracies/edited by Jan Grugel.

208 p. 15.6 × 23.4 cm. – (Routledge/ECPR studies in European
political science)

Includes bibliographical references.

1.Democratization. 2. Civil society. 3. Citizenship.
I. Grugel, Jean. II. Series

JC421.D4638 1999
321.8'09172'409049--dc21
98-53736 CIP

ISBN 978-0-415-19202-6 (hbk)
ISBN 978-1-138-96736-6 (pbk)

Publisher's Note
The publisher has gone to great lengths to ensure the quality of
this reprint but points out that some imperfections in the
original may be apparent

TO ANNA

CONTENTS

CONTENTS

CONTRIBUTORS

Edward Barnfield is a research student in the Department of Politics, University of Sheffield

Oda van Cranenburgh is at the Department of Politics, University of Leiden

Christian Freres is Director of Research in AEITI, Madrid

Jean Grugel is Lecturer at the Department of Politics, University of Sheffield

Petr Kopecky is Lecturer in Politics at the University of Sheffield

Geoffrey Pridham is Professor of Politics, University of Bristol

Francois Prikic is Researcher at CERN, University of Bordeaux

Hans Peter Schmitz is a doctoral candidate at the University of Konstanz

Katrin Sell is a doctoral candidate at the University of Berlin

Lucy Taylor is Lecturer in the Department of International Politics, University of Wales, Aberystwyth

ACKNOWLEDGEMENTS

This book has two separate origins. Some of the papers were first presented to a series of workshops comparing democratization and civil society in East and Central Europe and Latin America, organized jointly by the Department of Politics/PERC of the University of Sheffield and AIETI, Madrid in 1996 and 1997. Along with the other participants, I would like to thank the British Council and the Spanish Ministry of Education for making these meetings possible. I would also like to thank the participants, especially those who do not appear in this volume, for their contributions and suggestions for the book. The second source for this book is a workshop at the 25th session of the ECPR, 1997, *Democratization and the Changing Global Order*. Again, I would particularly like to thank those paper-givers whose work is not included here for their contributions and ideas. This book was a collective project; I would like, therefore, to thank all the contributors, not only for writing their chapters on time and making changes quickly and without complaint, but also for being prepared to discuss the ideas in the book in general. I would like to thank Petr Kopecky and Chris Freres in particular in this respect. Thanks are due, as always, to all my colleagues and all the office staff at the Department of Politics, University of Sheffield. Patrick Proctor of Routledge was a helpful and supportive editor in the early stages of this book, so thanks to him. And finally I would like to thank Martin Smith and Anna Grugel Smith for their help, entertainment and company throughout.

PREFACE

By the Series Editor

A decade ago the people of East and Central Europe put an end to state socialism and authoritarian rule in their countries. The so-called 'third wave' of democratization had returned to this region after its beginning in the 1970s in Southern Europe, and its spread over developing countries in several parts of the world. The fall of the Berlin Wall and the collapse of the Soviet Union mark the end of the Cold War and the system of bi-polar power structures. The new era would be characterized by the conclusive victory of capitalist economics and liberal politics. Finally, the 'invisible hand' behind free enterprise and market competition would 'make the world safe for democracy'. But as usual, reality and expectations proved to be different categories.

Optimistic and rather naive expectations about the chances for democracy to develop under clearly different social, economic, and cultural conditions are mostly rooted in variants of modernization theory. According to this line of reasoning, socio-economic development is highly correlated with the existence of democratic institutions. Although the exact nature of this relationship in causal terms is contended, the development of democratic decision-making procedures is widely seen as a kind of 'by-product' of industrialization and economic growth. In addition, these analogue economic and political developments are closely linked to the nation state as the most relevant and salient arena for democratization. Rival interpretations might change the structuralist focus of modernization theory and offer more voluntaristic explanations, yet the view that democracy and democratization are basically domestic phenomena was widely shared and considered self-evident until very recently.

The factual development of the 'third wave' made it clear that available interpretations are deficient in several respects. First, the use of a simple dichotomy between authoritarian and democratic systems suggests that a decline of authoritarian rule automatically implies a rise in democracy. However, democratization is a much more complex process than this would suggest, with more facets than a decline of authoritarian rule. In fact, one of the more interesting questions is how democratization advanced although aspects of authoritarian rule did not disintegrate in several societies.

Second, a traditional conceptualization of democracy restricted to state actors and institutions is much too limited for analyses of actual processes of democratization. Since organization is one of the very few resources open to the less-privileged groups in society, the rise of social movements and non-governmental organizations indicates that social engagement takes place outside the sphere of the (nation) state. Democratization, then, requires a broad conceptualization of citizenship to characterize the ways in which people show their involvement in 'civil society'.

Third, democratization increasingly depends on developments which are not bound by the borders of the nation state or by domestic phenomena alone. This can be observed in the internationalization of democratization, ranging from the growing impact of activities of the European Union to the obstacles experienced by non-democratic states in defending their status and position in the world.

The contributions to this volume are all based on the notion that democratization should be broadly conceptualized in terms of civil society instead of aspects of the state, and in terms of trans-national and international interdependencies instead of domestic forces alone. It is this combination of discussions about citizenship and civil society on the one hand, and internationalization on the other, which defines the unique character of this collection of essays.

While there is certainly no lack of research on democratization or on citizenship, there are very few publications aiming explicitly at a discussion of these developments from the perspective of increasing influences which go beyond the impact of the nation state. The contributors to this volume explore this complex area by selecting various approaches and objects. Most chapters pay attention to the conceptual and empirical complications of the process of democratization, following the seminal works of Lipset, Rustow and Huntington. These problems are discussed in a more extended way in Jean Grugel's introduction and in the attempt of Hans Peter Schmitz and Katrin Sell to confront and integrate the various aspects of democratization and developments beyond the nation state.

The second part of the volume contains a number of chapters on citizenship and the role of non-state actors is several parts of the world. For instance, Petr Kopecky and Edward Barnfield discuss the changing meaning of the concept of civil society in Central Europe, showing that there is no need for an uncritical acceptance of the presumed positive aspects of the rise of non-state actors. Very different examples of the relevance of international developments for domestic democratization are presented by Oda van Cranenburgh in her discussion of the attempts of the Dutch government to promote democracy in Africa, and by Francois Prikic in his analyses of military interventions by Nigeria. This broad variety of approaches and topics has much more common ground than might be expected on first sight: as Jean Grugel shows in her concluding chapter, democratization on the one hand, and transnational and non-state influences on the other, are linked in several very interesting ways. Her six propositions summarize the debate neatly, and are a badly-needed starting point for the development of further discussions and research.

Democratization, citizenship, and the role of non-state actors in the present world are too important for the well-being of people to be left to specialists in distinct areas. The extraordinary quality of the collection of essays presented here represents an attempt to improve conventional approaches towards democratization and citizenship, by taking the perspective of increasing transnational dependencies and the influence of non-state actors. The contributors show the need for a critical re-evaluation of our concepts, and underline the relevance for this task of differences within and between countries by analysing developments in Europe, Africa, and Latin America.

A decade after the revolution in Eastern and Central Europe, we might be watching the ebbing of the 'third wave', and we might be confronted with the paradox that democratization does not necessarily imply democracy. These problems cannot be understood within the actual and conceptual borders of the nation state or by relying on Western European experiences alone. What is needed is a rethinking of democratization from a global perspective, taking account of the rise of non-state actors, new concepts of citizenship, and transnational interdependencies. If traditional politics is identified with the national state, then a Polish graffiti painter neatly summarized the idea behind this volume with his or her request: 'Give us Democracy, not Politics'.

Jan W. van Deth, Series Editor
Mannheim, November 1998

Part I

THEORIZING TRANSNATIONAL AND NON-STATE INFLUENCES IN DEMOCRATIZATION

1

CONTEXTUALIZING DEMOCRATIZATION

The changing significance of transnational factors and non-state actors

Jean Grugel

'At this time in history, almost without exception, democracy of one type or another is the only legitimate form of political domination' (Schmitter 1995a: 19). The 'third wave' of democratization, which started in Southern Europe in the 1970s and which, in one form or another, spread to most of Latin America, East and Central Europe and parts of Africa and Asia, has continued unevenly through the 1980s and 1990s (Huntington 1991). The effect has been to create a major field of inter-disciplinary studies as academics have attempted to map, analyse and explain democratization while politicians, governments and a range of international organizations from political parties to religious communities, from the United Nations (UN) to aid agencies, have reacted to it. Opposition to, and the collapse of, authoritarianism unleashes struggles over the new political system and what kind of 'democracy' should be built. Democratization studies are an exploration of those struggles and offer ways of analysing the new regimes.

The so-called transitions to democracy have thrown up a rich variety of regime types in a range of different social, economic and cultural settings. Some have succeeded in establishing relatively stable new forms of government; others have failed. There is no uniform agreement as to why this occurs. At the same time, many new regimes are termed 'democratic' but do not conform to commonsense understandings of the term, except at best in formalistic ways. Some post-authoritarian regimes are termed 'limited' or 'partial' democracies as a way of indicating their democratic lacunae. Yet the academic world and the international community continue to describe global change as moving in the direction of democracy and most new regimes are awarded a label including the term. Are we right in labeling these new systems 'democratic'? Collier and Levitsky note:

Scholars . . . seek to avoid the problem of conceptual stretching that arises when the concept of democracy is applied to cases for which, by relevant scholarly standards, it is not appropriate. The result has been a proliferation of alternative conceptual forms, including a surprising number of subtypes involving democracy "with adjectives". . . [A]s democratization has continued and attention has focused on an increasingly diverse set of cases, the proliferation of subtypes and other conceptual innovation has continued.

(Collier and Levitsky 1997: 430–1)

As they indicate, the meaning of 'democracy' has been modifed in order to make a number of regimes fit in with the idea of an irresistible wave of democratization spreading across the globe. The poverty of political and academic language means that we tend to think of authoritarianism and democracy in binary terms: systems that appear to be dismantling old forms of authoritarianism are presumed to be constructing democracies. But it is not at all clear precisely what 'democracy' means in the democratization debate or the kinds of 'democracies' that are being created.

This book makes its contribution to clarifying the increasingly ambiguous concept of democratization by exploring certain aspects of what democracy and democratization mean in specific cases and regions for particular actors involved in the process. The authors set out to explore the various kinds of democratization projects in different regional settings from the perspective of a range of transnational and non-state actors in East and Central Europe, Africa and Latin America. Some chapters probe the significance of the current emphasis on civil society and non-governmental organizations (NGOs) in democratization; others explore transnational dimensions of political change, including the role of transnational political parties and international observers and, in one case, of a transnationally active regional state. One of the chapters is dedicated to the rich theoretical debate centering on the concept of democratization itself; another addresses the various ways European civil society organizations attempt to influence democratization outcomes.

This introductory chapter aims to set the studies contained in the volume in context in three ways. The first section deals briefly with how democratization has been conceptualized and explained. It offers a critical reading of the dominant approach in democratization studies, the 'transitology' or 'agency' perspective, on the grounds that it fails to reflect the contested nature of 'democracy' and ignores the meanings invested in the term for a number of important actors involved in the struggle to construct it. This leads to a simplification of the term. It becomes essentially a process of establishing of a set governing institutions generally modelled on or replicated from western societies, rather than the struggles to create systems which, independent of their institutional form, stress accountability, inclusion, representation and citizenship. As a consequence, transitology can sometimes mistake the existence of the institutions, such as elections or parliaments, for democracy itself.

A second criticism of the transitology perspective is that it does not pay sufficient attention to how the cultural, socioeconomic or historical legacies shape outcomes in countries experiencing changes of regime. These legacies can sometimes subvert institutions which appear to be democratic in form and turn them into unrepresentative and authoritarian organizations. Transitology ultimately offers us a pluralist analysis of politics and does not pay sufficient attention to the structures of inequality which can undermine formally democratic institutions.

The chapter goes on to examine the importance of the regional context in which democratization is taking place, the role of international actors in the process and the significance of civil society for democratization. I suggest that the kind of democratization project which results from the collapse of authoritarianism is in part determined by the regional context, where history and a shared geopolitical and socioeconomic environment have created an arena in which ways of understanding the world are broadly similar, obstacles to democracy are, in general terms, common and civil societies have comparable characteristics. Democratization also depends on the relationship generated by the complex interplay between forces outside the state-in-transition and actors based within it. All authoritarian regimes have, in different ways, felt the weight of international pressure to liberalize since the end of the 1980s. The kind of democratization which results from the collapse of authoritarianism, therefore, is shaped by a combination of the terrain (the region) in conjunction with the activities of actors, external and internal. The final substantive section stresses the importance of the transnational dimension of democratization and argues that all actors, state and non-state, increasingly operate in a transnationalized environment.

Democratization studies: from 'transitology' to citizenship

The emergence of democratic movements in 'third wave' countries challenged long-held convictions, amongst academics and political elites alike, about the suitability of democracy for societies other than advanced capitalist ones. If democracy required capitalism or market economies as a prerequisite, how could democratic movements have become so powerful so quickly in East and Central Europe? If it required solid middle classes, why has there been pressure to democratize sub-Saharan African states? And if it required dynamic economic growth, why did Latin Americans succeed in forcing authoritarian regimes to open up to democratic forces in the economically disastrous 'lost decade' of the 1980s? All of this led to an intellectual rethink of the paths to democracy.

Some of the fervour of the 1980s, as academics struggled to explain events which moved more rapidly than their own ability to construct explanatory frameworks, was due not to new thinking but to a revival of old schemas. Theorizing on the evolution of democracy drew much of its strength from the debates between different schools of thought. On the one hand were structuralist theories of democratization, especially the seminal work by Barrington Moore (1966) and the prerequisite school of thought such as the modernization literature of the 1950s and 1960s, and on the other was the searching agency-based critique of both approaches set out for the first time by Dankwert Rustow in 1970.

This debate is explored in detail by Schmitz and Sell in Chapter Two. Here the intention is simply to describe briefly the three fundamental approaches to democratization, to recognize the limitations of the modernization and structural perspectives, and to show how the dominant transitology view fails to engage with what democracy means or to acknowledge the importance of social and economic structures. Potter defines the three original positions as follows:

1 The modernization approach, emphasizing a number of social and economic prerequisites either associated with existing liberal democracies or necessary for successful democratization.
2 The transition approach, emphasizing political processes and elite initiatives and choices that account for moves from an authoritarian rule to liberal democracy.
3 The structural approach emphasizing structures of power favourable to democratization.

(Potter 1997: 10)

The modernization school of thought is associated overwhelmingly with the work of Seymour Martin Lipset (1960) which relates democracy to levels of economic development. However, it was not the emergence of capitalism *per se* which Lipset argued correlated with high levels of democracy but the indices of development, such as *per capita* income. This led to an assumption that the chances a country had to become democratic could be measured by empirically verifiable data. Countries where these conditions did not exist could not become democratic.

The Cold War context in which this research was carried out meant that it became a justification for the West supporting pro-western authoritarian regimes in the Third World on the grounds that they could not be expected to be democratic; they were 'not ready' for it. It also upheld a sense of western superiority since democracy was perceived as a higher form of government which many societies were unable to enjoy because their development levels were inferior. It followed that the best that the West could do, in order to promote democracy, was to encourage capitalist development since markets would create the prerequisites for development and therefore, by extension, the basis for democracy.

Barrington Moore (1966) and later Rueschmeyer, Stephens and Stephens (1992) also saw democracy as an outcome of capitalist development, but by no means an inevitable one. The structures of capitalist development could create the conditions for democratization but, in themselves, were not sufficient to guarantee democracy as an outcome. They argued that the nature of political regimes was a consequences of struggles between classes and social groups for control or influence over the state. The relationship between capitalism and democracy was, therefore, indirect and democracy would only result from economic development if political and social struggles changed the structures of power. Capitalist development could lead to democracy; but equally it might lead to the imposition of authoritarianism, as in Japan at the end of the nineteenth century or Latin America in the 1960s. Consequently, the paths to democracy, where it is established, would be different from country to country because political and social struggles are not solely determined by levels of economic development.

Nevertheless, for Barrington Moore and Rueschmeyer *et al.*, democracy always requires industrialization and the subordination of the landed aristocracy. According to Barrington Moore, this is achieved as the commercial classes become sufficiently dominant to be able to defeat the aristocracy in political and cultural terms. For Rueschmeyer *et al.*, the outcome of class struggles would be democratic only when the landed aristocracy was defeated by commercial and industrial interests *and* the urban working classes were able to force through a recognition of their rights on the bourgeoisie.

The modernization and the structural perspective share a view that the paths to democracy are determined, or at least shaped, by the process of economic development. In sharp contrast, the transition, or agency, approach sees democracy as created by conscious, committed actors, who possess a degree of luck and show a willingness to compromise. It is not, therefore, a question of waiting for economic conditions to mature or political struggles to be won. Hence the divide between transitologists on the one hand and structuralists and modernization theorists on the other turns on the roles of structure, culture and class relations in democratization and regime change. The transition school argues that both modernizationists and structuralists exaggerate the role of economy, history and development in determining political outcomes.

For structuralists and the modernization school, democracy is an exceptional outcome which has occurred in only a few areas of the globe. It cannot be reproduced in countries where either the required levels of development are absent or where the class or social structure is unfavourable to it. The attraction of the transition approach lies precisely in the fact that it questions these rather pessimistic assumptions. In the contemporary world, transitologists suggest, democracy is not structurally determined and can therefore be made independent of the structural context. The optimism of transitology accounts in large measure for its success, politically and academically. After all, this seemed to be precisely what was happening at the end of the 1980s.

The transition approach presumes that the chances for spreading democracy in the contemporary world order are good because the aspirations of people in the underdeveloped and ex-Communist world for change, better government and freedom are couched as demands for democracy. It hypothesizes successful outcomes for these movements so long as their leaders learn the 'right' way to proceed. By 1990, it had captured the mood of the moment, as authoritarian regimes did indeed appear to be giving way in regions of the world where the 'objective conditions' for democracy were lacking. Rustow's 1970 critique of modernization, which argued that the only condition for democracy was a relatively unified national state, was taken out, dusted down and infused with new life. Using this approach, a variety of scholars explained the outcomes of the collapse of authoritarian regimes in Southern Europe, Latin America and Eastern Europe in terms of the agency of elites.

In 1986 O'Donnell, Schmitter and Whitehead edited the seminal transitologist analysis of democratization in 1986, entitled *Transitions from Authoritarian Regimes*, which became the key reference for transition studies. It marked the beginning of a massive literature which focused on the processes of democratization by examining how interactions, pacts and bargains between authoritarian leaders and democratic oppositions lead to 'transition', a kind of half-way house between authoritarianism and consolidated democracy. In none of these cases does democracy appear as predetermined by the structural situation in which the struggles take place and pacts are made. Skillful leadership, aided by luck, was seen as producing outcomes leading to the establishment of democratic procedures for government. Above all, these studies emphasized the agency of elites (Higley and Gunther 1992).

Nevertheless, despite its popularity, transitology has a number of intellectual flaws. Democracy is visualized as a set of procedures for government negotiated by and between political leaders. In seeing democracy in this way, the transition approach separates it from its essential meaning as rule by the people and conceptualizes it principally as the establishment of a set of governing institutions, the outcome of elite pacts formal or otherwise. Its elitism consigns the mass of the people to a bystander role in the creation of new regimes. This ignores empirical evidence which points to the role of popular struggles in some transitions as the determining element in unleashing democratization in the first place (Grugel 1991).

Transitology also divided democratization into two discrete stages, transition and consolidation, with most research concentrating on the transition stage. By focusing mainly on short term changes, transitologists failed to examine deep-rooted obstacles to democratization over the long term. Democratizations that went wrong were, by implication, due to the wrong tactics. The transitology approach does not explain adequately why some democratizations fail except by presuming inadequate leadership styles or the adoption of incorrect policies. It does not distinguish between outcomes – all regimes are 'democratic' in some way once elections are held and authoritarian office holders are forced out – or explain why apparently democratic institutions can operate in non-democratic ways. And finally, it omits to analyse in any depth the roles of culture, development, history or the internationalization of politics in democratization.

In sum, transitology does not pay sufficient attention to structural contexts and constraints. As a result, it shows no interest in drawing on either political theory or historical and cultural studies to analyse how 'democracy' fits into 'democratization'. Yet as more authoritarian regimes collapsed in different parts of the globe, the concept of 'democracy' had to be stretched, confused and weakened in order to fit regimes that sometimes barely appeared to qualify for the label. At the same time, some 'transitions to democracy' for which hope was initially expressed ended very far from the democratic ideal.

Typically, the transitology literature sets out a straightforwardly institutionalist and electoralist definition of democracy, then quickly passes on to identifying mechanisms of regime change as the more interesting phenemenon. A good example of this is to be found in the detailed work on third wave regime change by Linz and Stepan (1996). In this 500-page study of Southern Europe, Latin America and Eastern Europe, the meaning of democracy is dealt with on page 1, and then ignored or confused with the creation of institutions for most of the book. The definition of democracy offered by Linz and Stepan is the following:

> A democratic transition is complete when sufficient agreement has been reached about political procedures to produce an elected government, when a government comes to power that is the direct result of a free and popular vote, when this government *de facto* has the authority to generate new policies, and when the executive, legislative and judicial power generated by the new democracy does not have to share power with other bodies *de jure*.
>
> (Linz and Stepan 1996: 1)

In the same vein, Terry Karl (1990: 2), sets out what she terms a 'middle range' definition of democracy in order to proceed to a detailed study of the processes by which this is achieved. She rejects the inclusion of elements of popular participation or the need for an absence of discrimination against some political parties as an essential part of democracy since this would restrict the number of states that could be included in comparative studies of democratization.

Karl built upon this position in a later article written with Schmitter. Here they attempt to lay out what 'democracy is . . . and is not'. They recognize that 'the specific form democracy takes is contingent upon a country's socioeconomic conditions as well as its entrenched state structures and policy practices' (Schmitter and Karl 1991: 76) and reject electoralism in favour of arguing that democracy must offer a variety of competitive processes and channels for the expression of interest apart from elections. However, they prefer to concentrate on democracy as a set of procedures for creating institutions and the government.

They argue that democracy is, in fact, too abstract a concept to tie down in any useful way. Instead, they suggest that it makes more sense to establish a 'procedural minimum' for a functioning 'democracy' and work from this.

As a result of these emphases, transitology has devoted little time to the analysis of civil society, associational life, social and political struggles and citizenship in the construction of democracy. In fact, rather than arguing that democracy needs an active civil society or social activism, some sectors of the agency school saw them as unimportant for democratic consolidation. Przeworski (1991) suggested that popular mobilization was actually detrimental to democratization since it threatened the interests of powerful elites who would close down any tentative opening that had emerged. Similarly, O'Donnell and Schmitter (1986) warned that the 'resurrection of civil society' would almost certainly give way to its demise, a process which they saw as a step towards consolidation rather than one that imperiled democratization.

Structuralism, by contrast, which failed to explain why the 'third wave' of democratization began, has proved more useful for examining the politics of the period after the collapse of authoritarianism. It is also more able to explain differences between national and regional experiences and outcomes. It conceptualizes democracy not as the result of luck, tactics and elite compromise, but as an outcome of social and class struggles. Democracy is a complex system of power relations between social groups and classes. Democracy is not therefore located in a set of governing institutions; the institutions mediate social and class conflicts. They are the expression of an uneasy compromise between social groups and make possible the resolution, however temporary, of the conflicts which are generated within capitalist societies.

Democracy is legitimized because most groups experience some material gain from the compromises which emerge – or believe that they have the possibility of doing so – or because democracies espouse values of tolerance, respect and rights which people hold to be desirable in themselves (Held 1996). Institutions make democracy functionally possible, therefore, but their mere existence does not guarantee that societies are democratic. Hence structuralism recognizes the central importance of society as a whole and social struggles for creating democracy. It allows for the analytical separation of democracy, as a concept, from the study of regime change (democratization) in a way that transitology is unable to do.

Using perspectives influenced by structuralism, a number of commentators have, since the early 1990s, asserted the importance of analysing the role of civil societies and social struggles in building democracies. This research is also influenced by the normative tradition of political theory. In particular, it recognises that, in order to be meaningful or substantive, democracy is required to have social as well as civil and political components. T. H. Marshall argued in the 1970s that the social component included 'the right to a modicum of economic welfare and security . . . the right to a share . . . to the full in the social heritage and to live the life of a civilized being according to the standards prevailing in society' (Marshall 1973: 71–2). Writing on the chances for democracy in the Caribbean, Huber (1993: 94–5) points out that the provision of 'basic services is not only important for the maintenance of formal democracy but crucial for any movement toward substantive democracy, that is toward a society where the many hold a real share of power and can use that power to improve the material conditions of life for those in the lower ranks of the social order'. Similarly, Hall (1995: 26) suggests that the value of democracy lies chiefly in its social practices.

As a result, much of the contemporary writing on building democracies is now far more aware of the importance of structures, history and culture than in the 1980s. For example, Waylen (1994) criticizes the institutionalist perspective for ignoring a number of societal dimensions of democratization, including the significance of women's mobilization for democracy. Grugel (1991) stresses the importance of incorporating a 'bottom-up' perspective into the literature in order to comprehend the political struggles which take place after the initial stages of the transition. Citizenship is placed at the core of democracy. Jelin and Herschberg (1996: 2) point out that the transition literature tended to overlook 'the multiple dimensions of democratization' and wrote that 'it is striking that the classic studies of democratization . . . have made no mention of authoritarian relations based on differences of gender, ethnicity or race'. They call for broader studies of democratization as the building of social citizenship. These critiques emerged in the first instance from students of Latin America and Africa, but were given new impetus by the debate on the role of civil society which surfaced after 1989 in East and Central Europe.

Democratization, in sum, cannot be seen merely as the establishment of sets of governing institutions but is, more fundamentally, the creation, extension and practice of social citizenship throughout a particular national territory. This approach directs the observer away from an excessive focus on the state in isolation from society and towards the examination of state-society relationships. It can be used to illuminate and explain ways in which regimes are, and are not, democratic; after all, there may be spaces of democracy and areas of authoritarianism which coexist. It also draws attention to how civil rights are understood and to the struggles to make them real in different contexts. According to Jelin (1996: 104), 'from an analytical perspective the concept of citizenship refers to a conflictive practice related to power – that is, to a struggle about who is entitled to say what in the process of defining common problems and deciding how they will be faced'.

Citizenship, then, is filled with meaning in concrete situations of struggle and through social practices which become embedded in society. Emphasizing the importance of citizenship directs our attention, above all, to analysing social relationships, power struggles and the quality of people's lives. Placing citizenship at the centre of democracy in this way transforms democratization studies. Democracy can be said to exist when there is popular consent, popular participation, accountability and a practice of rights, tolerance and pluralism; the existence of formally democratic institutions alone does not guarantee or indicate the existence of democracy.

As a result, democracy becomes a much more complex and contested phenomenon. Creating democracy means the elimination not only of authoritarian institutions but, just as importantly, of authoritarian social practices. This approach shares the structuralist belief that democracy cannot be achieved in a short transition period but requires long term and deeply rooted social changes. It is also a radical perspective on democratization in that it identifies the quality of life of ordinary people as the litmus test of democracy. Democracy has to be seen to operate at the micro-level of social relationships, not just at the macro-level of institutions. It must be substantive as well as formal.

Non-state actors and democratization

Our attention is directed towards analysing the role of local civil societies as soon as democracy is understood as citizenship. Civil society is the sphere of associations, of networks, of agency and of resistance to the state. It is also conceptually distinct from the market. Local organizations of civil society are now seen as important deliverers of services, as major players in all political systems and as increasingly active agents in the international arena. Identifying a central role for civil society in politics has led to the development of civil society theory. This points to the necessity of examining the role of ordinary people and their associations in any process of social and political change. According to Fine (1997: 9), 'the distinguishing mark [of civil society theory] is that it *privileges* civil society over all other moments or spheres of social life, on the grounds that civil society furnishes the fundamental conditions of liberty in the modern world'.

The importance of civil society, rather than the state, as the core of democracy is reinforced by the trend towards globalization and the transnationalization of politics which have reduced the autonomy of the state and diminished its capabilities (McGrew 1997). As a result, the significance of non-state actors for national and international politics has expanded. Held (1996: 358), for example, argues that democratization now requires 'entrenchment in regional and global networks as well as in national politics'. Non state actors increasingly engage in operations across state borders as a way of effecting changes within states. Freres, in Chapter Three, looks at the transnational role of European civil society organizations in democratization. Other chapters analyse the activities of political parties, local social movements and non-governmental organizations. We see these as the most vital of the civil society organizations in terms of supporting the establishment of democracies in the three regions under discussion.

Political parties have long been regarded as central to the construction of democracies. It is hard to imagine elections, governments and parliaments without the existence of a competitive political parties. In this sense, political parties are close to, (and in some cases penetrate) the state, and a number of observers are reluctant to include them as organizations of civil society. However, parties channel the aspirations of important sectors of the population for participation and operate within communities as well as in national parliaments. At the same time, a significant amount of external aid for democratization flows through transnational party systems (see Chapter Four). The aim of this assistance is not always to make the running of the state more efficient; it can be to encourage, train and educate party members, trade unions and community organizations in the practice of democracy. The role of democratic parties, therefore, is not merely to staff the institutions of democracy. It is also to aggregate and express popular aspirations.

The establishment of effective party systems has been identified as an important marker on the road to consolidating democracy in parts of Latin America and East and Central Europe; the general absence of a system of competitive and ideological party systems in much of sub-Saharan Africa is regarded as an obstacle to its creation. All three regions, however, have at times seen political parties fail to play the democratic role assigned to them. Parties have sometimes been corrupt vehicles for private enrichment, or for exercising authoritarian control over society. They have been machines aimed at promoting the careers of party leaders, or tools for the cooptation of the masses. In all three regions, therefore, society at large harbours some suspicions of political parties. Instead, there is evidence that trust, confidence and hope was placed, especially during period of opposition to authoritarianism, in local social movements, associational life and community, or even private non-market relationships. In East and Central Europe, democracy was initially thought to depend on the revival of civil society, the arena of non-marketized, non-politicized relationships. In Latin America, where the transitions to democracy frequently carried with them sharp overtones of class struggle, local social movements of the poor and economically marginalized played an important catalysing role in bringing down dictatorships. In sub-Saharan Africa, the existence of community and village groups has enabled individuals to support each other against arbitrary state power.

As authoritarian regimes collapsed, many of these social movements diminished in size, importance and impetus, and faith in the spontaneous role of civil society as an agent of democratization disintegrated. But as social movements lost prominence in the democratization debate, so non-governmental organizations (NGOs) moved to the fore. These were more formally constituted than social movements, and, in sharp contrast to them, were frequently staffed by 'professionals', and had better international contacts. Increasing attention has been paid to their role as the vehicles through which civil society could organize itself to influence new democracies as the 1990s have progressed.

NGOs have also become far more important in the international system since the end of the 1980s, as governments and even international bodies have sought expert advice from them or devolved functions to them. The number of

NGOs active transnationally has grown as their influence in defining the norms of international behaviour in arenas such as human rights, food security and the environment, has expanded. Some scholars have seen the growing influence of NGOs as a sign of the emergence of an 'international civil society', as globalization erodes the state system of the Cold War period. As states become less important, so internationally connected social organizations cooperate across borders and engage in international activism.

Despite their prominence in certain areas, it should also be remembered that civil society organizations and NGOs face structural pressures which can limit their effectiveness, both at the state level and transnationally. Freres in Chapter Three identifies substantial differences in the strength of civil society organizations and NGOs within Europe. Taylor in Chapter Nine demonstrates that NGOs in Latin America are subject to the same pressures as their European counterparts to become service-deliverers for governments trying to opt out of social provision. This in turn creates pressures on them to conform to what governments, who increasingly finance NGO operations, want from them. Parties are subject to similar sets of constraints, especially when in office. At the same time, local social movements which have survived the initial transition period are easily dismantled and are essentially fragile as instruments of change and transformation.

In other words, the activities of social organizations, even when transnationally connected, are bounded by very real limitations, including the power of states, limited financial and organizational resources, opposition and domestic conflicts. These limitations and the conflicts they frequently generate in democratization are documented in the book by Freres, Kopecky and Barnfield (on East and Central Europe) and Taylor and Grugel (on Latin America).

Civil society in a regional context

At the beginning of this chapter it was argued that we should not see democratization as a global process creating uniform sets of political systems and similar state-society relationships. Democratization is a blanket term which can obscure complex and different sets of changes in the state and the relationship between citizens and the state. These changes are very different in their form and their content. Indeed it could be said that they share little more than the tendency to have the term 'democracy' attached to them.

If 'democratizations' are qualitatively different experiences in different states and regions, so too are civil society organizations, their relationships with states and with each other. As with other aspects of democratization, the activities of civil society organizations are shaped by their context. Under authoritarian systems, the main aim of citizenship organizations was to draw attention to the absence of democratic rights. Once a political opening has appeared however, their goal is to give meaning to the legal rights people have acquired. The kind of abuses committed by authoritarian states varies. Communism deprived and repressed civic freedoms while insisting at the discursive level that citizens had economic and social entitlements; the military dictatorships in Latin America inaugurated states of terror but recognized market freedoms. Thus, the themes around which these organizations emerge differ, and they attempt to address different problems as regimes liberalize.

Latin American civil society organizations, whether parties, social movements or NGOs, by and large now operate in a context created by a relatively long history of popular mobilization and resistance to oligarchic and military domination. Challenges to domination and demands for political incorporation, social rights and economic entitlements became features of Latin American politics from around the 1930s, with social and political struggles intensifying in the 1960s in particular. These demands were expressed by social movements and popular organizations as well as by political parties of the left. This capacity for popular resistance contributed to the waves of repression, violence and disappearances and the emergence of the national security state. The brutal dictatorships of the 1970s and 1980s were set up partly because elites were unable to create stable hegemonic political systems and refused to create inclusive ones. Landed elites, the military, the rich and the privileged did not wish to share out either political power or social and economic resources as the popular movements demanded.

In many Latin American countries, therefore, social movements and NGOs draw on a history of organization and a tradition of mobilization. Because they have developed in contexts of acute class conflict, Latin American civil society organizations are frequently classist and overtly politicized. According to Oxhorn (1995: 251), this means that Latin American civil society has a particularly rich potential for acting as a vehicle for democratization.

A distinguishing feature of Latin American civil society groups is that they forged early links with actors outside the state. There were intense and repeated contacts between Latin American popular movements and European parties on the left from the 1970s as part of a strategy of resistance and opposition to the authoritarian regimes. This early internationalization has given rise to a dense network of relationships on which the social movements and local NGOs draw. Human rights is probably the most clearly defined issue area in which Latin American NGOs, social movements and political parties have developed transnational contacts. According to Brysk (1993: 261), Latin American human rights groups have used transnational networks 'to survive, save lives, delegitimize the state and foster new mechanisms and institutions'. Latin American feminist and women's organizations are also considerably internationalized.

In other areas, however, Latin American civil society organizations have been poorly or weakly organized. Environmental and indigenous rights, for example, have only recently been put on the agenda in any serious fashion. The links between NGOs and political parties, the tendency of the civil society organizations to seek to influence the state through pressure or penetration, and the orthodox Marxist tradition of the Latin American left, can restrict the scope

15

of the different groups. They have not always taken up social issues for which there is no easy or immediate solution or which cannot be dressed up as a consequence of peripheral capitalism and class exploitation. The problems of the aged, for example, have received relatively little attention, the rights of children have been ignored, and racial and ethnic tensions have, on the whole, been subsumed as part of a general political struggle.

Latin American local social movements responded ambigously to the onset of democratization. For some observers, their reaction to the scale of deprivation Latin Americans suffer has been remarkably muted, in view of the openings created by democratization (Little 1997: 192). For Oxhorn (1995), this is due to the subordination of social movements to the political parties. Other scholars have pointed, in contrast, to the contemporary dynamism of Latin American local groups and associational life (Pereira 1993; Cook 1997). Their relationship with the formal institutions of the new political systems has become more problematic, however, and the distance between civil society and political society has broadened. It is not clear what effect this will have on democratization. On the one hand, more groups and greater associational activities make for more demands and more mobilization; on the other, this distancing may also point to greater ineffectiveness in terms of civil organizations' capacity to deliver social change.

Nearly a third of the world's independent states are located in sub-Saharan Africa. The diversity, in terms of state–society relationships and social traditions, is therefore immense. It is far harder to speak of an 'African' pattern of social organization than it is for Latin America. African societies reflect much higher degrees of ethnicity as a defining feature of society. Socially, politically and economically women are also considerably more disadvantaged than men and gender difference is more marked than in Latin America, although in both regions the social exclusion of women is mediated by other factors such as income and status. This has affected the kind of themes around which civil society organizations have formed and mobilized, especially since women frequently take a prominent role in citizenship organizations. It has thus limited the depth of these organizations' penetration into society.

Owing to the linguistic and cultural diversities which characterize the region, civil society organizations have also had less contact with similar groups in other states in the region than in the case of Latin America. The excessive dependence Africa has exhibited since Independence and in particular during the crisis years of the 1980s has led, instead, to high levels of contact with groups from the West, especially Western Europe. In some cases, this relationship has been marked by almost total financial dependence (Ndegwa 1996). Financial dependence on this scale carries with it two dangers: first, that NGOs will carry out an agenda which reflects international demands not local needs; and second that they will become distanced from local communities as their staff internationalizes through repeated contacts with the outside world.

Although civil society has been described as embryonic in much of sub-Saharan Africa (Haynes 1997:109), organizations have in fact mushroomed, especially since the 1980s. Social groups are strongest where they reproduce tra-ditional loyalties (Hintjens 1996). One of the causes behind their recent expansion is the collapse of the state in much of the region. Local groups have taken on responsibilities that once, theoretically at least, were carried out by the state. The inability of the state to deliver services or to resolve developmental issues is intensifying the traditional distrust felt towards Africa's generally weak states and traditional elites.

The collapse of local states has also increased the flow of external assistance to local movements and NGOs, as donors have sought ways to channel aid effectively. Van Cranenburgh and Prikic analyse the impact of state collapse on democratization in certain states of Africa in Chapters Six and Seven. As a response to the weaknesses of the African state, external forces, especially aid organizations, have espoused local social movements and civil society organi-zations as the channels through which development and democracy should emerge. This has created expectations that it is difficult for African groups to live up to. NGOs cannot replace the state, and they certainly cannot express local demands and at the same time exercise relatively autonomous powers, as states do. NGOs and social movements represent only a part of civil society; they cannot lay claim to representing the nation or replace the state. Additionally African states have tried to harness local initiatives for their own benefit. Using local social organizations is a rational response for states that are unable to draft or implement policies, especially if they see that the civil society organizations receive external support. Consequently, the relationship between social and political society is more blurred in sub-Saharan Africa than might initially seem to be the case.

The tradition of civil society is different again in Eastern and Central Europe. It was difficult for social groups to organize openly outside the auspices of the authoritarian state; civil society therefore became a banner of freedom around which loosely organized oppositional groups and intellectuals mobilized rather than an active player in undermining authoritarian societies over the long term.

Nevertheless, as citizens retreated into the private sphere during the commu-nist period, the concept of civil society as the original source of freedom and rights was strengthened. In some cases, popular organizations took on an important role in dismantling authoritarianism. The trade unions and the orga-nizations of the Catholic Church became the bastion of the opposition in Poland in the 1980s. In East Germany and Czechoslovakia, the overthrow of Communist rule drew more on apparently spontaneous and sudden rebellions which were in fact rooted in long term disillusionment with the state.

Hence, in one way or another, the transitions to democracy inaugurated after 1989 were presented as the triumph of civil society. For leading democratic intellectuals such as Michnik in Poland and Havel in Czechoslovakia, civil society was a term with almost magic powers: it combined a political project of freedom, an economic project of growth, a form of international insertion and the basis for building democratic institutions. In other words, there appeared to

17

be no inherent contradiction between finding and building democracy through civil society and institutionalizing it formally, between growth through marketization and civil and social rights.

While this created a strong intellectual tradition for the civil society project, it left organizations on the ground weak *vis-à-vis* the political elites who dominated the transition negotiations and were responsible for creating the formal institutions of the new democracies. Organizations such as Solidarity in Poland and the Civic Forum in Czechoslovakia were unable to maintain their coherence and unity in the post-Communist period. Also, because civil society organizations were expressly political and addressed issues concerned with 'high' politics and the form of the state, environmental, ethnic and gender problems were largely ignored. This has weakened the foundations for building these concerns into post-Communist societies now. Corrin (1993: 136) noted, for example, that after 1989 women simply 'disappeared from view'. The political traditions of East and Central Europe, for example the strong state and the persistence of ascriptive identities, have also undermined the creation of civil society. As Seligman comments:

> while civil society as "democracy" does provide an alternative to state socialism, the existence of the necessary preconditions for civil society – based on the autonomous individual (freed from communal identities) as moral agent – cannot be taken for granted . . . It is not the apotheosis of the individual that vitiates the civil (and communal) pole of civil society but the continued existence of strong ethnic and group solidarities which have continually thwarted the very emergence of those legal, economic and moral individual identities upon which civil society is envisioned.
>
> (Seligman 1992: 162–3)

The result is that the project of democratization through a strong civil society appears to be in retreat. This is discussed in Chapter Five. It has been hastened by the distinctive way external aid and cooperation have been channeled into Eastern and Central Europe. In contrast to Latin America and Africa, external actors have chiefly directed their efforts towards building a new state and cooperating with state elites. Hence their partnerships have been with actors from political, not civil, society. Political parties dominate over other forms of political organization and have taken the lead in channeling participation. Nevertheless, they remain, with only a few exceptions, strongly elitist and low voting levels in elections are a source of concern. The danger is that this will lead to the incorporation of the party system into the state and the continuation of state domination over the realm of civil society.

To sum up, civil society organizations and the concerns they express differ considerably from region to region. The terrain on which they operate, and the kind of relationships they sustain with the state and with actors outside the state, are also very different. However, in all three areas they now exercise, or are expected to exercise, a significant political role. They are seen as having a potential for bringing about social and political change. This is relatively new. In all three areas, they challenge norms that were until very recently accepted almost without question: the domination of the state, and those groups in control of it, over the individual and even over the collective interests of society. In Latin America, Africa and Eastern and Central Europe, civil society organizations try and challenge the fear, deference and patterns of social subordination which upheld the authoritarian hierarchies and which made possible the creation of authoritarian rule. This is, perhaps, their major contribution to democratization.

The transnationalized context of democratization

All the original debates about democratization presumed that the main forces were domestic. Either they were structural factors, the development of capitalism, or the emergence of a strong middle class or an articulate and combative working class, or democracy would be the work of imaginative and courageous political leaders. Even as late as 1994, Pinkney's study of democratization in the Third World did not contemplate external factors as a principal explanation of transitions anywhere Whitehead (1990) identified the possibility of democracy by imposition but limited it to a very few cases in which it might be imposed upon an excessively dependent state or a non-sovereign territory, as in the case of Puerto Rico. However, globalization, or the growth of deeper interconnectedness between societies, citizens and organizations across state boundaries, brought a new possibility with it: could democracy be encouraged or created from outside?

The studies in this book recognize and demonstrate the impact of the transnationalization of international relations on the democratization process. Indeed, many democratizations in Latin America, sub-Saharan Africa and Central and Eastern Europe were initiated as a result of international pressures or the activities of actors from outside the states concerned. Democratization emerged as a global trend in large part due to international pressures from a range of global actors: the US, the European Union, the World Bank, and internationally significant aid agencies and non-governmental organizations. International factors are also shaping the outcomes and the political struggles which are taking place as democracy is – or fails to be – consolidated. Democratization also frequently has two faces: one internal and one for the international community. It is 'not just about internal change, political participation and reform or national reconciliation. It is also about satisfying powerful international observers . . . that acceptable political systems are taking shape' (Grugel 1995: 238).

Democracy has thus become 'globalized'. It is intimately tied up with pressures generated at the international level and the agency exercised by a number of transnationally active groups and organizations. To win international acceptance and success in the contemporary global order states must, it is generally assumed, create systems that can plausibly be called 'democratic'.

The globalization of democracy takes on a particular form at the regional level: as struggles for democracy get underway in a particular region, authoritarian states in the region can find the costs of isolation too great a price to pay. It becomes difficult for them to use arguments that democracy is a foreign import when their immediate neighbours are trying, perhaps successfully, to introduce it. At the same time, civil society organizations imitate or learn from tactics from neighbouring countries or even further afield, and external agencies frequently apply 'recipes' or 'best practice' formulae that are regional in their assumptions and prescriptions.

It can no longer be argued that the international aspect of democratization is 'the forgotten dimension' (Pridham 1991a:1). Identifying the importance of the transnational dimension has led to a significant output of research on the activities of states or suprastate bodies, such as the European Union, and the role of international bodies such as the World Bank and the IMF, which have imposed economic and political conditionality on states in transition. There is less detailed research about how non-state actors operate at the transnational level in support of democratization. Studies of the interactions between domestic groups in states in transition and external non-state actors are even fewer. The elucidation of this complex and significant relationship therefore remains a major task in democratization studies.

Most work on transnationalism has remained at the macro-level of hypothesizing that, in a globalized environment, powerful organizations will be able to use their resources to produce the outcomes they desire. Given the hegemony of capitalism economically and the West culturally and geopolitically, it is likely that this will result in the global imposition of a limited and formalistic version of liberal democracy. One important aspect of Van Cranenburgh's chapter is to look at the imposition of electoral democracy in sub-Saharan Africa. Prikic stresses how the democratization agenda can be cynically manipulated and act as a cover for the retention of authoritarian government. In contrast, some of the other chapters emphasize how a variety of non state transnational actors interact with domestic groups, not to impose an agenda of limited, partial or formal democratization but in the attempt to create an alternative based on citizenship values and participation. The relationship between western activists and their counterparts in the developing and post-Communist worlds is by no means an easy one, however, and it is fraught with structural impediments and misunderstandings, limiting cooperation between social actors who themselves operate in unequal relationships. This points to the importance of examining the context and structural constraints in which transnational relationships take place for defining the agenda of democratization itself.

Academic attention has emphasized the 'Washington consensus' of formal democracy coupled with liberalization of markets as an example of transnationalization in democratization. However, not all transnationally active actors accept the Washington consensus as the way to democratic consolidation. European political parties, for example, have, on the whole, perceived democratization and economic liberalization as conceptually separate processes (Grugel 1996). They have emphasized the importance of a stable socioeconomic context for strengthening democratic institutions alongside, or even instead of, liberalization of markets. As Pridham's study here demonstrates, for most European parties, democracy requires economic progress and the development of forms of popular participation. European non-governmental organizations tend to go even further (Macdonald 1997; Grugel 1999). Their vision of democracy is much closer to the citizenship approach and their allies are generally local social movements or local NGOs. These transnationally active actors have emphasized the role of civil society in building democracy over either economic reform or the building of institutions and the introduction of elections.

Transnational democratization networks thus promote more than one way of understanding democracy and in some cases external actors offer competing visions of what democracy should be. But how successful non-state transnational networks are depends in large measure on the reception of ideas about citizenship and the strength of their local partners on the ground. In other words, external non-state actors need conduits and partners inside the democratizing country in order to realize their vision. These relationships are examined here in chapters by Freres, Pridham and Grugel.

The organization of the book

The book is organized into three sections. In addition to this introduction, the first section contains two theoretical or overview chapters. Hans Peter Schmitz and Katrin Sell set out in detail the development of the debate on democratization. They point to the growing interest in transnational factors and the importance of broadening theories of democratization to include the period of consolidation as well as the transition to democracy. Christian Freres' work analyses the development of traditions of civil society in Europe and in particular the transnational activism of European civil society. It contextualizes the later chapters which detail the activities of particular organizations of civil society in specific regions.

The six chapters that follow, Section Two, are organized by region. Pridham (Chapter Four) and Kopecky and Barnfield (Chapter Five) offer analyses of transnational and civil society activism in Central and East Europe. Pridham explains the central importance external contacts have for the political parties there. Kopecky and Barnfield trace the history of the concept of civil society and its importance in democratization in the region. Van Cranenburgh (Chapter Six) and Prikic (Chapter Seven) focus on sub-Saharan Africa. Van Cranenburgh offers a critical analysis of the work of the international community in terms of its emphasis on the introduction of formal democracy in the region. Prikic's chapter looks at the example of Nigeria's regional policy to point out how

21

democratization can be placed on the agenda in unforseen ways, but also to indicate its limitations in an area where some states have virtually collapsed. Taylor (Chapter Eight) and Grugel (Chapter Nine) examine different aspects of the roles of NGOs in Latin America. Using the examples of Chile and Argentina, Taylor shows how local NGOs are increasingly subject to government pressure as democracies are consolidated. Grugel argues, somewhat in contrast, that NGOs are part of increasingly active transnational networks which, despite their ties with states, are participating in creating ethical networks for global change and substantive democracies. Her work focuses on the role of Northern NGOs trying to support Latin American democratization from outside.

In the third section, the Conclusion, the significance of the empirical work presented on the regions for how we can conceptualize the role of non state and transnational actors in democratization is assessed.

2

INTERNATIONAL FACTORS IN PROCESSES OF POLITICAL DEMOCRATIZATION

Towards a theoretical integration

Hans Peter Schmitz and Katrin Sell

Introduction

The recent global trend towards democratic governance, labelled the 'third wave' of democratization by Samuel Huntington (1991), left the academic debate in many of the social sciences in considerable confusion. Emanating from Southern Europe in the 1970s and diffusing into Latin America during the 1980s, the wave finally reached Central and Eastern Europe, Asia and Africa at the end of the 1980s and the early 1990s. True, this wave of democracy (like its predecessors) left many countries virtually untouched, while others experienced an authoritarian backlash after initially implementing democratic reforms. In other states the outcome of liberalization and democratization is still uncertain. However, in a great number of the affected countries the democratizing impact of the wave has led to sustained domestic change and has substantially increased the total number of democratic regimes in the world.

The countries affected cannot be identified as belonging to a distinct group of nations in social, economic or cultural terms. They differ considerably with respect to their basic structural background conditions such as income levels, education or urbanization. Hence, the wave constitutes an important research focus for the social sciences and casts serious doubts on long-held convictions about the likelihood of democratization under 'structurally unfavorable conditions' in either a material or a cultural sense.

In the early 1980s, the growing gap between theory and empirical reality led to an intellectual shift away from the macro perspective of the modernization paradigm as a means to explaining democratization towards a descriptive 'micro' view that puts more emphasis on the role of agents in initiating and managing political transitions to democracy. Based on the intellectual groundwork provided by Dankwart A. Rustow (1970; see Anderson 1997), this approach was pioneered by a collaborative project led by Guillermo O'Donnell, Philippe Schmitter and Laurence Whitehead (1986) and originally centered on the early cases in Southern Europe and Latin America (see also Pridham 1984). Once the Eastern bloc and other countries began to follow suit, agency-centered approaches found a wide range of new cases to work with.

However, the modernization paradigm did not disappear and scholars influenced by modernization also sought confirmation of their assumptions from the new cases. According to Karen Remmer (1991: 481), the initial responses to the 'third wave' varied widely. They included: first, offering modernization theory as an old answer to new questions; second, rejecting theory altogether and linking political outcomes, at best, to 'choices of particular political elites' and, at worst, to '*virtù* and *fortuna*'; third, advocating 'barefoot empiricism' in order to generate a new agenda; or fourth, dismissing the developments as insignificant or a mere 'wave in the cyclical alternation of democratic and authoritarian regimes'.

This is an unsatisfactory state of affairs for an area that aims at establishing itself as a new sub-discipline within comparative politics (Bernhard 1994: 50; Schmitter 1994). However, there is also some hope in these developments. The debate on structure versus human agency, for example, which opened up in the aftermath of the study by O'Donnell *et al.* (1986) falls within a wide-ranging discussion of the nature of the social order and places democratization studies within the mainstream of social science research.

The modernization camp is concerned with structures and assumes that agents' behaviour is epiphenomenal and ultimately reducible to material or other external conditions. The voluntaristic or agency view of democratization asserts that political change and democratic consolidation are outcomes primarily determined by the process of transition itself and the interaction of choices made by individuals or groups. Both approaches have weaknesses. Structural theories cannot usually account for similar results emanating from different material conditions (Karl and Schmitter 1991: 269; Ruhl 1996: 9), whereas agency-based approaches fail to explain why individual actors or groups initially decide to support democracy in situations of great uncertainty. Furthermore, both positions share a consistent 'domestic bias' when it comes to explaining democratic transformations. Modernization is a fundamentally inward-looking perspective while agency-based approaches tend to neglect international factors or treat them as a constant and unchanging background condition (see Diamond 1993).

We argue here that research should be carried out to identify more precisely the linkages between the 'inside' and the 'outside' of domestic political change (Almond 1989), supplementing existing studies (Collier 1993; Pridham 1991b; Pridham and Vanhanen 1994; Whitehead 1986, 1991; and Segal 1991). In terms of its treatment of international factors at least, we suggest that the agency-based literature offers a more promising start and could constitute the basis for a more unified analysis of democratization processes across regions and time.

This chapter will argue that the 'third wave of democratization' is global in character. In order to study democratization in all its stages - liberalization, transition, and consolidation - it is important to identify and integrate the impact of international factors on the process. International norms, models of democracies from outside, and processes of transnational cooperation provide specific inputs to the domestic arena in different phases of democratization. Thus, they not only serve as crucial links between the existing material conditions or actor constellations and the overall process of democratization; they are themselves also potential actors that can shape perceptions and direct behaviour. International influences, such as pressures generated from political conditionality and internationally based norms and models, may actually change the course of domestic politics. It is important therefore to understand how the international arena supplies domestic actors with ideas about how to construct and re-construct democracy (Tilly 1995: 368). We therefore propose integrating the 'forgotten dimension in the democratic transition' (Pridham 1991a: 1), namely international factors, into democratization as an ongoing social process.

Democratization is understood here as a process of regime change that is directed towards a specific aim: the establishment and stabilization of substantive democracy. The final outcome of democratization, therefore, is more than the establishment of a set of institutions; it is the extension of meaningful rights to all citizens. In that sense, democratization is an ongoing process.

The transformation of a political regime from authoritarian to democratic can be analytically divided into three identifiable but overlapping stages (Baloyra 1987b: 9). In the *liberalization* phase, the elites in power abolish old rules and introduce new ones – often civic rights for individuals and groups – in order to overcome a crisis of legitimacy within the autocratic system (O'Donnell and Schmitter 1986: 7). Liberalization is a gradual process in which the authoritarian system disintegrates as a result of the redefinition and enlargement of political rights and the expansion of the societal space for political manoeuvres (Przeworski 1986: 61). *Transition* comprises the time from the breakdown of the old regime to the formal establishment of a new government. During this stage, the new rules of the political game are defined (O'Donnell and Schmitter 1986: 6).

In the third phase, *consolidation*, the new political regime is established, institutionalized and legitimized so as to make democracy durable and resistant to crises (Morlino 1995: 573). It is in this phase that democracy is extended beyond its formal aspects (mainly free elections) to become truly meaningful for the majority of citizens and takes on specific national characteristics. These stages represent ideal types which can later be used to describe empirical cases of democratic change. The use of this typology is strictly analytical and should not be understood as implying an evolutionary logic. Not all democratizations end up as substantive democracies.

In each stage, different kinds of political action become relevant. During liberalization and transition from authoritarian rule, changes of the status quo are at the centre of political development. Consolidation cannot be understood as the mere continuation of these reforms. Though part of the process of political regime change as a whole, the process of consolidation aims at *solidifying* the new achievements, *routinizing* the new forms of political interaction and *deepening* the nature of the new democracy. Consequently, the analysis of consolidation processes shifts interest away from the search for catalysts or preconditions of change to the study of factors that enable or constrain the stabilization and legitimization of new democracies.

Until recently, research concentrated mainly on the first two stages of democratization. Due to a minimalist understanding of transformation processes, it was generally argued that the consolidation of the new regimes is an automatic result of the establishment of democratic institutions (Di Palma 1990). Consolidation was therefore seen as the least interesting and most automatic of the stages. However, although an 'institutional transition' (Kößler and Melber 1993) may be the *conditio sine qua non* for the further development of democracy (Heller 1988), a merely formal regime change does not 'automatically' imply substantive democratization (Kaase 1994: 110), understood as the participation of the majority of people in the political process. Only when the values and ideas inherent in the new democratic institutions are accepted throughout society is democracy both substantive and stable.

In the following section we discuss the current state of the research on democratization. We divide scholarly output basically into either structural or agency-based approaches[1]. Our aim is to identify some of their basic disagreements, strengths and weaknesses in explaining the democratization process, and to clarify the nature of the debate. We will then go onto offer a way to integrate international factors more fully into the analysis of democratization.

State of the art: structural and agency-based explanations of democratization

A number of authors argue that the recent global surge in democracy has verified the causal link between economic development and democracy (Diamond 1992: 110; Londregan and Poole 1996). In this way, modernization theory claims that it can explain outcomes from democratization. According to Lipset *et al.* (1993:157) the correlation between both development and democracy was stronger and 'more pronounced [by] the early 1980s than in the late 1950s' when Lipset's original study was carried out. According to Diamond (1992: 126), democracy will, sooner or later, follow on from continuous economic growth, provided that improvements are broadly distributed among the population and that they lead to adequate 'human development'. The structualist argument also drew strength from the apparent ebbing of the third wave in the 1990s (Diamond 1996). This seemed to vindicate the theory (Lipset *et al.* 1993: 158) in that the countries where democracy was not consolidated were judged to be those where the prerequisites were absent.

Consequently, there are now signs that the modernization paradigm is gaining ground in academia, as well as within policy-oriented studies which have always been a modernization stronghold.

Adrian Leftwich's work represents perhaps the most forceful contemporary restatement of modernization. He argues that 'what the West should do is to support only those dedicated and determined developmental élites which are seriously bent on promoting economic growth, *whether democratic or not*. For by helping them to raise the level of economic development it will help them also to establish or consolidate the real internal conditions for lasting democracy' (Leftwich 1996: 329, emphasis in the original). Thus, as in the heyday of modernization theory thirty years ago, some scholars remain convinced that economic conditions create the 'superstructure' of political epiphenomena; that democratization will follow in an automatic fashion from economic growth.

None the less, overall, the appeal of functionalist or structuralist conceptualizations of social change to scholars has declined. In a bid to win the high ground and persuade academics of the continued relevance of the modernization paradigm, some adherents have sought to improve their analysis and refine the original claim so as to tighten its explanatory and predictive value. In particular, the use of quantitative methods has been introduced into the debate. Some authors have used their data to confirm modernization (Burkhart and Lewis-Beck 1994; Helliwell 1994) while others have introduced modifications to the orignial claim (Arat 1991; Gonick and Rosh 1988; Hadenius 1992; Vanhanen 1990). A third tack has been to suggest a reversed path of causality: to argue that democracy leads to economic growth, not vice-versa, as was orignally presumed. However, studies which claim that democracy had a positive impact on economic growth have only become popular in the wake of the 'third wave', a fact that Przeworski and Limongi (1993) attribute largely to ideology rather than research.

Refining modernization has also meant the introduction of a broader perspective on socio-economic development. Issues such as literacy rates, urbanization and exposure to mass media have been brought into the debate and tested in order to clarify the idea of social differentiation. Urbanization and exposure to mass media (Lerner 1958), presumed to be the key to social change in the original modernization literature, were largely rejected as the main link between economic growth and democracy. Education and literacy have fared better (Hadenius 1992: 88f.).

The modernization argument now is that, with development, societies turn into such complex entities that 'the system can no longer be effectively run by command' (Przeworski and Limongi 1997: 157). However, the fundamental weaknesses of the approach remain. These include most notably the failure to explain contradictory evidence – where development does not lead onto democratization – and the systematic neglect of a micro-perspective of political change.

As a consequence, a second line of argument consciously reduced the claims made by Lipset. The emphasis was on describing a *milieu* favorable to democracy rather than arguing for strict causality. Vanhanen (1990: 195) argued that socio-economic development 'is only an intervening variable that correlates positively with democratization because various power resources are usually more widely distributed at higher level than at lower levels of socio-economic development'. Arat (1988: 30) also supported a milder version of the modernization paradigm: 'on the basis of these findings it can be concluded that increasing levels of economic development do not necessarily lead to higher levels of democracy, even for the less developed countries'.

In sum, research has led to a growing theoretical and empirical differentiation within modernization rather than the strengthening of its core assumptions. Despite improved data-sets and methods, there has been no substantial agreement with respect to research design, measurement, or individual variables. At the same time, not all studies live up to the highest methodological standards and measurement errors often seriously limit their value (Bollen 1991, 1993). In particular cross-national statistical correlations are often misused (Huber *et al.* 1993: 72). Single observations at a particular point in time are not sufficient to show a causal relationship between the independent variable 'economic growth' and 'democracy' as its dependent. As Rustow (1970: 342) pointed out, 'correlation is evidently not the same as causation – it provides at best a clue to some sort of causal connection without indicating its direction'.

Another error has been to use the data to draw conclusions about the emergence *and* the chances of survival for democracy. It might well be that democracy is more likely to survive in a wealthy nation, but this claim is logically different from suggesting that democracy is the necessary result of economic development (Przeworski and Limongi 1997: 156). In their own recent statistical work Przeworski and Limongi (1997) concluded that even a threshold of $4000 US income per capita was not enough to make dictatorships go away. They therefore rejected the idea that the downfall of authoritarian regimes was connected with income levels.

Structural explanations and the 'macro-view' of society have been criticized more generally for their mechanistic approach to politics. Modernization seldom allows for an appreciation of detail. Przeworski (1991: 96) sums up this critique in the following way: 'in this formulation the outcome is uniquely determined by conditions, and history goes on without anyone ever doing anything'. Przeworski and Limongi use their review of the literature to mount a general attack on the use of quantitative studies to predict the outcomes of democratization. They see such studies as haunted by the methodological fallacy of an endogenous case selection. 'Whenever observations are not generated randomly, quasi-experimental approaches yield inconsistent and biased estimates of the effect of being in a particular state on outcomes' (Przeworski and Limongi 1993: 63). This means that the explanatory variable has possibly been affected by the chosen dependent variable at a prior point in time and that this leads to an endogenous case selection (Collier and Mahoney 1996: 60; also King *et al.* 1994: 185f.). It is essential that theory 'not only relates variables but gives immediate insight into the motivational forces which link them' if it is to be useful (Eckstein 1966: 285). Hence Przeworski (1991: 97) concluded that structural explanations are 'satisfying ex post' but 'useless ex ante'and that modernization is of no real predictive value.

To sum up, modernization theory suggested a causal link between socio-economic development and democracy. However, most of the sweeping claims made in its early days have not stood up to in-depth scrutiny. As research stands today, it is safe to assume no more than '(1) the probability that a democracy is born is widely scattered with regard to the level of development, rising at lower levels, and declining at higher levels; (2) the probability that a democracy dies declines monotonically with the increase of per capita income; and (3) as a result, the probability that a country has a democratic regime increases with the level of economic development' (Przeworski and Limongi 1997: 172).

Modernization theory also fails to explain why authoritarian regimes begin the process of *liberalization*. Sometimes economic growth precedes this; sometimes it occurs in the midst of economic crisis. Even more confusing is that the 'third wave' has brought liberalization to places where modernization theory was completely unable to predict any such development.

With regard to *transition* as the second phase of democratization, the modernization school is basically silent. Transition as a process of defining the new rules of the political game and establishing formal democratic institutions involves mainly decisions by individual actors or groups. As a variant of functionalism, modernization theory simply does not provide the tools for micro-level analysis, nor indeed is it designed to do so.

The analysis of *consolidation* as the most complex part of democratization must take into account economic issues and overall welfare levels. It is certainly true that consolidation under unfavorable economic conditions will be more difficult than during times of economic growth and prosperity. However, there is no deterministic link between economic conditions and political change and the legitimacy of a new democracy does not exclusively rely on economic performance. Insights from modernization theory may be useful for understanding consolidation but ultimately cannot explain exactly why consolidation occurs or fails to occur.

Basic to the difference between modernization and agency-based approaches is 'the concept of choice in political action itself. For structuralists, choices represent calculations in light of given preferences and institutional constraints. For process-oriented scholars, choices are caught up in a continuous redefinition of actors' perceptions of preferences and constraints' (Kitschelt 1992: 1028). Empirical evidence from the 1960s and 1970s challenged the structural link established by the modernization paradigm, especially for a variety of Latin American cases (Smith 1991: 610). For example, the middle classes in Latin America did not behave as modernization had predicted. Instead they joined with the ruling strata and created authoritarian regimes.

29

This led to two kinds of revision in theoretical approaches. First, some scholars attempted to refine structural analysis and move beyond modernization theory in order to identify its shortcomings or errors, while sticking to the basic claim that structural factors play the most important role in explaining political change and shaping choices. The *dependencia* perspective, in which politics was introduced into the debate through class analysis and a discussion of external linkages, was the most notable outcome of this line of research (Cardoso and Faletto 1979). The trend towards authoritarianism in Latin America in the 1970s thus seemed to support the need to revise structuralism from within (Collier 1979).

Once democratization began to take root in Latin America, Eastern Europe and Africa, however, research moved into a new phase, and the focus shifted away from structuralism. Academics were no longer interested in clarifying the role of structures in democratization and indeed tended to dismiss the idea that it was even possible to identify them. Karl (1990: 19) argued, for example, that 'rather than engaging in a futile search for new preconditions, it is important to clarify how *the mode of regime transition (itself conditioned by the breakdown of authoritarian rule) sets the context within which strategic interactions can take place because these interactions, in turn, help to determine whether political democracy will emerge and survive*' (emphasis in original). Suddenly, simplistic prescriptions for how to micro-manage transitions (Robinson 1994) were in great demand while macro-perspectives became non-sellers (Weiner 1987: 861). The agency-based approach began to dominate the democratization debate.

Authors like Schmitter, Whitehead, Di Palma, Przeworski, Karl, O'Donnell and others took up the ideas originally developed by Dankwart Rustow in 1970 and began to challenge structural explanations of transition processes by moving their research focus towards actors, political entrepreneurship, and the processes of change. This demand-driven movement addressed issues that structural explanations had ignored. While earlier studies of societal change tried to identify the 'necessary and sufficient conditions' (Shin 1994: 140) or 'prerequisites' for transition and consolidation , more recent studies tend to ignore these socio-economic and cultural bases and dissociate democratic politics from the wider context (level of modernization, class structures, cultural values etc.). 'The characteristics of societies that have become democratic are sufficiently diverse to suggest that less attention should be paid to conditions and prerequisites [and] more to strategies available to those who seek a democratic revolution' (Weiner 1987: 863).

Herbert Kitschelt identified three fundamental premises which have been questioned by more recent agency-based scholarship on democratic change. First, the process of transition is much more decisive than structural preconditions. Second, democratic norms and orientations are not a prerequisite, but rather an outcome of transitions. Democracy is often the result of a societal stalemate reflecting the resources not the values of significant actors (the original Rustow argument). Third, recent transitions to democracy have shown that the literature focusing on preconditions was simply empirically wrong (Kitschelt 1993: 413).

The four-volume study by O'Donnell, Schmitter and Whitehead (1986) represented a focal point for an agency-oriented explanation of political change. Since then, a variety of approaches within this school have emerged which offer slightly different perspectives on transition processes (Higley and Burton 1989; Przeworski 1986; Przeworski 1991; see also Bos 1994). Desfor Edles (1995: 357) distinguished three approaches within the 'pact school': O'Donnell and Schmitter (corporatist), Przeworski (rational choice) and Higley and Burton (elite unification).

They all start from the assumption that political liberalization and democratization are the direct or indirect consequence of 'important divisions within the authoritarian regime itself, principally along the fluctuating cleavage between hard-liners and soft-liners' (O'Donnell and Schmitter 1986: 19). For O'Donnell and Schmitter (1986: 16) the *blandos* (soft-liners) are motivated by the 'consensus of this period of world history' and seek to secure 'some form of electoral legitimation'. Higley and Burton, on the other hand, share an emphasis on elites with Schmitter and Whitehead but argue that elite settlements, although rare, represent the basis for a slowly emerging democratic consensus. Disunited elites exist 'when [their] members share (1) few or no understandings about the properties of political conduct, and (2) engage in only limited and sporadic interactions across factional or sectoral boundaries' (Higley and Burton 1989: 19). This leads to unstable regimes which oscillate between democracy and authoritarianism. Consequently, Higley and Burton understand democratization not as a process of elite stalemate and 'destructive struggles' but as one of converging expectations and interests. 'There is substantial evidence . . . that by taming and institutionalizing elite competitions, settlements unleash a dynamic that gradually disperses cartels and fosters the emergence of modern democracy's procedural features' (ibid.: 98-9).

Przeworski sides with O'Donnell and Schmitter in emphasizing competition rather than unity or shared understandings. Using a rational choice perspective his work is much more precise than other agency-based scholars with regard to the sources of change and the different interests significant actors develop during subsequent stages of democratization. 'What matters for the stability of any regime is not the legitimacy of this particular system of domination but the presence of preferable alternatives' (Przeworski 1986: 52). Relevant actors emerge in moments of regime crisis and their perceptions, strategies and actions determine the process and the outcome of democratization (Merkel 1994: 316). These strategies are dictated by cost-benefit calculations of the collective actors: the 'opposition' and 'regime elites'. If the expected gains for the opposition (more freedoms, material well-being and political participation) are higher than the risks (danger to life, imprisonment etc.) then it will continue to press for change. In turn, the regime elite is most likely to split into hard- and soft-liners proposing the two basic alternatives, either to suppress the opposition or to regain legitimacy by using a strategy of liberalization.

31

Successful transition is most likely when soft-liners ally with the opposition and are transformed in this process into reformers. The introduction of democratic procedures is an almost natural result of an emerging situation of uncertainty, where significant actors agree on democratic procedures because no one can unilaterally dominate the process and determine outcomes. If outcomes are uncertain (as in elections) and power is already diffusing, then the best choice for everyone is to charge democratic institutions with as much power as possible and hope that elections will bring one's own group eventually (back) to power (Przeworski 1991: 19).

In sum, agency-based approaches have challenged the structural paradigm by establishing actors, their preferences, behaviour, and interactions as the most relevant units of analysis. Agency theories do not simply represent a supplement (Lipset et al. 1993) to conventional modernization theory but rather constitute a self-supporting alternative based on a 'micro-perspective' of societal change. In its rational-choice variant, a commitment to methodological individualism makes it irreconcilable with a structuralist analysis. However, the theoretically more stringent rational-choice perspective also makes for a number of problems which come from its emphasis on methodological individualism and assumption that actors act rationally. In particular, it does not clarify how and why initial power shifts occur and why actors chose to follow a democratic path once those power shifts have led to the emergence of overall uncertainty; why is democracy the 'rational' outcome for authoritarian actors in situations of uncertainty? In this respect, Higley and Burton, despite their narrow perspective, have a more interesting approach in that they point to the importance of elite convergence or settlement and to how beliefs change over time.

The rational-choice variant of democratization linked the micro perspective of political change to a well-established intellectual tradition within social science emphasizing methodological individualism and rational action. Agency-based approaches thus gained additional standing within the field of comparative politics, and methods such as game theory were introduced to democratization studies. However, the search for greater analytical rigour also brought with it some of the long-standing empirical and theoretical problems associated with rational choice.

Rational choice assumes that actors have a clear idea about what their preferences are and act strategically by adjusting their behaviour to the actions of others. How far this has been successfully demonstrated in democratization is a matter of some doubt. It remains unclear how and why initial power shifts occur and why actors chose to follow a democratic path once those power shifts have led to the emergence of overall uncertainty. Hence it fails to explain why obviously new preferences for change emerge. How do we account for élite confidence in insitutions which do not yet exist, if agents are expected to trust and pursue nothing but their own self interest? Furthermore, as in all agency-centred perspectives, actors are seen as divorced from their social and cultural bases.

Neither O'Donnell and Schmitter nor Przeworski can ultimately explain why democratic change sets in and why, as a consequence, actors become 'progressively mesmerized by the drama they are participating in or watching, and gradually [are] becoming committed to playing more decorously and loyally to the rules they themselves have elaborated' (O'Donnell and Schmitter 1986: 66).

To sum up, both modernization and agency theories of political change have used the 'third wave' as an opportunity to refine their theoretical approaches and both have claimed victory in terms of explaining democratization. What is striking is their emphasis on different aspects and stages of democratization and their different methodological approaches. They differ not only in their approaches to democracy and democratization however; they are also fundamentally different ways of perceiving the social world and represent different ways of carrying out social science research. While there are strengths and weaknesses in both approaches, neither has paid sufficient attention to the international context in which democratization in the contemporary order takes place. It is to this issue that we now turn.

Integrating international factors into the explanation of democratization

Since international factors crucially contribute to the process of democratization, it is important to understand more precisely how they work. International factors influence changes of political regime by providing ideas and models of democracy; these are gradually internalized by domestic actors and induce a process of converging perceptions, and general acceptance of 'codes and rules of political competition' (Higley and Burton 1998: 98). Political conditionality also contributes to shaping the emerging democratic regime.

While an agency perspective (as opposed to structuralism) is a precondition for a meaningful and in-depth analysis of democratization understood as a process of subsequent *liberalization, transition and consolidation*, democratization cannot be understood by referring only to strategic and rational interest calculation at a particular point in time. It is the result of a complex interaction of international and domestic factors where initially competitive claims about the better social order are exchanged, and significant pro-democratic actors appear. In the course of time a gradually emerging democratic setting slowly re-frames the interests and behaviour of actors.

Throughout the whole process, international factors can provide varying and specific support for democratic change. In the periods of *liberalization* and *transition* it is important to understand why representatives of once dominant élites suddenly feel uncertainty about their own future and concern about the capabilities of the opposition. One of the reasons may be that international factors support domestic forces for change. Knowledge about the source of uncertainty is important if we are to understand its possible effects. In the *consolidation* period, also, a domestic perspective on agency is too limited to explain the process.

Although scholars now make frequent references to the international context in analyses of democratic transformations, the systematic integration and operationalization of international factors is still rare. Due to the 'domestic bias' in transition research, democratization is often defined as an exclusively domestic affair aiming at the transformation of the *internal* political system. Both the modernization school and the agency-based explanations of regime change argue that international factors have little influence. Democratization is seen, first and foremost, as a process of delegitimizing the old and legitimizing new *national* political structures. Analysts usually assume that the sovereignty of each nation-state prevents major interventions in its internal affairs from the outside (Morlino 1995: 587). This ignores sharply increasing levels of interactions on the global scale and the many more subtle influences which cross national borders.

The global wave of democratization in Africa, Latin America and East and Central Europe showed that the course of events in a national political system can be affected decisively by external factors. Consequently, the recent literature identified what has been termed a 'conjuncture for democracy' (Drake 1994: 1) and began to take the 'external dimension' of transformation processes explicitly into account (Hyde-Price 1994; Niklasson 1994; Pridham *et al.* 1994). Until this point, only a few publications had examined the international influences of regime change (Pridham 1991b; Tovias 1984: Whitehead 1986). But instead of producing a more theoretically-driven argument, international dimensions of democratization were integrated in the analysis as residual categories only. Authors argued either that they have merely reinforcing effects (Huntington 1991; Schubert *et al.* 1994) or that they figure as a catalyst for transition processes (Burton *et al.* 1992a). Even theories that explicitly build their explanatory power on the influence of international factors (most prominently the *dependencia* approach), have failed to provide a nuanced picture of the recent global surge for democracy, largely because the international arena is conceptualized as a force that prevents rather than enables democracy in developing countries. Hence, they fail to account for the dynamics and variations of different transition processes (Hartmann 1997).

In sum, we still need a more systematic conceptual integration of international factors in the analysis of democratization. As the current notion of the 'globalization of democracy' indicates (Diamond 1993), the concept of *globalization* has been introduced into discussions in reaction to economic developments towards a 'global economy' (Hirst and Thompson 1996). This suggests one way to describe forms of international influence on the processes of democratization provided that we disaggregate the abstract concept of globalization into distinct processes of interaction between the local and the global. Those processes systematically link global structures and international actors with democratization within states at all stages of democratic change: liberalization, transition, and consolidation.

While definitions of globalization still vary widely, there is a basic consensus that there is a growing interdependence between different parts of the world. National borders lose some of their meaning and the autonomy of the state in domestic decisions decreases (Altvater and Mahnkopf 1996). Globalization, therefore, results in the 'disembedding' of social relations from the local context (Giddens 1990). In terms of democracy, globalization suggests that the examples of political, economic and social interactions offered by one country can widen the range of options in another by introducing a 'change of familiar alternatives' (Wiesenthal 1996: 3).

This idea is not completely new: The 'domino theory', invented as a justification for US military interventions in Asia, argued that a communist take-over in one country would lead to similar take-overs in its neighbours. In the end the theory was right, but the cases selected were wrong: sustained political change started with the prolonged transformation in Poland which began in 1981, indicating that the realization of 'western' pro-democratic norms, ideas and values was possible in an 'eastern' context as well. Subsequently, neighbouring countries fell to democracy more and more quickly, culminating in the Romanian revolution in which only ten days were needed to oust the Ceaucescu regime (Garton Ash 1990). Hence the Central and Eastern European region illustrates one possible way that international factors exert influence over democratization: through the diffusion of 'western' values, such as personal liberty, pluralism, the right to political expression and a market economy, as well as the spread of specific models, strategies and tactics of democratization. The result is the *socialization* of domestic actors (Diamond 1993: 53).

The diffusion of ideas and the adoption of models from outside have been linked to various factors. One is international cooperation such as trade, student or cultural exchanges, and the learning processes about institutional models emanating from this collaboration. Developments in communication technologies that enable short-wave radio broadcastings, the reception of long-distance television programmes and, in recent times, the distribution of democratic ideas via the internet, have also played a role. A third factor is the activities of transnational issue networks in the area of human rights and democratic governance (Keck and Sikkink 1998; Risse *et al.* 1999).

Due to the diffusion of political values, then, democracy becomes an aim in its own right. However, the passive diffusion of values is only the supply-side side of the story. The domestic demand-side is characterized by the active adoption, selection and also rejection of ideas offered in the international context. This is particularly relevant in later stages of consolidation and institution-building. Governments might actively search for institutional models, hoping to facilitate and complete the necessary transformation in their countries. The Spanish transition in particular has been explicitly used as a model for democratization elsewhere. Baloyra (1987a) denied that Spain was a model for Latin America, but argued that it was influential in Central and Eastern Europe: many of the newly elected politicians from post-Communist countries went to Spain for discussions and seminars during the transitional phase in Eastern Europe. The *Moncloa Pacts*, one of the main agreements concluded during the Spanish transition, were even translated into Hungarian and used as an example of how governments could mitigate social conflict. Thus, while once democracy was seen as a contingent outcome of national struggles for power (Rustow 1970: 353), globalization has led to an international recognition of the democratic idea (Franck 1992). Institutional models or policies may be imported from other countries to be used as strategies for dealing with domestic policy problems.

As a result of external influence, a kind of 'preemptive' institution-building took place in East and Central Europe in order to force their adaptation to Western European standards. This process was stimulated by the need to create conditions which would attract financial aid and investment from the West by offering potential donor states a familiar institutional framework (Wiesenthal 1995). Possible membership of the European Union (EU) was also an incentive.

The neo-institutionalist approach explains this voluntary *adaptation* to international standards through the need to reduce the costs of international interaction (North 1989). The end of the Cold War and the 'victory' of market capitalism mean that western economic and political models have become the international standard for regimes wishing to integrate into the global order. Western-style democratic systems consequently function as prototypes for institution-building in transition states (Ágh 1996a; Kurtán 1993). The logic of this argument is that political and economic institutions will converge over time. Thus globalization, understood as a disaggregated process of interactions between the local and the global, enlarges the sphere of democracy and market economies.

Globalization has shaped the process of democratization through the importing of institutional models not only in East and Central European countries but in Latin America and South Africa as well. This can be seen in the establishment of tripartite institutions, so-called 'Councils for Interest Reconciliation' inspired by western models including the Austrian social partnership scheme or the *Moncloa Pacts* of the Spanish transition. Such councils are increasingly widespread. They form a mediating system with the aim of regulating conflicts in the economic sphere, bringing together representatives of government, trade union confederations and employers' associations to discuss wage developments and labour-related policy measures. Their task is to maintain social peace in times of socio-economic difficulties by sharing responsibility between the social partners and the government.

Adaptation to international models is the second way in which influence is exerted. Here, globalization is understood as a channel for disseminating alternative models of political, economic and social structuring. Actors in search of solutions may adopt these ideas or modify them to fit their domestic context. A transfer of institutions will not invariably generate success. In fact, these transfers can be inherently problematic. But our point is that actors transcend their domestic context and turn to the international arena in a search for ways and means to stabilize democratization.

Apart from these voluntary modes of influence, a more coercive interpretation of globalization is also conceivable. Both *dependencia* and *neo-realism* interpret globalization primarily as a process of increasing power asymmetries. Growing interdependence weakens the periphery and increases the control of the centre. Thus, processes of adaptation in East and Central Europe and elsewhere are seen simply as reflections of the new power realities after the end of the Cold War and not as voluntary convergence towards common values and norms.

Influence via *pressure* is most obvious in the economic sphere. Due to the effects of international trade, the rising growth of imports and exports and the interdependence resulting from debt and credit-structures on international financial markets, the economic sovereignty of states is diminishing. National governments can no longer independently control the volume of external trade or the interest and inflation rates, and consequently are now restricted in policy terms (Wiesenthal 1996). This may well apply to all countries but it is particularly so for developing states. The debt crisis and subsequent austerity policies designed by the IMF and World Bank forced many countries to implement neo-liberal structural adjustment policies and to reshape their economic institutions through, for example, the creation of independent central banks. Even in the political sphere, the concept of 'good governance', including the introduction of a free press and elections (World Bank 1991), increased the coercive influence of international organizations over developing states.

In sum, three different modes of influence can be identified, with competing theoretical concepts broadly derived from a realist, a liberal and a constructivist perspective on international relations. Neo-realist thinking primarily understands the globalization of democracy as an issue of *pressure* coming from international economic or geo-political conditions. The target countries have little choices but to adapt to the new power realities. In contrast, neo-institutionalism accounts for voluntary *adaptations* to international standards as a result of the desire to reduce transaction costs. Finally, the concept of *socialization* is derived from a constructivist perspective, where norms, values and ideas have an independent influence on the way actors use the international arena to affect domestic change. We argue that these three modes of influence should be understood and conceptualized as competing explanations, although it is also possible that they might all be present at different stages of political transitions.

These three modes of influence, *socialization* via the diffusion of ideas, norms and values, the *adaptation* to concrete institutional models and the *pressure* from the international environment impact upon different sectors of societies in transition. While the diffusion of ideas translates domestically into a 'bottom-up' process of change, both instrumental adaptation and pressure highlight 'top-down' processes of elite learning. A systematic analysis of the influence of international factors on the process of democratization requires the simultaneous recognition of all three possible modes.

The domestic impact of international influences can invariably be understood as a form of *institutionalization* in three ways. First, the diffusion of democratic values and norms *institutionalizes* new ideas in a given national context, thus making available images of alternative regime types and influencing the changes in the actors' preferences and choices. Second, the adaptation to alternative political models and the standardization of economic mechanisms shape the processes of *de-* and *re-institutionalization* in new democracies. The pressure to adapt to international standards converts democratic and market economic institutions into prototypes for *institution*-building in liberalizing and democratizing regimes. Finally, the integration of newly democratized countries in international institutions contributes to the process of *institution*-building and development. This third step reinforces both the diffusion of ideas and the spread of institutional models. So, just as 'ideas do not float freely' (Risse-Kappen 1994), the three modes of influence can be conceptualized through the mechanism of institutionalization. This indicates that the influence of international factors is not restricted to any particular phase of a political transition.

In each of the three stages of democratization, liberalization, transition and consolidation, international factors can play an important role. Initially the general diffusion of norms dominates, while specific outside models play only a limited role as general reference points in the struggle for power. In the transition phase, importing specific institutional models moves to centre stage. Finally, in the consolidation period, global influence can be detected in the general international support for the new democracy: in a global environment of democratic states, democracies are more easily accepted as partners than autocracies or dictatorships (Drake 1994). Newly democratized countries are also generally more likely to be accepted in important international organizations. Ideas do not only influence the democratization process in the liberalization stage. It is possible to imagine a permanent, even reinforcing mode of influence via the diffusion of ideas after the first steps in the direction of democracy have been carried out. In this sense, even liberalization enables a growing and widened flow of international values and ideas into a given domestic context.

The same is true for the adaptation to international models. Following the transition phase when the initial effort in institution-building takes place, a number of secondary institutions, minor laws, etc. have to be adapted to the new democratic constitution. Here again, it often proves attractive – and easy – to adapt to international patterns. Finally, since even authoritarian states are members of international organizations, they experience pressure through the structures of international cooperation not only in the phase of consolidation but also during liberalization and transition.

The three modes of influence must be understood as additive and mutually reinforcing, although some factors are more important in one phase of democratization than in others. The influence of international factors and globalization on the process of democratization, manifested through the role that institutions play in the transformation, can be understood as a process of *institutionalizing institutions*. Starting with the more fluid institutional character of ideas, values and norms, international influences become more concrete when translated into models of adaptation, and can finally lead to the sustained involvement of new democracies in the very international institutions that previously represented the ideas, values and norms necessary to initiate change.

Conclusion: perspectives for future research

The global character of the 'third wave' of democratization highlights the importance of both actors and international factors in explaining processes of political democratization. This chapter has offered an agenda for further research by presenting a model that conceptualizes the international influence as a set of institutional factors ranging from rather informal channels of information exchange to more inclusive structures of cooperation. In an effort to give a more systematic account of the different channels, we divided the process of democratization into three phases: *liberalization, transition,* and *consolidation.* In each of those periods, distinct exchanges between the domestic and the international arena are possible. We argue that those exchanges become more and more institutionalized and formal as the process of democratization passes through all three stages. We have also addressed the question of differing modes of influence. We identified *socialization, adaptation,* and outright *pressure* as three dominant types. International norms, models of democracies, donor requirements for good governance and processes of institutionalized international cooperation provide specific inputs for the domestic arena in each particular phase of democratization. However, international factors should not be understood as determining domestic change. The challenge for scholars is to identify the mix in particular case studies.

So far, the 'third wave' has left us with only a small (but nonetheless significant) number of success stories, and a whole range of countries that progress only slowly or even regress back to authoritarian forms of governance. Only a minority of countries proceeded directly from liberalization to stable consolidation within a short period of time. In order to understand where individual countries stand at present idealized typologies of the democratization process are useful as initial heuristic devices. Nevertheless democratization is not a one-way street. The idea of *channels* and the modes of influence can be used to describe external influences on democratization processes. Thus, we would like to suggest that a more systematic recognition of international factors is helpful in cases where democratization is in doubt as well as where it is successful.

Globalization complicates or undermines existing structures of (national) democratic accountability. It is a particular problem for newly democratized countries where national institutions lack overall acceptance and legitimacy anyway. As a result, the 'preemptive institution-building' that has occurred in most democratizing countries may lead to structures and organizations that are 'empty', although they are formally democratic. They are frequently created before they are really needed and do not respond to domestic political requirements. Instead they are a copy of ideas from outside or from international cooperation partners. The development of institutions affecting industrial relations in Central and Eastern Europe and the unsuccessful attempts to copy the Spanish *reforma pactada* through formal social pacts in various Latin American countries are examples of the failure of 'preemptive institution-building' to adapt to distinct national settings (Wiesenthal 1995: Sell 1997b). Historically, one can also point to the fate of many democratic institutions in newly independent countries in Asia and Africa, which were hastily introduced by the colonial powers during the period of decolonization.

The 'ebbing of the third wave' (Diamond 1996a) and the emergence of so-called 'hybrids' (Weffort 1995), like delegative, unconsolidated, limited or pseudo-democracies (Burton, *et al.* 1992b; O'Donnell 1994) indicate that the consolidation of new democracies is not an automatic result of the transition from authoritarian rule. The power of international donor organizations and their rather formal and minimalist criteria of democratic governance may actually increase the stability of the 'hybrid' regimes. Donor-driven institution-building can lead to the establishment of formal reforms that simply mask the continued dominance of the old regime. In some African countries donor-driven institution building has ever been used by elites (for example in Kenya since 1991/92) to ignite ethnic or religious rivalries with disastrous consequences for human rights (Schmitz 1999). Rather than supporting democratization, therefore, international influences may actually weaken or stall it. This has policy implications in that if external influences are from only one source and are based on a 'top-down' approach they are likely to fail. Transnational and societal support for democracy is a necessary condition for sustained change.

To conclude, the effects of globalization are identifiable and should be examined systematically in more detail. This chapter has proposed a conceptual framework for this task. This model does not reflect a conviction that all countries will become democratic but serves as a heuristic device which enables comparisons in the first place. It does not mean that we understand globalization as an explanatory variable for the emergence or the survival of democracy. It is a context variable situated at the macro-level of a given system. We argued that globalization is a complex process of various interactions between the local and the global. Academic understanding of this process is most likely to increase if we disaggregate these interactions and identify relevant actors and structural features. Globalization cannot explain democratization, just as the macro-structural approach cannot explain political and institutional change in specific countries. But it can help in understanding the pressures and adaptations which are at work in new democracies and how domestic actors respond to the pressures and opportunities generated at the international level.

Notes

The ideas in this chapter were first presented to the Twenty-Fifth ECPR Joint Session of Workshops, Bern, February 27 to March 4 1997. We would like to thank all the participants in this workshop for helpful comments. Section 2 is partly based on Schmitz (1998), section 3 on Sell (1997a).

1 In contrast to Chapter One which defined three approaches to democratization, structuralism, modernization and agency or transitology, we identify only two: structuralism and agency approaches. We define modernization as the most important of the structural approaches. Our discussion of structuralism therefore refers principally to the modernization paradigm.

3

EUROPEAN ACTORS IN GLOBAL CHANGE

The role of European civil societies in democratization

Christian L. Freres

Introduction

Academic research has made considerable progress in the last decade in terms of understanding how and why democratic systems emerge as a result of democratization. Most authors now agree that there is no single path to democracy. For some countries the passage has been turbulent while for others it has been relatively smooth; some transitions result from elites transferring power to new groups while in others the elites simply change the regime but remain in power (see Mainwaring 1992: 317–26). In most democratization processes a variety of actors are involved, some briefly and peripherally while others play a central role and their presence is sustained throughout. Clearly, of all these actors, the national and sub-national ones (political parties, trade unions, grassroots organizations, business associations, etc.) are most important. In the end, 'progress toward democratization or the lack of it, is a home-grown phenomena' (Barkan 1997: 395).

There are a number of issues where uncertainty still predominates. In particular, the role of international actors in democratization remains unclear. Although significant in some specific cases, they are usually understood to play a secondary role. Nevertheless, over the long-term their influence – the combination of the separate efforts of many different agents – may be more relevant than has been recognised so far, even if it is the hardest to gauge (van Klaveren 1994: 32–3; Huntington 1991: 85–99).

This chapter will focus on how one group of international actors, civil society organizations (CSOs), contributes to democratization. The discussion here will be fairly general although it is based on research into the particular role of European CSOs in Latin America. It should be remembered, therefore, that while these activities may provide useful lessons for actors in other parts of the

42

world, not all the implications of European activities in Latin America can be exported elsewhere. Also there are considerable intra-regional differences both within the promoting region, Europe, and in the democratizing region, Latin America, which make even generalizations about 'European' activity in 'Latin America' difficult.

The starting point for our analysis will be the nature of democratization in Latin America itself, the context to which CSOs from Europe must respond. One of main challenges for deepening democracy in Latin America is how to strengthen civil society: this is the main issue of the chapter. It is in the context of this central question that the particular role of European CSOs will be explored. In sum, this contribution, which is based on a literature review and to a more limited extent on empirical research (see Freres 1998), is meant to bring out the main concerns related to European CSOs' attempts to strengthen Latin American civil society.

Latin America: trying to link democracy and development

Latin America has been a fertile area for research because of the relative success of 'third wave' democratization in the region. Formal democracy has become the norm in most Latin American countries where not so long ago dictatorships were the order of the day. Nevertheless, there have been – and in some cases there continue to be – serious problems in consolidating democratic institutions. In some countries there have been clear regressions, as in Peru where a democratically-elected president has installed a regime with many authoritarian elements.

Social violence is on the rise in Latin America, corruption continues to prevail in many areas, the judicial systems are woefully inefficient and human rights are still being violated throughout the region, albeit on a much more limited scale and often in more complex ways than previously (see Sikkink 1996: 158–160). All of these are obstacles towards deepening democracy. Moreover, it is evident that the Latin American economies are not growing sufficiently fast to deal with the many challenges to sustainable and equitable development. It is particularly worrying that the number of poor in the region has grown by some 30 per cent since democratization began over a decade ago, largely due to the programmes of structural adjustment initiated in the mid-1980s.

These problems have contributed to an overall dissatisfaction with democracy within the region, because as Diamond (1996b: 112) notes, 'democracy will not be valued by the people unless it deals effectively with social and economic problems and achieves a modicum of order and justice'. This was confirmed in a 1997 public opinion poll of 17 Latin American countries (MORI Chile 1998, *Latinobarómetro*), which found that 65 per cent of the region's population is dissatisfied or not very satisfied by how democracy works. Over 60 per cent of those polled believed democracy to be preferable to any other political regime, but this figure is actually quite low compared to levels of support for democracy in consolidated democracies. For instance, in Spain – which only rid itself of the Franco dictatorship some two decades ago – democracy is the preferred system for over 70 per cent (Hartlyn 1994: 32).

Nevertheless, it should be noted that most political and business groups and even sectors of the Armed Forces are now convinced that democracy should be irreversible. Some reforms are being put in place which over the long term should strengthen democracy. Decentralization of public administrations in a number of Latin American countries, for instance, should have a positive impact. In the past ten years or so, municipal and regional governments have emerged as increasingly important actors. Local governments have democratic legitimacy since most are now popularly elected (some for the first time) and have resources and jurisdiction over growing areas of public policy, particularly those which are chief concerns of citizens: health and education. Over time, the strengthening of this level of government should have positive implications for democracy, particularly as it is the closest level to the population at large (see Schmitter and Karl 1991: 51).

The challenge in Latin America is how to make the socio-political system more responsive to citizens' needs and desires; in other words, how to improve the distribution of democracy in the region. This requires understanding not just the political components (free and fair elections, free association, freedom of the press, etc.), but also the socio-economic dimension of democracy, in the sense of equity and social justice. In effect, it is based on the assumption that democracy and development are intimately linked. As one specialist noted, 'just development . . . demands that equity, democracy and social justice be paramount objectives, alongside the need for economic growth' (Clark 1990: 23). However, this begs the question of how to obtain a more complete (or 'consolidated' or 'socially equitable') democracy. Apart from the efforts to strengthen democratic institutions, and to establish the rule of law – both of which are certainly important goals, but by themselves insufficient – there are several other more or less direct channels.

Towards 'distributing' democracy

Among these channels, two in particular should be stressed. First, the fabric of civil society can be strengthened through the creation of mechanisms for greater citizenship participation in the democratic process. Second, governments can adopt policies that contribute to a more equitable distribution of income and permit new groups to have a minimal level of participation. Figure 3.1 illustrates how these channels may contribute to a fuller democracy (although recognising this may not occur in all cases), and identifies the mechanisms through which this occurs. Civil society is an important actor in both cases. In the first channel strengthening and deepening its presence is an immediate goal. In the second it is an *agent* used to produce another goal; in this process, it may gain organizational strength that enables increased

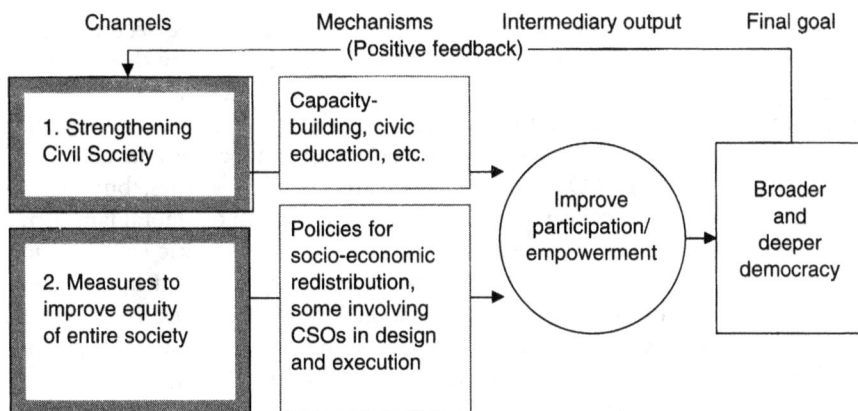

Figure 3.1 Two main channels for 'distributing democracy' through civil society organizations (CSOs)

participation, 'the principle defining quality of democracy at the level of civil society' (Oxhorn 1995: 268).

In relation to the first channel, the term civil society refers to the 'realm of organized social life that is voluntary, self-generating, (largely) self-supporting, autonomous from the state, and bound by a legal order or set of shared values' (Diamond 1996c: 228). This goes beyond Gramsci's idea of civil society as the 'totality of social institutions and associations, informal and formal, that are strictly production-related, non governmental or familial in character' (Huber 1995: 172). Linz and Stepan (1996:7) also include individuals within civil society, although in our view this comes close to confusing civil society with society in general and, as Diamond insists, the concept is not a substitute for society. It is qualitatively different in that it involves the collective activities of citizens who 'in the public sphere . . . express their interests, passions, and ideas, exchanging information, achieving mutual goals, make demands on the state, and hold public officials accountable' (Diamond 1996c: 228).

Civil society, then, does not have a concrete shape. Instead, it can be seen as the set of private associations that operates in the public domain without forming part of the political system, and which does not have achieving economic goals as its primary objective. It is not, however, separate from the rest of the social system; on the contrary, its importance depends to a large extent on its relations with other actors. Moreover, for civil society to function adequately, it is necessary to ensure its autonomy; the state must guarantee civil rights and a mixed economy should exist to allow for independence and vitality (Linz and Stepan 1996: 14).

Civil society is particularly important in the context of democratization in Latin America because, for the marginalized groups in the region, 'organization is their only source of power' (Huber 1995: 173; see also Haynes 1997 and Oxhorn 1995). Where there are few social organizations, civil society is weak. Munck (1991) argues that, in Latin America, the importance of civil society is such that 'the only democracy that will in all probability be secure is that which is supported by a greater mobilization of the civil society that has been the case in Western democracies'. Nevertheless, we should not overstate the contribution of civil society to democracy: Chalmers (1997: 148) notes that CSOs do not always contribute to strengthening democracy and according to Offe (1997: 103) CSOs at times 'cultivate not civil virtues, but, to the contrary, [can pursue] collective selfishness, particularism or amoral familism'.

It has generally been expected that the process of democratic consolidation should contribute to a 'broad resurrection of civil society' (Valenzuela 1992: 84). A working democracy is expected to generate 'social capital', which according to Putnam (1993: 167), comprises 'features of social organization, such as trust, norms, and networks, that can improve the efficiency of society by facilitating coordinated actions'. Social capital is 'not the private property of any of the people who benefit from it; rather, it builds social cohesion for all' (CIVICUS 1998: 1). In practical terms, building social capital is the same as strengthening civil society, which, as it has been conceived here, signifies the support for the creation of new organizations, the improvement of the institutional capacity of existing associations, aid to networks, and other activities such as civic education, which enable the public to participate more in democracy.

The second way to make democracy more just, introducing mechanisms and implementing programmes aimed at improving socio-economic equity, goes beyond simply applying macro-economic policies. It implies the implementation of redistribution policies in order to stimulate balanced and sustainable growth which contributes to a reduction in poverty. Besides their effects on equity, social policies may also bring political benefits: for example, a series of studies carried out in a large number of countries found that the level of education is the strongest determining factor for explaining attitudes of 'participant citizenship' (Nelson 1979: 131).

In Latin America (as elsewhere), CSOs are frequently asked to participate in the design, monitoring and execution of these social policies (Gonzalez *et al.* 1995). This was, for example, one of the premises behind the Law of Popular Participation in Bolivia, where power has traditionally been centralized and municipal administration weak. The Bolivian government assumed that increased participation would empower local groups and contribute to reducing poverty over the medium to long-term. To sum up, therefore, in both channels, strengthening civil society is seen as a means to strengthening democracy and achieving a more equitable and just society, not as an end in itself.

What is the situation of civil society in Latin America today? While this is not an easy question to answer, in general we would argue that it has historically been weak. A fundamental reason for this is the 'extreme geographical and social concentration of power resources which has stifled the emergence of vibrant civil societies' (Oxhorn 1995: 253). As a result, the public space necessary for civil society to develop 'has been lacking, or is far more restricted, with the state a bulwark of social and economic exclusion' (Foweraker 1995:

31). In addition, civil society has suffered 'because of the fragility of the associational culture in the region' (Pearce 1997a: 263).

In view of this it is perhaps surprising that so much is expected from it. Vilas (1992) for example, speaks of the 'hour of civil society' as though its moment in Latin America's history has arrived. What has happened is that the transitions toward democracy have diminished the authority of traditional political parties in most countries, and the structural adjustment policies implemented in the 1980s have weakened the labour movement (which had, in any case, only ever been significant politically in a few countries). In this context, dispersed 'pockets' of activism and confrontation with the state, often at the local or regional level, have been seized on as signs of a major resurgence of social movements across the region (see Petras 1997). In fact these movements face enormous problems, including their lack of institutionalization and the tendency of political parties to coopt them.

The weakness of social movements has opened up wide spaces for non-governmental organizations (NGOs) in the public sphere. There are now more than 10,000 NGOs in the region, largely due to the explosive growth of this sector in the 1980s and 1990s. But the NGO world in Latin America is complex and fragmented. There seems to be a broad division between two groups. On the one hand are those that support (although perhaps not very explicitly) the general tendency of government policies, including privatization, and are willing to become 'intermediary organizations'. On the other are those that believe they must remain loyal to their bases. These are sometimes termed grassroots organizations or GROs (see Pearce 1997a: 270; Biekart 1996: 11). The distinction, then, is between NGOs that seek to make a wider impact which requires direct collaboration with the state, and those that give primacy to the participatory approach which is oriented towards specific communities and give greater attention to the poorest and weaker social groups. To complicate this picture even more, there are also 'governmental NGOs', which (although contradictory by definition) are created by people closely linked to government, generally without recognising their dependence.

For the most part, international cooperation has focused on the first group of organizations. Some argue that the strengthening of NGOs goes hand-in-hand with the weakening of government agencies and grassroots organizations (GROs); these authors even claim that in the case of Bolivia, NGOs may have weakened democracy (Arrellano-López and Petras, cited in Pearce 1997a: 272). Although these conclusions may be somewhat exaggerated, they introduce a key issue: to what extent do NGOs – whether from the North or from Latin America – contribute to deepening democracy?

The role of international cooperation in strengthening civil society

Although the task of fortifying civil society is mainly the responsibility of the governments and societies of Latin America, organizations of international cooperation are attempting to carve out a role in this area. Bilateral official donors as well as non-state actors are giving increased attention to this issue (Barkan 1997). The donor community, since at least the end of the Cold War, has come to see NGOs and GROs 'as vehicles for democratization and essential components of a thriving 'civil society'. Essentially, this is part of what has been termed the 'New Policy Agenda' (Hulme and Edwards 1997a: 6; see also Chapter Seven).

This new agenda has two main elements: first, the market and private initiative, and second, 'good governance'. Both are seen as fundamental for economic development and democracy. In both cases, NGOs and GROs – seen as integral parts of civil society – play key roles. This approach is new because at the beginning of the interest in good governance, civil society hardly received any attention in the donors' documents (Robinson 1996: 202). In the early 1990s donor agencies realized that the 'macro' focus of their democracy promotion efforts – concentrated on the electoral system and state institutions – was inadequate; it lacked a component to strengthen citizen participation.

In the light of this, the Development Assistance Committee (DAC) – the bilateral 'donors club' - of the Organization for Economic Cooperation and Development (OECD) created a working group on Participatory Development and Good Governance in 1994. One of the objectives of the aid agencies, according to this group, was to promote the cooperation of developing country governments with civil society organizations (Sand 1996). On the basis of the efforts of this group the DAC, in its strategic document for the twenty-first century, admitted that the success of development assistance requires – among other things – 'enhanced participation of all people, and notably women, in economic and political life, and the reduction of social inequalities' (OECD 1996: 20). The message was not only that foreign aid should be used to promote civic participation, but also that participation was a necessary condition for international cooperation to work well. The World Bank, through its 'partnership strategy' advanced the same idea shortly after, as did the Inter-American Development Bank (see Wolfensen 1995; Synergos Insititute 1996)

The European Union (EU), a major aid donor, has developed various policies to promote democracy. In relation to Latin America, the introduction of a 'democracy clause' as part of the EU's third-generation cooperation agreements in the 1980s was particularly important (Crawford 1997: 5–6; Freres, van Klaveren and Ruiz-Gimenez 1992: 113). The resolution of the European Council on democracy, human rights and development of November 1991 enshrines the Community's policy in this area. It draws specific attention to the need to support efforts to ensure the pluralist nature of societies in developing countries. The EU also called for a 'decentralized' approach in the management of the aid programme. A number of budget lines are now aimed at strengthening civil society in Latin America. Between 1990 and 1996 close to 15 million Ecus were spent on supporting the development of civil society, making it the third most important area within the field of democracy and human rights (European Commission 1997: 13).

Most of the European programmes for democratization in the South are actually carried out by European non-governmental development organizations (NGDOs) and sometimes by local NGOs, which have increasing access to European funding. Northern NGDOs are a more or less specific set of organizations with certain common traits. They are 'altruistic organizations' that, through their cooperative activity, have a specific objective which is to provide a benefit for third parties (which in this case could be to help the poor and marginalized groups) and/or to provide a public good, for example, to promote democracy and peace. They aspire in some way to produce 'social transformation with wider effects' beyond the direct material benefits accrued for those involved (Funes 1995: 30). A variety of Northern CSOs seek to help the poor in the South, while only a small subset considers the promotion of democracy as their central objective (see Diamond 1997a: 314–29). In terms of their number and their weight, the NGDOs are by far the most significant and have come to be seen almost as a substitute for civil society in general (Freres 1998: 15).

There is growing international commitment to building civil society as part of democratization and European CSOs/NGDOs see themselves as part of international civil society. They have therefore begun to implement programmes of cooperation aimed at strengthening their counterparts in the developing world. Their role is certainly much less evident than that of the official development agencies, largely because their work is at a much more 'micro' level within the developing countries. Nevertheless, as we shall see later, the official donors channel a large part of their efforts in support of civil societies in the South through the Northern CSOs and more concretely, the Northern NGDOs. As a result, the activities of European CSOs/NGDOs cannot be totally separated from the donors' policies.

Northern CSOs/NGDOs were providing help to their Southern counterparts in the years before the New Policy Agenda emerged. Private organizations from the US and Europe, for example, supported human rights organizations and the democratic opposition in Latin America, during the last wave of authoritarian regimes. Their role was clear: to help maintain the democratic forces in those countries suffering under dictatorships. As Vilas (1994: 48) notes, referring to the case of Central America, 'the incredible invasion of non-governmental organizations from Europe and North America which the zone experienced during the seventies and eighties was key for opening the social system and political debate'. In fact, many donors – such as the Netherlands and Sweden – could only carry out their aid programmes in Latin American countries under the dictatorships of the 1970s and 1980s indirectly, through the CSOs (Freres 1993).

With the return of democracy, however, the role of the Northern CSOs became much less clear. Although their 'humanitarian interventionism' and solidarity was considered internationally legitimate while the dictators were in power, their justification for carrying on 'political' tasks such as monitoring human rights can more easily be questioned by elected regimes in the region. Although Latin American governments now recognise in public the importance of pluralism, in practice national CSOs are often perceived as suspect or even subversive institutions, particularly when in receipt of international funds. This has led a number of governments in the region to step up efforts to 'register' the CSOs as a form of control over them.

Main ways in which Northern CSOs operate in the South

European CSOs/NGDOs work in Latin America in basically the same way all such Northern organizations operate in the developing South. They engage in three kinds of operation, each with distinct effects on the strengthening of civil society in the developing country in question: implementing development projects, support for civic and organizational activities, and international campaigns for advocacy and protest. What these operations imply is developed below.

Development projects. The main functions are: implementation of socio-economic development projects (health, agriculture, micro-enterprise, etc.); serving as intermediaries for obtaining finance; providing technical assistance; and in some cases, the direct execution of activities. These functions are directly related to poverty alleviation and the provision of basic needs. They are the most common type of activity carried out by NGDOs. One area which is specially relevant is the work in favour of institutional capacity, through funds not directly attached to a specific development project, for activities such as training or the purchase of computers.

Support for civic activities. Northern CSOs also provide assistance to activities involving civic education or community organizing by the Southern CSOs. Examples of this are educational campaigns, denouncing human rights violations, courses for community leaders, and legal assistance for local grassroots organizations seeking formal recognition. In general, these activities are carried out by a small sub-sector of the Northern CSOs/NGDOs.

Advocacy. A few CSOs/NGDOs also engage in advocacy campaigns that aim to pressurize Southern and Northern governments, international organizations or multinational corporations to take certain decisions (or not to take them, depending on the case), normally in collaboration with Southern partners. A recent example was the international campaign to end production and trade in antipersonnel mines.

Northern CSOs are themselves divided as to the extent that they should be directly supporting democracy in the South. Some agencies do not see that they can play any direct role in promoting democracy, and prefer to avoid activities that require getting involved in 'political' issues. Other organizations believe they have a role to play in establishing democratization through their support of civil society. For the more activist organizations, activities of the second and third types – civic/organizational and/or advocacy/protest – as well as creating and developing existing networks are generally the preferred form of activity.

Within Latin America, we can point to the support provided by a number of NGDOs and GROs that seek to empower poor groups through programmes of *conciencizacion*. For example, in Chiapas, Mexico, European organizations are engaging in *conciencizacion* within the indigenous communities. An example of the operation of advocacy networks is the campaign carried out by European NGDOs because of human rights violations in Chiapas perpetrated by groups reportedly linked with the Mexican government. They put pressure on the EU to implement the 'democracy clause' contained in the recently-signed framework agreement between the EU and Mexico. This would have implied imposing sanctions on Mexico by reducing or even ending EU cooperation.

Even in those organizations which are most inclined to be involved directly in pro-democracy work, there is sometimes a tendency to conform to the official donor's orientations. As various authors have noted (see, for example, Pearce 1997a), the donors decide which issues are the main priorities and NGDOs who are largely dependent on them for funds have little choice but to adapt their activities accordingly. This does not mean that there is no room at all for NGDO autonomy, but it depends on the level of commitment of each organization to its own principles and goals, and on its abilities to raise other funds. It is also important to note that in many cases there is a gulf between rhetoric and reality in the NGDOs. That is, even though these organizations claim that their goal is to strengthen civil society in Latin America, they may not have a clear strategy for achieving this or they may not perform well in the field. Not all CSOs/NGDOs actually do what they say or think they do.

The project: a 'necessary evil'

'Traditional' development projects are seldom seen as making any direct contribution to consolidating democracy, at least in the short term. The Northern CSOs which concentrate on developing these kinds of activities expect their role to be limited, and the projects affect a relatively small number of people and institutions. Nevertheless, they can bring specific benefits to the poor, and in the long run may contribute to increasing their possibilities of participation in the social, political and economic spheres of their country.

If projects become the central feature of NGDO work in the South the perception of the organization is inevitably narrowed. It can end up isolating or ring-fencing the projects from society and institutions at large. This approach can contradict an emphasis on democratization which has to be seen as a long and continuous process, not easily divisible into small pieces, and not straight-forwardly the result of any particular project financed from the North. As Fowler points out:

> Simply put, as a tool, projects are not appropriate for all but the most technical types of development initiative, such as building roads. Where altering human behaviour is concerned, the less appropriate projects

51

become. Many limitations to NGDO effectiveness stem from this fact . . .
They are time-bound, pre-defined sets of objectives, assumptions, activities
and resources which should lead to measurable, beneficial impacts
. . . The central assumption of the project approach is that it is possible to
construct a defined future but this does not reflect how societies change.

(Fowler 1997: 17)

Despite this and many other criticisms of 'projectitis', 'the project mode is
unlikely to be replaced by something more suitable' (Fowler 1997) because of
the way in which Northern aid to the South is financed; donors wish to see
concrete results and to obtain demonstrable 'value for money' for their
aid, which is most easily achieved through funding projects. This creates a
structural limitation on how far the Northern CSO/NGDO can contribute to
long term change in the South, even when this is actually their goal.

This presents a major challenge for Northern CSOs seeking to go
beyond a limited and localized impact and contribute in a direct way to
broadening participation of their Latin American counterparts and, by
extension, of the poor in general. They need to find new types of relationships that overcome the limitations of the project. A case where the
project approach has led NGOs to see their interventions in completely
different terms from the beneficiaries was highlighted by Biekart. As a
result of a participatory evaluation in Central America, he discovered

That donors [European NGOs] and beneficiaries were using different
definitions of impact and performance. Donor NGOs tended to
overemphasize financial management and short-term material out-
puts; beneficiaries tended to look for modest changes in organizations
over a longer period of time.

(Bierkart 1995: 66)

Going 'beyond' the project approach is not easy, however, partly because the
accountability demands of the official donors and of the individual
contributors require that Northern CSOs operate in this way. Donors want
to see what has been done with the money. Edwards and Hulme (1995b:
223) suggest that NGOs are unable to solve the dilemmas of accountability; they learn to manage them which frequently means bridging a gap
between what donors demand and what CSOs/NGOs wish to achieve.

The success of the NGOs as an obstacle for their pro-democracy work?

As Edwards and Hulme (1996: 964) note, there is evidence that individual
NGOs have become effective in some service-provision areas, such as micro-
credits, basic health and development of appropriate technology for agricultural

production. These successes, among other factors, have persuaded bilateral donors and governments to channel increasing amounts of funds to local NGOs. This may be counterproductive if it obliges NGOs to 'scale up' their operations. This means departing from work which involves direct contact with the poor in favour of an approach that concentrates on building intermediary organizations. This may undermine their capacity to develop those qualities which are most useful to promote democratization: independence from external interests, closeness to the poor, and a commitment to confronting the powerful. Efficient providers of social services do not always work best as agents of democratization (Edwards and Hulme 1996: 965).

At the same time, foreign NGOs (NGDOs) may actually be undermining democratization in the South because they can weaken and even replace local groups and the state by taking on increasing responsibilities for designing and carrying out social policies. Strengthening civil society may actually come at the expense of governmental credibility or capacity, reducing the legitimacy of the state.

European civil society and democratization in Latin America

Despite the difficulties which European NGDOs face in carrying out their pro-democracy work, their role in this area is expanding. This raises the question how far a 'European' approach to democratization through support for civil society can be identifed. European NGOs are increasingly coming together in terms of the broad principles guiding their operations, but this does not mean that there is a single 'European' approach to development.

Each EU member state has its own organizational and political culture within which the NGDOs have developed. For example, the corporatist culture of the Scandinavian countries, which prioritizes consensus in public decision-making, is quite different from the system prevalent in France, Italy and Spain where the tendency is for conflicts to be managed differently (Smilie 1992: 17). Another difference is that associational life in each European country has different levels of intensity. In the UK it is particularly strong and private organizations were precursors of the welfare state with the result that charities are largely self-regulated. The development NGOs of Spain, Greece, Portugal, and to a lesser extent, Italy, do not have such a long tradition; this reflects their recent histories and the relative weakness of their civil societies. Nevertheless, there has been an extraordinary growth in associations in the last decade or so throughout Southern Europe. For example, in Spain the National Platform, which includes a large proportion of the NGDOs, had fewer than ten member organizations when it was founded in the 1980s; today it has about a hundred members.

Although Latin America is not a priority zone for the international activities of European CSOs/NGDOs – sub-Saharan Africa is the main priority because of its greater poverty, its geographic closeness and a more recent colonial past –

they maintain an important presence in the region. In fact in most European countries NGDOs give more importance to Latin America than do their governments (except in Spain where the interest is more or less the same). Apart from funds that they receive from donations, private foundations, membership fees, sales of publications, goods (usually 'fair trade') and services, European NGDOs benefit from central government funding and, in some countries, from funds from municipalities, provincial and regional governments. Another important source for financing their development activities is the European Commission. In effect, the data available from the Commission gives an idea of the amount of funding European NGOs receive. Between 1992 and 1995, the European Commission co-financed over 4000 projects in Latin America presented by European NGDOs, for a total subsidy of 203 million Ecus, which represents between 50 and 70 per cent of the total costs of these projects (Freres 1998: 27, 52–4).

All these projects require European organizations to have Latin American counterparts. This is seen as a way to support civil societies in the region. However, it is difficult to work out exactly how, and how effectively, these projects *do* in fact contribute to civil society in Latin America or to democratization. It is very difficult to break down the data available so as to obtain concrete information about how many projects are directed toward institutional strengthening, how many are poverty-related and so on. Measuring effectiveness is also practically impossible. From the European NGDOs' own discourse, it would seem that the increase in community participation is a priority, but few make the effort to explain how this links with democratization (even if they make the implicit assumption). Biekart (1995: 66) notes that it is practically impossible to assess 'whether European NGO assistance has contributed to higher levels of participation and to the strengthening of GROs'.

Final reflections

The issues discussed here are quite complex and it might not be useful to try to present them in brief conclusions. Instead, I will focus on the central issue of the role of European civil societies in democratization in Latin America. In addressing this question, another one arises: what specifically do European civil societies have to offer which is of 'added value' in comparison to CSOs from other areas, particularly from the US? Answering this question goes some way to suggesting the *potential* Europe has to play a positive role in democratization in Latin America, and indeed in the South in general.

In terms simply of development assistance and funding, European agencies can contribute nothing that is particularly distinctive. There is a convergence between all Northern organizations working in the South around a common set of principles. There are no really meaningful international differences. It might be that US organizations tend to serve US government interests more readily than is the case in Western Europe but, increasingly, even this distinction makes less sense as European governments channel ever greater funds through NGOs, thereby increasing governmental leverage over development agencies.

There are significant differences in how European and US NGOs think about democracy and democratization, however. Our argument here is not so much that European ideas are superior, but that they may be more appropriate to the Latin American context and perhaps even to the context of developing countries in general. European CSOs may be better placed in some circumstances to influence democratization positively. Given the dominant intellectual and cultural influence of the US in Latin America, seen as the alternative perspective on democracy presented by European groups can be valuable to Latin Americans who seek diversification as a means to reducing their external dependence.

US organizations tend to suggest that democracy should be built on confrontational politics and that institutions should balance each other out: a powerful executive 'balanced' by Congress and an independent judiciary. In Latin America, political polarization has consistently undermined attempts to build democracy; this suggests that the US approach, which is chiefly about getting the institutions 'right', is not appropriate because it does not attempt to change the dominant political culture of the region. European CSOs, on the other hand, have less of a set formula for democratic institutions and tend to see pluralism and consensus-building as central features of democratic politics.

In Europe, civic organizations do not generally question the importance of the state as a provider of services and mediating force in social conflicts; this is not the case in the US where the role of the state is contested by a number of civic organizations. Despite reforms throughout Europe cutting back the role of the state, it remains an essential social actor. This consititutes an important model for Latin America. There, the state historically has offered very limited provision to society at large, has not served as a mediator in social conflicts, and has not ensured equal rights for all citizens before the law. Emulating the US 'minimal' state and further weakening the state in Latin America may well be counterproductive for democratization and for civil society in the region. Thus the European view of the state may actually offer more to Latin America than the US view and CSOs may be important channels through which this view can be transmitted.

The same is true of the European view of civil society. The prevailing view in the US is that civil society is either opposed to the state or serves as a counterbalance to it. In both cases, civil society is seen broadly as part of the 'non-state', along with, and closely linked to, free enterprise institutions. In other words, North Americans tend to suggest that there is a symbiotic relationship between civil society, capitalism and democracy. In Western Europe, in contrast, civil society is often seen as linked to the state, although without forming a part of it; the state is not a 'necessary evil' but plays a key role in providing a space for civil society. Suspicion of the state is much deeper in Latin America than in Europe, in part because of the authoritarian legacy, in part because of its inefficiencies and class bias. However, there is a growing recognition among civil society leaders that CSOs cannot function well if the state does not fulfil its minimal obligations and guarantee the existence of public and private spaces.

Finally, European CSOs may contribute to Latin American democratization and to civil society in the region through their appreciation of the value of regional integration which has become a fundamental fact of life in the European Union (EU). Although there are certainly differing views on how well European integration has gone, the general consensus is that it has been valuable for promoting peace in the region and increasing exchanges amongst the countries and peoples involved.

The EU also favours the principle of economic and social cohesion among the members and provides resources to the poorer regions and countries. Latin America is currently embarked upon a project of regional and sub-regional integration which is explicitly seen as a way of promoting peace and democracy in the region. European CSOs have already become involved in a number of initiatives to strengthen subregional networks of NGOs in the context of growing integration. Central America provides an example of their work. As one Central American NGO leader noted, the sub-regional network *Concertación*, which has received considerable assistance from European NGOs, helps:

> participating NGOs to be able to strengthen each other in order to confront the challenges of thinking and acting in Central America as a region. And to support the democratization and participation processes of grassroots initiatives with an expanding Central American dimension.
>
> (W. Rueben, cited in Macdonald, 1997: 157–8)

Nevertheless, despite the appeal of the European model, it would not be wise to overstate the role or importance of European CSOs/NGDOs in Latin American democratization. In part this is because, as we have noted, many NGOs still fly their national flags; it is also due to the structural limitations of European contributions to political developments in Latin America.

Much more reflection is needed in order to understand the past and current contributions of European CSOs/NGDOs to democratization in Latin America and how they might improve their efforts in the future. It would be very useful to have a much broader selection of empirical studies than is available at present. Even if European CSOs/NGDOs can only make a modest contribution, it is important that it be a relevant and positive achievement which helps to distribute democracy to the majority of Latin Americans who have yet to benefit from the introduction of democratic regimes in the region.

Part II

CASE STUDIES

Transnational and non-state actors
in East and Central Europe, Africa
and Latin America

4

THE EUROPEAN UNION, DEMOCRATIC CONDITIONALITY AND TRANSNATIONAL PARTY LINKAGES

The case of Eastern Europe

Geoffrey Pridham

Introduction: focusing on democratization within regions

Studies on democratization have sometimes referred to 'waves' of regime change from authoritarian rule to constitutional democracy (Huntington 1991: 13–26). Such 'waves' may either acquire a regional focus (in the area study sense), or they may represent a more cosmic phenomenon with democratic transitions occurring simultaneously in different parts of the world.

The notion of 'waves' of democratization has, however, limited analytical merit. If it is viewed simply as an observation of a process occurring contemporaneously in the same or different parts of the world, then the term has a descriptive value. But it provides small insight into the dynamics of regime change, the causes of which must include domestic factors however much international influences play a part. An advance on this notion is the use of concepts like 'contagion', 'diffusion' and 'demonstration effect' (Whitehead 1996: chapter Two) which all, in different ways, begin to convey how transnational influences pressurize domestic system change.

It is easier to imagine such interaction when focusing on regions, not merely because of geographical proximity but also because structured relations may exist between states in a given region that directly channel – indeed, may strengthen – such transnational influences. The most articulated and intensive form of such structures is presented by the European Union (EU), although other European and international organizations have played a significant part in the democratization process in Eastern Europe. As Przeworski has noted, the

59

EU provides not merely expanded economic opportunities in the form of integration in regional markets, but also pressures for democracy and integration in European-level political institutions (Przeworski 1995: 9).

The concept of 'conditionality' captures the essence of this form of interaction. It also reflects how much more deliberate international actors have become in their promotion of democracy , rather than relying on the indirect and perhaps fortuitous effect of democratizing influences in the international environment. 'Conditionality' can assume a more concrete form when we consider patterns of transnational collective action. In a recent essay, Tarrow (1996: 19) suggests typologizing transnational interactions in the following way: unified social movements that cross national boundaries; the diffusion of national movements across international boundaries; transnational political exchange between groups of national actors; and transnational issue networks which target international institutions. It is important also to consider whether such interactions are temporary or sustained and integrated.

In this chapter, after a brief look at the EU's potential for influencing democratization, discussion turns to its application of 'democratic conditionality' while comparing its influence with that of other organizations that seek to apply this. In order to examine this strategy more closely, we look at transnational party linkages developed by the European Parliament (EP), EU-wide party organizations and national member parties with political parties in Eastern Europe since the transitions to democracy began there in 1989. Such linkages provide a very specific focus for studying international influences on democratization, and incidentally, relate to a crucial component of liberal-democratic systems, namely the guarantee of political pluralism.

European integration and democratization

The EU possesses an institutionalized regional framework which readily transmits the kind of influences and pressures that may affect the course of democratization, deliberately or otherwise. It is now seen as the most important external actor in Europe, particularly because of its expansion of policy concerns in the past two decades and its increasing international political weight. Its potential influence in encouraging democratization was already evident at the time of the Southern European transitions in the late 1970s, but is more widely recognized today with respect to regime change in Eastern Europe.

Whatever the degree of cross-national variation in the impact of the EU on regime change, its influences are most likely to be long-term. Schmitter has usefully summarized how they occur:

> First, EU membership is expected to be permanent in nature and to provide access to an expanding variety of economic and social opportunities far into the future. Second, it is backed by a 'complex interdependence', an evolving system of private transnational exchanges at many levels and

involving many different types of collective action (parties, interest associations, social movements, subnational governments etc.). And, finally, it engages in lengthy, public, multilateral deliberation and is decided unanimously in the Council of Ministers and by an absolute majority in the European Parliament. This requirement enhances the 'reputation' or 'certification' effect beyond the level attainable via unilateral recognition or bilateral exchanges where other criteria (i.e. security calculations) may override the democratic ones. More than any other international commitment, full EU membership has served to stabilise both political and economic expectations. It does not directly guarantee the consolidation of democracy; it indirectly makes it easier for national actors to agree within a narrower range of rules and practices.

(Schmitter 1995b: 524)

For this reason, it has been commonly assumed in the democratization literature that the influence of European integration increases with time, peaking during democratic consolidation rather than at the outset in the transition phase which is in any case usually short-lived (Pridham 1991: chapter 11). One variation on this, expressed in a study of the Greek case, is that the EU helped to underwrite democracy following consolidation rather than exporting it there in the first place (Tsingos 1996).

It does not, however, follow that the influence of European integration is negligible at the early democratization stage. In fact, there is now more reason for arguing that its influence is not merely evident in new member states but also in prospective ones still undergoing initial regime change. Recent experience in Eastern Europe (especially with the more dynamic transitions in the region) suggests the EU's importance here may be greater than with previous democratizations elsewhere in Europe. It should be remembered, too, that the transitions in Eastern Europe have, though with considerable cross-national variation, lasted distinctly longer than earlier ones; this political change has combined with economic transformation and depended to a large extent on outside assistance.

One of the less explored areas of evolving EU links is that of political rather than socio-economic influences on prospective member states. In many (although hardly all) cases these have also been countries undergoing transition from authoritarian rule. The then new democracies of Spain, Greece and Portugal, which eventually joined in the first half of the 1980s, showed that the prospect of membership – an overriding strategic priority of their governments – exerted influence through various channels. These included involvement in transnational networks and various forms of economic support from Brussels, as well as different elite-level pressures and influences (Pridham 1991: 213).

Newly evolving links with the EU and its member states can affect policy options and economic interests. They can also impact on élite mentalities in a

61

prospective entrant, especially as a country emerges from international isolation and ever closer contacts are made with élites from established democracies. In post-1974 Portugal, for instance, the priority accorded EU entry provided a common platform on which parties supporting the then fragile new democracy could unite against domestic opponents of the transition (Pridham 1991: 226–7).

With the prestige it enjoyed in these countries, the EU became a symbolic reference point for successful democratization. It had been viewed as a source of moral support in pre-transition years through its identification with democratic values which was demonstrated, for instance, when it discouraged gestures of rapprochement from Franco's Spain. Much rhetoric was voiced about EU entry strengthening democratization; and, as later in Eastern Europe, expectations were raised to levels that were probably unrealistic. In Greece, prime minister Karamanlis visibly linked the prospects for the new democracy there with successful early entry to the EU and this theme reappeared in official Greek statements from 1975, not least as a means for forcing the pace of negotiations (Pridham 1991: 226). It has to be said, however, that this view was a matter of partisan contention between the main political forces in Greece, with PASOK regarding EU entry at this time with hostility (Tsoukalis 1981: 110).

There are obvious limits to the extent of the EU's influence. Brussels can affect developments, but is in no position to alter the course of regime change if domestic conditions worsen, as the attempted military coup in Spain in 1981 demonstrated. The same goes for the rather more difficult transitions in Eastern Europe, despite the commitment of élites there to the 'return to Europe'. By the time of these transitions, however, the EU had developed more mechanisms for assisting and influencing prospective member states. It was also more ambitious about strengthening the trend towards liberal democracy that had emerged in Europe and elsewhere.

Democratic conditionality and the EU

Among the various notions of international influences in democratization, 'conditionality' is the one most resonant of deliberate efforts to determine the process's outcome through external pressure. This is achieved by specifying conditions or even preconditions for support, involving either promise of material aid or political opportunities. It is a method adopted increasingly by several international and European organizations, and parallels the greater international attention to minority rights since the collapse of Communism in Eastern Europe (Jackson Preece 1998: 20ff.). However, it is the EU that has come to be most associated with democratic conditionality since the prize is no less than eventual membership for new democracies.

The term originated with respect to economic conditions demanded by international financial or aid organizations, such as the International Monetary Fund (IMF), entailing sanctions for governments that did not comply with policy prescriptions. Political conditionality is a fairly recent extension of the more familiar economic conditionality, with governments of the industrial countries and the World Bank making aid conditional on the elimination of corruption, protection of human rights, limits on arms expenditure and, in some cases, steps towards democracy (Przeworski 1995: 6). The term has subsequently entered the debate on democratization. In this connection, it has acquired quasi-official status in the EU relating to new democracies seeking membership, although the term is not widely used outside the EU institutions. In fact, so far as conditionality has become a rigorous practice, it has been largely confined to Europe.[1]

Various aspects of the principle of conditionality have become clearer over time. First, it involves multilateral pressure which is seen as more acceptable than pressure from one particular foreign government, that might be viewed as tantamount to a patronñclient relationship. For instance, the move of new Southern European democracies like Greece and Spain in the 1970s from a client status *vis-à-vis* the USA to a multilateral relationship with the EU resulted in more balanced external links and ones more conducive to liberal democracy.[2] It is a matter ultimately of international legitimation, for the EU's offer of an official relationship and eventual partnership as a member state is widely considered as a firm seal of approval on a country's new democratic credentials. That gives Brussels significant leverage over such countries in making conditions. The prestige and respect accorded the EU in Eastern Europe suggest that in most countries there multilateral pressure will carry weight, provided of course that EU entry is not bitterly contested between the political parties.

Second, there is the strategic question of when to apply the democratic criterion, which has led to contrasting arguments. On the one hand, it has been maintained that early recognition of democratic credentials helps the transition process, a view often voiced by applicant states determined on membership. However it has more often been argued, notably by the EU itself, that certain preconditions should be met before recognition is granted. The former view has not however disappeared among international organizations, as shown by the Council of Europe's acceptance in recent years of membership for Romania and Russia.

In the debate in the Council's Parliamentary Assembly in September 1993, supporters of Romania's membership argued this would strengthen democracy there while delay would weaken it. Many doubts were expressed by others, especially over the situation of minorities, the system of justice, the lack of constitutional guarantees and the arbitrariness of public administration in that country. The decision in favour was, in the end, coupled with the warning to the Romanian authorities that their actions would be followed with 'critical attention', and with recommendations for improvements, notably in the rights of minorities, which would be regularly monitored by the Assembly (*Frankfurter Allgemeine*, 29 September 1993).

The debate over Russia was similar, although geostrategic considerations also entered the debate. In this case, a greater urgency was attached to the argument that membership would strengthen democracy, or rather prevent its further destabilization. In 1995, the Parliamentary Assembly had voted to suspend Russia's application in protest against the Kremlin's brutal suppression of the Chechen separatists. In January 1996, however, the same body voted by a large majority (164 to 35) to allow Russia to become the thirty-ninth member. Doubts were again voiced about Chechnya, human rights abuses and the absence of the rule of law, while some delegates saw acceptance of such a fledgling democracy as premature. Nevertheless a vote in favour was seen as consistent with the West's support for Yeltsin against his political rivals, whose commitment to democracy was not clear-cut. It was significant that nationalism was mentioned as a factor in the debate, but one that might make Russia 'more aggressive' if membership were rejected (*Financial Times*, 26 January 1996).

Third, conditionality entails the imposition of specific democratic conditions for membership of a European organization. The EU has tended to be particularly rigorous, especially in the past half-decade, but other organizations also lay down entry terms. An entrant to the Council of Europe is required to observe its 'European standards', involving a democratic system of state organs, guarantees of human rights, recognition of the law as the main regulator of state-citizen relations and guarantees of a market economy (Sokolewicz 1995: 251–2). As we have seen, it can sometimes apply such standards rather flexibly, and it cannot always monitor developments in member states in a rigorous fashion. Membership of the Council of Europe involves a fairly straightforward procedure, but this also makes it relatively easy to expel a member for flagrant abuse of democratic values.

The EU is a rather different organization from the Council of Europe and other bodies by virtue of its integrative element. Entry to the EU is a lengthy and elaborate procedure with negotiations for membership lasting several years following a preliminary exploratory period. The time taken before membership is finally agreed allows for ample observation of democratic conditions, and any serious setback in these may possibly abort or delay negotiations.

While the EU has always made clear that membership is only open to European states that are liberal democracies, it has defined the conditions only very gradually over time. This is partly because the major integration treaties, such as the Rome Treaty of 1957 (article 237), did not specify these terms of membership and were content with general statements.[3] The first enlargements in 1973 did not include new democracies, so there was no compelling need to be more specific. It was not until Greece, Spain and Portugal showed a clear interest in membership early in their transitions that the EU began to define its democratic conditions (apart from the traditional emphasis on fundamental rights).[4] The criteria applied then were: genuinely free elections; the 'right' balance of party strength (a predominance of pro-democratic parties); a reasonably stable government, led if possible by a credible figure known in European circles; and, of course, the inauguration of a liberal democratic constitution (Pridham 1991: 235).

During the past two decades, the EU has moved beyond formal criteria (e.g. free elections, separation of powers, rule of law) to the conditions which characterize what is usually called 'substantive democracy'. The latter refers to the quality of democracy, including the social function of constitutions and the way human rights are perceived, how far political parties provide a means for political participation, the role of the media and whether they represent broad political debate, the transformation in public administration and the existence of an active civil society (Kaldor and Vejvoda 1997: 66–67). Issues of human rights have featured prominently at times, notably in debates in the European Parliament over developments in Turkey, which pressed for EU membership in the late 1980s. An EP debate in 1991 on growing links with East European countries undergoing transition underlined new forms of cultural cooperation to boost democratization there. It stressed the 'renewal of society', which was 'at least as necessary and at least as difficult as the introduction of a social and ecologically oriented market economy' (*Official Journal of the EC*, 1991).

It was the transitions in Eastern Europe from 1989 that prompted Brussels to define in greater detail the democratic conditions that are required. The Europe Agreements granting the new East European democracies association status with reference to possible future membership provided the occasion. These have been signed with most of the post-Communist states in Eastern and Central Europe, including Poland, Hungary, the Czech Republic, Slovakia, Romania, Bulgaria, Slovenia, Estonia, Latvia and Lithuania. In proposing an association relationship, the Commission envisaged these countries 'giving practical evidence of their commitment to the rule of law, respect for human rights, the establishment of multi-party systems, free and fair elections and economic liberalisation with a view to introducing market economies' (European Commission 1990).

The Europe Agreements provided for 'political dialogue', an innovation in EU agreements with outside parties. This involved regular meetings at the highest executive and parliamentary levels, including association councils at ministerial level as well as parliamentary association committees. These bodies were to embrace all subjects of common interest including progress with political and economic reforms as well as bilateral, European (CSCE) and international issues (European Commission 1995a: 3). The last involved systematic consultation with these new partner countries on positions taken by the EU within international organizations. The new partners were also entitled to participate as observers at certain European Political Cooperation (EPC) meetings (European Commission 1993: 3). Working groups on policy issues, including experts, were also provided for. The general idea behind the institutionalization of links with East European countries was to develop 'structured relations', and thereby create 'a pre-accession atmosphere' through the progressive involvement of these new democracies in the business of the EU (Maresceau 1996: 131–2).

The Europe Agreements laid down a variety of conditions for eventual accession to the EU. These included 'the stability of institutions in the candidate country guaranteeing democracy, the rule of law, human rights and respect for minorities' (European Commission 1993: 2). The increasing insistence on political conditions can be seen by comparing the first such agreements (Poland and Hungary) with the second round of agreements (Czech and Slovak Republics, Romania and Bulgaria), which including references to the Helsinki Final Act and the Charter of Paris for a 'new Europe' (Cremona 1996: 155). Indeed, pressure was put on Romania at one stage over the treatment of political opposition by delaying the Agreement.

These conditions became criteria for criticizing any significant political deficiencies by East European signatories. Slovakia was severely upbraided by a demarche from the EP in late 1995 for its treatment of the Hungarian minority in measures such as the recent language law. This led to sharp polemics on the occasion of the meeting of the EU-Slovakia Joint Parliamentary Committee (JPC), one of the bodies set up under the Europe Agreement). The Slovak government reacted defensively to the EP criticism, claiming that the West misunderstood the Slovak situation. Opposition parties used the opportunity to stress the problem of minorities there and to express the hope that Slovakia would not be excluded from eventual EU membership as that would only strengthen nationalist tendencies (*Daily News Monitor*, 23 and 24 November 1995). In its declaration, the JPC meeting noted: 'With regard to the development of civil society and democracy in Slovakia, the JPC insists on the need to conduct an in-depth, open and continuing dialogue in order to ensure support for the process leading towards Slovak accession into the EU' (EU-Slovakia Joint Parliamentary Committee 1995: 4).

These JPCs are seen in Brussels as a test of multi-party representation. In several cases, opposition parties are suitably represented in the national delegations, even providing the chair or vice-chair in a few cases. Slovakia's delegation proved a problem, for contrary to assurances, one of the vice-chairs was not from the opposition (Harris, interview, 1996).

Slovakia was one of the few East European applicants criticised seriously by the European Commission's official opinions on accession. While the Slovak constitution was regarded as suitably democratic, 'the situation is unsatisfactory both in terms of the stability of the institutions and of the extent to which they are rooted in political life'. This referred to the government's disregard for the rights of the opposition, persistent conflict with the President, ignoring of decisions by the Constitutional Court, and its use of the police and secret services, as well as the lack of full independence in the judicial system (Agenda 2000 1997). As a result, Slovakia's membership of the EU is seen as increasingly unlikely unless there is a substantial improvement in these areas.

There were also some serious reservations about democracy in Bulgaria and Romania, but in both cases recent alternation in power was seen as progress towards satisfying political criteria. In all other cases, criteria for membership were regarded as largely satisfied (demonstrating 'the characteristics of a democracy, with stable institutions guaranteeing the rule of law and human rights'), although improvements in the operation of the judicial systems and intensifying the fight against corruption were still necessary (Agenda 2000 1997).

EU policy towards prospective entrants from Eastern Europe was not restricted to political monitoring. It was complemented by a series of economic and training programmes designed to facilitate these countries' transformations after Communist rule. The most relevant of such programmes from our viewpoint was the PHARE Democracy Programme, originally established in 1989, whereby the European Commission was charged with a new international role in coordinating Western aid to sustain the political and economic reform process.

The aim of PHARE is:

> to support the activities and efforts of non-governmental bodies promoting a stable open society and good governance and focusses support on the difficult or unpopular aspects of political reform and democratic practice, where local advocacy bodies are weak and professional expertise is particularly lacking.
>
> (Phare Democracy Programme)

The PHARE programmes for Hungary and Poland, for instance, mention civil society and aim to involve 'intermediate non-state bodies, associations and organisations', such as trade unions, employers' associations, professional associations, consumer bodies, local authorities and environmental non-governmental organisations in its development (Pinder 1997: 122). This democracy programme, administered by the European Human Rights Foundation in Brussels, includes provision for training in a variety of political tasks. These include parliamentary techniques and organization; improving the transparency of public administration; the development of non-governmental organizations and independent, pluralistic and responsible media; the transfer of expertise about democratic practices and the rule of law to professional groups; promoting public awareness about democratic concepts; an, furthering minority rights, equal opportunities and non-discriminatory practices.

The PHARE programme, limited as its resources are, is undoubtedly significant in promoting democracy, particularly when related to other EU activities towards Eastern Europe. Relatively small sums were often much appreciated among resource-starved political activists in Eastern Europe. This was true of the Robert Schuman Institute for Developing Democracy for Central and Eastern Europe, a Christian Democratic training academy based in Budapest; the PHARE Democracy Programme was 'one of the most important financial resources necessary for the functioning of the Institute' (Szalai, interview, 1995).

Another European organization that has played an active part in supporting transformation in Eastern Europe has been the European Bank for

Reconstruction and Development (EBRD). According to the first article in the EBRD statutes:

> In contributing to economic progress and reconstruction, the purpose of the Bank shall be to foster the transition towards open market oriented economies and to promote private and entrepreneurial initiative in the Central and Eastern European countries committed to and applying the principles of multiparty democracy, pluralism and market economics.
>
> (EBRD 1990)

Political (i.e. democratic) considerations were taken seriously and steps were taken to implement them, while cooperation with the Council of Europe was seen as strengthening the Bank's political mandate. An EBRD document on this mandate emphasized human rights and listed various factors on which progress should be reported. These included the familiar formal criteria of liberal democracy as well as fair criminal procedure, the right to form trade unions and to strike and freedom of speech, peaceful assembly, conscience and religion and of movement. Sanctions were even envisaged in the case of countries not meeting such requirements (EBRD 1992).

The political mandate was an innovation for international financial institution, although the World Bank has since moved moderately towards political conditionality. In practice, however, the political mandate of the EBRD has gradually weakened as its operation, originally confined to just seven countries with reasonable prospects of democratization, has been extended to as many as twenty-six. It was the collapse of the USSR in late 1991 which opened the way for this development, as a result of which political conditionality was in effect downplayed.

It is now recognised in EBRD circles that a strict application of democratic criteria to its client states would be impossible. The Bank now acts more like a private sector institution, guided by the 'Washington' institutions of the IMF and the World Bank (EBRD interviews, 1996 and 1997). Its political department was disbanded for cost-cutting reasons, so that political assessments are now made by its shareholders. However, the drift towards forms of authoritarianism in former Soviet central Asian republics threatens to jeopardize its lending policy to the area, showing that political criteria are still present (*Financial Times*, 31 May 1995).

Compared to other European or international organizations, the EU has increasingly stood out as the one with the most comprehensive approach and effective policy in pursuing democratic conditionality. NATO, which now offers a security framework for countries in Central Europe, may be seen as a more powerful organization, but it has been in the past rather lax about democratic conditions. Countries like Portugal, Turkey and Greece were or remained members despite their regime changes and authoritarian rule.

The Council of Europe is committed in its statute to democracy as a condition of membership, but the EU has more political weight and economic attraction for prospective entrants. This gives it significant leverage over new democracies so long as their interest in closer links and eventual membership is a compelling strategic need.

Transnational party linkages and democratization in Eastern Europe

As mentioned above, the EU's goal of democracy-building and its search for wider influence are matched by the desire for EU entry and resources in the East. This interdependence provides the context in which transnational networks can develop with some effect. This is an important dimension of East/West 'convergence' that is complementary to official links that have intensified over recent years. The PHARE programme has, indeed, given a priority to non-governmental actors in new democracies. We focus here on transnational party linkages as a particular means for underscoring democratic conditionality.

Transnational party linkages have operated in several parallel ways. They function as parliamentary groups in the European Parliament (EP) but also through transnational party federations, such as the Party of European Socialists, the (Christian Democratic) European People's Party and the European Liberal Democrat and Reform Party, with equivalent organisations for other political tendencies. The traditional international groups (Socialist, Liberal and Christian Democratic) overlap with European federations, but their membership is not confined to EU member states or indeed Europe. Finally, one should not forget the range of bilateral links between national parties in different countries. Such bilateral cooperation is all the more influential if it involves parties from the European organizations.

While normally peripheral to national party development, these linkages may acquire a more general significance in the early stages of regime change, since new party systems are more open to international influences than long-established ones. This is especially true if the linkages form part of a wider programme of support for democratization. All the same, their influence may at best be secondary and depends primarily on internal developments and what opportunities they present.

One should not forget the countries in Eastern Europe by and large lacked democratic traditions at the mass level when they embarked on democratization in 1989. Transnational linkages cannot be expected to inculcate democratic values on a wide scale, nor to permeate down through party structures and out into the wider political arena. Such linkages are formed by elites and activists and only a few people are directly involved in transnational exchanges, including training programmes for party activists.

Transnational cooperation between parties in Eastern and Western Europe has taken various forms, including training, moral and material support as well as political monitoring. The possibilities for influence may cover party identity and early programmatic development, the acquisition of political experience and expertise, and building up organizational mechanisms. These various activities have occurred at the same time, although the emphasis on training in the first phase of democratization in Eastern Europe has shifted more recently towards policy discussion against the background of growing official links with Brussels and the prospects of EU membership.

This cooperation commenced in a rather dramatic way given the unexpected and rapid series of regime collapses in Eastern Europe in the autumn of 1989. There had been hardly any transnational interaction of this kind beforehand, if we discount the presence of exile groups in West European contries and the covert links maintained by dissident groups (Pridham 1996: 195–96). But there was a burst of activity once the first free elections were held, all within the few months of March to June 1990. There was a sudden desperate demand for expertise in democratic political methods, not least in running election campaigns.

In the following years, transnational linkages became more institutionalized through programmes of mutual visits, common policy seminars as well as by associate or observer status with full EU and EP membership in mind[5]. Joining the EP party groups was clearly not possible until the countries entered the EU, although informal links with them were established and delegations from Eastern Europe to the EP have grown markedly in recent years. Parties were allowed to send delegations to the Parliamentary Assembly of the Council of Europe, once their countries joined that organization, and party elites have acknowledged the valuable parliamentary experience gained there. Membership of bodies such as the Internationals was already possible.

These developing links had various gradual effects. Perhaps more significant than the cross-fertilization of overtly democratic political methods and practices were less obvious influences. Transnational intensification of party and personal links was a form of political socialization, albeit one-sided, where the assumptions of elites in established democracies rubbed off on new party leaders and activists – many with no previous political involvement – from Eastern Europe. Networking along ideological lines was sometimes quite institutionalized between bilateral partners, especially when their countries had a common frontier. Such cooperation could extend to links developing between regional or even local branches of the parties in question, a practice clearly modelled on the European practice of town-twinning. This was seen, for instance, in the activity of Austrian parties in other Central European countries like the Czech Republic, Hungary and Slovenia, occasioning reference to a 'Habsburg dimension' to transnational activity (Pridham 1996: 211). In organizations like the Socialist International (SI) there was often a division of labour between its member parties and fraternal allies in particular countries.

While party-political motives were bound to dominate in these developing transnational links, they did not have to be exclusive of deliberate or incidental democracy-building. Often the two motives intermixed, as expressed for instance in the statute of the Robert Schuman Institute at Budapest, the aim of which was:

> to support and promote the process of democratic transformation on the basis of European values in the spirit of Robert Schuman in Central and Eastern European countries; to help the flow of information and making contacts between East–East and West–East, to fulfil the idea of United Europe and to prepare the countries of the region for governing
>
> (Schuman Institute 1995, Statute 1/1)

The Institute's training programme aimed at helping Christian Democratic parties to win elections, but it also contributed to developing democratic practices and ideas. The activity of political foundations linked to individual parties in West European countries was geared to the broader purpose of democracy-building as well as to promoting ideological allies in Eastern Europe. This was notably true of the German foundations, the wealthiest and most active in the region, which were funded by the German state. Their brief was broad and included political education for democracy-building, even to the extent of offering training to those from different political leanings (Pridham 1996: 202).

One basic obstacle was a sense of cultural distance, deriving from the isolation of the Cold War period. Interviews with people involved in transnational organizations suggest this was greater with elites from the former USSR and, in some cases, Balkan countries than from East and Central Europe. There were problems of political mentality rooted in the Communist period. There was also the special question of former ruling Communist parties, mostly now renamed 'Socialist', which sought recognition by the SI as a central element in their own legitimation.

For this reason, the role of transnational party organizations in political monitoring is especially important if democratic conditionality is to succeed. Various procedures were adopted by the Internationals and the EU party federations to vet the democratic commitment of prospective members or associates. The SI in particular acted cautiously, having made some hasty mistakes over certain partners at the time of the 1990 elections. It therefore established a special European Forum for Democracy and Solidarity to filter such links, especially with ex-Communist parties. As one national party source indicated, SI member parties 'are not prepared to admit them until they have gone through hoops, jumped a lot of hurdles, and demonstrated their commitment to democracy and human rights, social democracy' (Rodgers interview, 1993).

Undoubtedly, this provided an extra pressure on applicant parties to adhere to their democratic credentials and, in the case of the former regime parties, to strengthen their reformist tendencies. Heinz Fischer, chairman of the European Forum, identified four main criteria for judging applicants: their programmes;

the credibility of leading figures in these parties; electoral legitimation (i.e. strength); and, 'how they handle their past'. The last aspect was tested in various ways, including declarations by party leaders, embassy reports and experience through contacts with these parties as in seminars organized by the Forum – 'how they react, how they behave' (Fischer interview, 1995).

The Forum was quite thorough in its procedure. Its secretary-general, based in Brussels, revealed how strict the procedure could be with regard to democratic commitment, particularly as some members were cautious about admitting the parties of the former regimes. Formal requirements in terms of accepting democratic values, freedom of speech, freedom of religion and of the media were 'not enough', for it was necessary to 'look at day-to-day behaviour, such as how they treat minorities, the media, how they develop the new constitution' (Toresson interview, 1996). Regular contacts with aspiring member parties from the East provided a close test for 'this cooperation develops in the course of years, and SI membership is the result of this – there is an inter-relationship somehow' (Gaugl interview, 1995). An official of the Austrian Social Democrats' international office elaborated:

> One cannot make a 100 per cent judgement of what impression one has of [East European] representatives one meets at SI meetings, in the Socialist group of the Council of Europe, for example – of how they conduct themselves, how they behave when votes are taken, what sort of proposals they make, of the policies they make when in government in their countries . . . from this one attempts to form an opinion. That one can make a mistake here goes without saying. One doesn't live in the country itself. One judges it from outside without getting to know the country really well.
>
> (Gaugl, interview, 1995).

Nevertheless, such regular cooperation provided the best means available for guaranteeing democratic commitment and therefore assisted the EU's strategy of democratic conditionality.

Other transnational party organisations applied very similar criteria although in varying degrees and with differing emphases. The Christian Democrats – not surprisingly – placed a special importance on freedom of religion. The European People's Party (EPP) and its linked organization, the European Union of Christian Democrats (EUCD), had various difficulties over its strict adherence to certain democratic conditions. The Hungarian Smallholders' Party was suspended by the EUCD council because of its increasingly nationalist line.

The Albanian Democratic Party's application for EUCD membership was another difficult decision. The application was only accepted after close examination of the party's stand on some crucial issues and following visits by EPP/EUCD officials to the country to talk with representatives of different church communities (Moslem and Orthodox) and investigate the situation of the Greek minority. Membership was made conditional on improvements for the latter and these were introduced, suggesting a direct influence of transnational linkages. At the same time, the EUCD took account of special problems in Albania for 'you can't judge the situation in Albania after the Hoxha regime and expect that they are like in Germany or Great Britain!'. Yet, 'the fact that they have been excluded from international life for such a long time gives it such a high value'. This, as the EPP/EUCD secretary-general admitted, allowed his party organisation a special leverage in the Albanian case (Welle interview, 1996).

Altogether, this transnational activity has played a not insignificant although low-profile part in the democratization process at the level of party development. Its precise impact is difficult to measure since it mixes with other influences occurring at the same time. Interview respondents tended to agree that transnational party cooperation of the East/West variety was, among other things, a useful agent of democratic conditionality.

The fact that transnational linkages dovetail with other pressures at the official EU level probably enhances their impact on party elites in Eastern Europe. These transnational contacts are increasingly seen as informal channels for promoting entry to the EU and establishing influence in Brussels once that occurs. The executive secretary of the conservative European Democratic Union (EDU) saw these links as providing a form of 'political groundwork' for eventual accession (Wintoniak interview, 1995). Significantly, there has been some interchange between party officials responsible for transnational contacts and government positions following government changes in some of the countries in Eastern Europe.

Conclusion

A report from the National Democratic Institute (NDI) in Washington, one of the American foundations involved in fostering transnational links in Eastern Europe, commented aptly: 'It is often easier to begin a democratization process than to exercise its reality on a day-to-basis' (NDI 1992). This recalled Vaclav Havel's much quoted remark that 'we have done away with the totalitarian system, but we have yet to win democracy'. Clearly, embedding new democracies and thus strengthening their chances of persistence is a long and sometimes frustrating political task.

Our examination of both official European efforts and transnational party linkages offers a special approach to the democratization process. While there are limits to transnational collective action as well as to the potential influence that may be exerted from outside by the EU, this study has nevertheless shown that external factors can have an impact provided the domestic conditions are favourable. In particular, it throws light on the cross-fertilization of political ideas and techniques and possibly also deeper influences. The interaction between official and party-level activity is shown in a number of ways with respect to the latter: political monitoring as a pressure to strengthen democratic credentials, regular cooperation as a means for guaranteeing democratic commitment; and, various other ways in which transnational action may lend practical support to the EU's strategy of democratic conditionality. At the same time, the EU has become politically more influential and more ambitious than it was during previous European transitions to democracy. This has undoubtedly strengthened the impact of transnational party cooperation as a channel for influencing developments in young democracies.

This study illustrates how the EU's influence can be exerted with respect to countries that are not yet member states and have not even formally commenced negotiations for entry. In general, it may be said that such transnational linkages are a significant indication of the real influence of European integration on political motives, ambitions and behaviour in such countries. They also illustrate in microcosm how international efforts at democratic conditionality operate and what kind of obstacles they encounter.

Finally, focusing on this approach also demonstrates that democracy-building is not taken for granted by outside actors in Europe. German political elites, who have played a central role at both levels, are particularly aware of the magnitude of this task, sensitive as they are to their own country's history. It is also clear that the EU has developed the strategy of democratic conditionality well ahead of any other international organization. And this has most of all occurred during the recent period of transitions in Eastern Europe.

Notes

This chapter draws on research carried out for the ESRC-funded project on Regime Change in East-Central Europe under its East-West Change Programme. Elite interviews on transnational party linkages were conducted between 1993–6 in several Eastern and Western European countries.

1 Przeworski (1995b: 504) notes signs that such regional organizations as the Organization of American States, the British Commonwealth and even the Organization for African Unity have begun to discuss the issue of collective security to prevent 'unconstitutional' regime change. It is understood the IMF rarely made democracy a condition but if it did the demand was kept confidential in order not to offend national sovereignty or dignity.

2 This point was underlined by the American link being identified in the countries concerned with implicit if not overt support from Washington for the previous dictatorships, and this became a controversial matter during democratization. In the case of postwar Italy, the adoption of a client status vis-à-vis the USA at the outset of the Cold War remained an issue of deep controversy along Left-Right lines in that country's politics for a generation. It helped to complicate Italian politics, although there were other factors behind the difficult consolidation of Italy's post-Fascist democracy (Pridham 1995: 173–77).

3 Even the Maastricht Treaty on European Union (1992) is suitably bland:

> ' . . . its member states, whose systems of government are founded on the principles of democracy; the Union shall respect fundamental rights, as guaranteed by the European Convention for the Protection of Human Rights and Fundamental Freedoms . . . and as they result from the constitutional traditions common to the member states, as general principles of Community law'.
>
> (article F)

4 The 1962 Birkelbach Report of the Political Committee of the European Parliament, which became EC policy, stated: 'Only states which guarantee on their territories truly democratic practices and respect for fundamental rights and freedoms can become members of the Community'.
5 The European People's Party Congress at Toulouse in November 1997 made it possible to offer associate membership to parties from countries which have applied for membership of the EU (*EPP News*, No. 134, 1998).
6 Interview respondents in transnational party organizations in Brussels remarked on the 'spiritual damage after Communism' and difficulties among some party visitors from Eastern Europe in developing 'an ability to open up, even to be confident in talking'. Another quoted Milos Zeman, the leader of the Czech Social Democratic Party, as saying that 'everyone over 40 years old is contaminated' (Interviews in Brussels, January 1996).

Sources

As well as the references listed in the bibliography, this chapter draws on the following interviews and sources:

EBRD (1996 and 1997) Interviews with an official of the EBRD, June 1996 and January 1997.

Fischer, H. (1995) European Forum, Interview, Vienna, November.

Gaugl, S. (1995) Austrian Social Democratic Party, International Office, Interview, Vienna, November.

Harris, G. (1996), European Parliament Secretariat, Brussels, January;

Rodgers, N. (1993) International Office, British Labour Party, Interview, London, November.

Szalai, M. (1995) deputy director of the Robert Schuman Institute, letter to Jan Carnogursky, leader of the Christian Democratic Movement in Slovakia, 2 October.

Toresson, B. (1996) European Forum, Interview, Brussels, January.

Welle, K. (1996) Secretary-General of the European People's Party and the European Union of Christian Democrats, Interview, Brussels, January.

Wintoniak, A. (1995) Executive-Secretary of the European Democratic Union, Interview, Vienna, November.

The Daily News Monitor (1995) press agency of the Slovak Republic, Bratislava.

5

CHARTING THE DECLINE OF CIVIL SOCIETY

Explaining the changing roles and conceptions
of civil society in East and Central Europe

Petr Kopecky and Edward Barnfield

> What we may be witnessing in Eastern Europe, without quite
> realizing it, is the birth of a new democratic structure of norma-
> tive thought. Never in previous transitions to democracy has the
> proper constitution of civil society been made so central – not in
> Southern Europe, not in Latin America, not even in the resis-
> tance to Fascism and Nazism.
>
> (Di Palma, 1991: 31)

Di Palma captured accurately the prevalent mood of 1989 in East and Central
Europe (Poland, Hungary and the Czech and Slovak Republics). The revolutions of 1989 were presented at the time as the triumphant victory of civil
society over the communist one-party states. The key terms which were used
to analyze and explain the peaceful Polish, Hungarian and Czechoslovak transitions were 'civil society', 'a return the commonwealth of democratic
European nations', and 'the forging of close links with the Europe and
the European Union (EU)'. The transitions were carried out in the name
of civil society; the related terms 'citizen' and 'citizenship' were used
constantly to describe the kind of political systems which, it was hoped, would
be erected.

Inevitably, therefore, once the ban on free association and organization was
lifted, there was an explosion of civic assemblies, civic movements, civic parties
and citizen's initiatives throughout the region. So popular was the notion of
civil society, not only among politicians but also on the streets, that mass movements such as Civic Forum in Czechoslovakia and Solidarity in Poland were
swept into power on a wave of goodwill in the first free elections after more
than forty years of communist rule. In sum, the triumphant re-appearance of an
independent, autonomous and self-organized social sphere was seen as an

important factor behind the collapse of communism, as well as the ground on which to build stable and healthy democratic politics.

Nevertheless, with the benefit of hindsight, Di Palma's predictions on civil socity and the expectations surrounding its (re)emergence in the region may have been too optimistic, both in relation to the ascendancy of *civil society as a theory*, that is a normative conception in political discourse, and also in regard to *civil society as an empirical reality*. Building 'civil society' was a major aspiration of the transitions in the East and Central Europe but politics in the new democratic states since then has not been about releasing the energies of 'civil society'.

Even a cursory exanination of the region reveals that the debate on the civil society project in these new democracies is very different from ten years ago, and it is certainly nowhere near as prominent as it once was. Outside the narrow circles of Eastern European intellectuals, the original breeding ground of the project of democratization through civil society, the concept frequently encounters opposition, not least from those who see behind it the rise of disruptive and destabilizing pressure group and social movement politics.[1]

At the same time, other writers have identified the lack of a robust and lively society in the region as one of the major shortcomings of the new democracies and an obstacle to further progress in the democratization process (see Nelson 1996; Green and Skalnik Leff 1997). These critics argue that, instead of strong civil society, there is a strong political society, composed of elite organizations (such as political parties) which penetrate the state. They monopolize the decision-making processes, and either actively suppress or simply ignore the groups organized beyond their auspices.

It is important, therefore, for understanding democratization in East and Central Europe to clarify the state of civil society in the region. Our discussion will focus first on the diffusion of the idea of civil society. We hope to show that both the current decline of the civil society project, as well as the problematic formation of civil society itself are in fact unsurprising. They can be explained by the context in which the project was initially formulated and later transformed, and by the social, political and economic context in which civil society is actually shaped.

The first part of the chapter, then, traces the idea of civil society back to the opposition movements, identifying it as a concept specifically formulated for the struggle against the communist regimes although of course the tradition of western political theory in the genesis of the project is recognizable The second part of the chapter analyses the post-1989 period and explains the evolution of civil society movements as a result of the bifurcation of post-communist societies into their political and civil components.

We argue that the original conception of civil society in the region could not survive once the totalitarian context, the essential backdrop against which it was positioned, disappeared. We will also suggest that the civil society project, meaning a new and more moral form of politics (see, for example, Isaac 1996), paradoxically left such a negative legacy that it significantly undermined

77

the possibility of achieving the aims it had set for itself. This, together with the impact of international agencies and the legacy of an individualized and alienated society, has produced new democracies in the region in which the state and institutions take precedence over the citizenship organizations.

Civil society before 1989

In one form or the other, the notion of civil society had become the key ideological weapon of the Eastern European opposition movements by the late 1970s. While civil society itself, in the sense of a mass organized social sphere, remained weak on the whole (with the exception of Poland), civil society in the sense of a declared ideology and political programme gradually grew more and more powerful. The most outspoken theorists among the East European dissidents were Adam Michnik in Poland, Vaclav Havel in Czechoslovakia, and Janos Kis in Hungary.

Civil society became the *leitmotiv* of the various opposition movements and was given international validation through the network of international human rights organizations which sprung up in support of the anti-Communist movements. As a result, the notion of civil society became an articulated political theory of opposition to totalitarianism. It was envisaged primarily as a strategy of opposition against the communist regime; but it was also presented as a programme for a post-communist society, and possibly even a 'post-democratic' one.

In many ways, the vision of civil society built on classical western liberal theory and the traditions of the Enlightenment, preaching individual liberty, limits on state authority and accountability for governments, the inviolability of private life, and an emancipated public sphere, independent of the state and economy (see Geremek 1992). Yet it was also a conception that envisaged a more radical form of democratic political praxis, an alternative form of politics, which would extend beyond a set of standard liberal institutions. It was to be a form of politics that would nurture civic initiatives and self-management movements in order to offset the bureaucratic and consumerist tendencies inherent in modern liberal and market societies (see Arato 1993; Isaac 1996).

Clearly then, the concept of civil society as it was used within the political discourse of the opposition was multidimensional (see Jorgensen 1992). The crucial dimension was the critique of state power. Experience of suppression and underlying anti-totalitarian tendencies led many dissidents to conclude that East European states were to a large extent defined by their hostility toward organizations outside state control. Jacek Kuron (1990: 72), a key member of Solidarity, saw the Communist regimes as 'an attempt to command all social life'. The degree of state infringement was seen as having a negative effect on social dynamism. The state could rely only on coercive measures to motivate the citizenry into any kind of social project.

For those outside the state, the lack of inclusive mechanisms and the impermeability of official institutions meant that there was very little motivation toward a positive engagement with society. The general experience of East Europeans under Communism was atomization and a retreat into the private sphere. The fact that large sections of the population had no sectional or emotional attachment to the state thus suggested to the dissidents the possibility that an alternative sphere within society could draw support simply by virtue of its existence. In the words of one commentator, 'they seized on what they saw as (to paraphrase Lenin) the weak link of the Communist system' (Smolar 1996:26).

It therefore became possible to present civil society as an actor in competition with totalitarianism, and ultimately as its antithesis. Geremek (1992:4) articulated this conception clearly, writing that 'the idea of a civil society – even one that avoids overtly political activities in favour of education, the exchange of information and opinion, or the protection of the basic interests of the particular groups – has enormous anti-totalitarian potential'.

The role the dissidents envisaged for civil society was broad. Initially the role was almost exclusively social and it was argued that the various constituent organizations could develop support networks across society while at the same time defending society against injustices. It was also thought that this would set in motion a process of gradual encroachment into the territory of the state and its eventual enclosure by the 'parallel polis' of civil society. The peaceful evolution of an 'independent society' would thus hollow out the power of the state, usurp its role, and leave the Party as leaders in name only.

The autonomous associations which re-emerged in the 1970s were seen as the building blocks for a post-totalitarian society in that these organizations would help to reconstruct authentic social ties which had been damaged by communist social engineering and the state's permanent surveillance of society. For a few, it was even possible to envisage the organizational form of these associations as providing a social blue-print for a genuine democracy. Havel was the most prominent advocate of civil society as the essence of democracy itself, writing, 'are not these informed, non-bureaucratic, dynamic and open communities that comprise the "parallel polis" a kind of rudimentary prefiguration or symbolic model of those more meaningful "post-democratic" political structures that might become the foundation of a better society?' (Havel 1991: 213).

It is interesting to note that in some dissident literature of this period the critique of state power tends to blur the distinction between the private sphere and civil society which is central to civil society theory[2]. Kuron, for example, came close to denying the validity of distinguishing between private life and civil society when he argued (1990: 72) that the state's 'monopoly is so total that if citizens gather and discuss freely a matter as simple as roof repairs on a block of apartments, it becomes a challenge to the central authority'. Any social activity outside the state was interpreted as opposition to it. Any shared complaint, no matter how trivial or random, was viewed as a complaint about the nature of state control. Irrespective of the nature, size or political content of social organizations, the mere fact that they represented association outside the state was valued in itself. The fact of 'association' at any level was given primary importance over its political content (Foley and Edwards 1996). It even became possible to present the general retreat into family life as a 'conscious reaction of society in defence of its acquisitions' (Wojcicki 1991: 102).

The definition of civil society as the antithesis of totalitarianism and the zero-sum logic that saw all actions detrimental to the state as conscious attacks on state power combined to conflate civil society with opposition *per se*. As a result, the conception of civil society in most dissident writing was unclear and amorphous. Actions committed on an entirely personal level were reinterpreted as oppositional and appropriated into the sphere of civil society. In part, this conception was possible because the critique of the communist state expressed through the idea of civil society was accompanied by a fierce critique of power in general. There was a conscious downgrading of the importance of the political in the traditional sense, and emphasis was placed instead on moral categories and imperatives.

Within this critique was a vision of a new form of politics which, fused with the new morality, was thought to be capable of recognizing the needs of individual people. In place of any consideration of difference and sectional interest, universal and pre-political concepts were emphasized. Tischer (1984: 4,16) preached that 'authentic solidarity . . . is the solidarity of consciences' and that its virtue was derived from being 'an expression of human goodwill'. Humanity's innate awareness of the distinction between good and evil, the necessity of dignity and the importance of truth and living in truth are recurrent themes across dissident literature. Indirectly, this supplied a way of denying the legitimacy of a public realm under the communist system, although it created false expectations that democracy implied overcoming difference, rather than living with it.

'Politics' and traditional political terminology were conflated in the popular mind with the negative experiences of authoritarianism.[3] Thus, use of conventional terminology implicated the speaker in the illusion of a 'people's democracy', and effectively forced him or her into being a 'player in the game' (Havel 1991: 137). The rhetoric of morality offered dissenters the opportunity to oppose the state outside its chosen terms of debate, and allowed them to frame the demand for political rights in the context of a higher moral purpose. No one was a more outspoken proponent of what was termed 'anti-political politics' than Havel, who wrote:

> I favour "anti-political politics: that is, politics not as a technology of power and manipulation, of cybernetic rule over humans or as the art of the useful, but politics as one of the ways of seeking and achieving meaningful lives, of protecting them and serving them . . . anti-

political politics is possible. Politics "from below". Politics of people, not of the apparatus. Politics growing from the heart, not from a thesis.

(Havel 1988: 396–8)

Finally, as Smolar (1996) emphasizes, the concept of civil society served as a way of redefining 'us' and 'them'. This applied not only in the sense of authority – we the citizens and they the authorities – but also as an antithesis of the dominant ethnic concept of the nation which, in the eyes of many dissidents, threatened the very existence of East and Central European states. In other words, the civil society project also functioned as a way to place the rights of individuals above national rights and above the values of the ethnic community.

This use of civil society became particularly important after 1989 when the region was caught up in a resurgence of national conflicts. A number of former dissidents began to employ the notion of civil society in their anti-nationalist rhetoric (see Michnik 1996; Urban 1996). Havel argued that:

the greatness of European integration on domestic foundations consists in its capacity to overcome the old Herderian idea of the nation-state as the highest expression of national life . . .European integration should . . . enable all nationalities to realize their national autonomy within the framework of a broad civil society created by the supranational community'

(Havel 1997: 130)

The strategy for democratization of the dissidents, therefore, was to unlease the rich potential of automous social groups and give free rein to civil society. The impact of this approach was of course different from country to country. This, in turn, influenced not only the political thinking of the opposition, but also the way in which the communist regimes were dismantled (see Bernhard 1993). Some would even argue that it helped shape the situation of civil society after 1989 (see Frentzel-Zagorska 1990).

In Poland what Michnik formulated as 'new evolutionism' enjoyed, in comparative East European terms, an unprecedented success. It began with the foundation of the Worker's Defence Committee in the late 1970s, an independent organization to defend victims of repression by the state in the aftermath of a wave of strikes. It gradually inspired the creation of other organizations, such as the independent trade union Solidarity, which contested state policy and pressed the party-state for legal recognition. Such was the power of the massive working-class movement(s) that legal recognition came as early 1980, the year Solidarity was actually founded. The reconstitution of civil society in Poland was disrupted shortly after by the imposition of martial law in 1981, which made Solidarity illegal once more. However, owing to its strength, it was able to organize as an underground movement, effectively pressing the

81

state until it was legally recognized once again in 1988, this time with permission to enter the round table negotiations with the party-state and, ultimately, to legally contest the first (partially) free elections.

The important point here is that, unlike Hungary and Czechoslovakia, the emergence of a robust civil society in Poland largely preceded the formation of legal systemic structures in which it was later to operate. In both Hungary and Czechoslovakia, the institutional framework emerged first, created from above, and was then filled (or was supposed to be filled) with the emerging civil society. Nevertheless, there were important differences between these two countries.

In Hungary, the reformist wing of the Communist party played a critical role in the reconstitution of civil society in that it encouraged the formation of independent groups in order to acquire a partner in negotiating reform. The round table negotiations in the late 1980s set up the basic legal framework for societal organizations outside the control of the state. The process of rebuilding civil society, put in motion by the party leadership, began to bear fruit at about the same time. Nevertheless, these organizations were generally weak.

In Czechoslovakia, civil society remained the project of a very narrow circle of dissidents and was not taken up by any sector of the communist leadership. One of the most conservative minded in the region, the party held tightly onto power until 1989 when it was overthrown by a spontaneous popular insurgence. The proto-civil society – the mass movements of Civic Forum in the Czech area and the Public Against Violence in Slovakia – organized astonishingly quickly, started to negotiate with the communist party, and agreed to create the basic rules which were to guide the reconstitution of state-society relationships.

The process of resurrecting civil society was by no means uniform in East and Central Europe. Civil society's rule in the transition varied from couuntry to country and in two at least (Hungary and Czechoslovakia), it was certainly not the driving force behind democratization. Also, while there can be no doubt that the dissidents helped to popularize the idea of civil society and undermined the legitimacy of the communist monopoly on power, the transitions generally occurred as the Communist leadership across the region was softening its attitude towards the opposition. This change was stimulated, it should be noted, mainly by the external factors, especially the impact of Gorbachov's reforms and increasing international pressure.

In other words, democratization cannot be attributed to the strength of civil society in the region. It is worth considering, even for the case of Poland where organization outside the state predated the reform process, precisely what the debate on civil society contributed to social organizations in the post-Communist period. Equally, we should ask to what degree the claims of Hungarian, Czech and Slovak civil society to autonomy are now compromised, given that they were at least partly nurtured by the state in order to fill the vacuum in the reform process (see Ekiert and Kubik 1997a).

Civil society after 1989

It is clear, therefore, that civil society experienced difficulties in take-off in the post-communist years, despite the optimism expressed by the dissidents. What follows here is a tentative explanation of why this should have been. Of course, for those scholars who adhere to a minimalist and procedural understanding of democracy and stress the existence of structures and processes, the weakness of civil society presents no problem for democracy in East and Central Europe. But for those who understand democracy as more than procedures, institutions and rules, who stress the importance of participation in democracy, the active exercise of citizenship, and the expansion of the political realm to the wider public, the post-communist democracies in the region can at best be seen as half-way houses.

Similarly, there is debate and division over the significance of the increasingly consolidated parties and party systems in the region, the activity of trade union movements, and the existence of various consumer associations and environmental groups. It is unclear whether these signify the emergence of a civil society and a healthy system of democratic representation, or whether there is a lack of real participation in the post-communist structures and organizations. It has been suggested, for example, that there is a distinct lack of activity at the local level and that the input into decision-making processes of social movements and organizations is low. Grass roots activism is also patchy and weak (see, for example, Nelson 1996).

The official information on social organizations tends to mask this weakness. According to the available information, associational life appears to have mushroomed with the collapse of the communist regime. In Czechoslovakia, which had 306 legally registered interest associations in 1989, for example, this appears to be the case in both constituent republics of the former Federation.

Slovakia had 3,167 interest associations and 38 trade union and employers' associations in 1990; these had risen to 11,870 interest associations and 86 trade union and employers' associations by 1996 (Malova 1997). The boom in social organizations thus almost reached the peak of the inter-war period when 16,000 educational, sporting, religious and other associations were registered in Slovakia alone (see Butora et al. 1997). In the Czech Republic, there were 4,000 civil associations registered in 1990; this increased to over 32,000 by the end of 1994 (see Green and Skalnik-Leff 1997).

Similarly in Hungary, Miszlivetz (1997: 28) refers to the existence of 'statistically strong civil society'. He presents a overview of the historical development of nongovernmental organizations (foundations and associations), claiming that there were 14,365 in 1932, merely 100 at the peak of Stalinism in 1952, and 30,507 by 1992 after the fall of communism. Finally, Ekiert and Kubik (1997b:10) report that, by the end of 1994, 'civil society in Poland was comprised of 47,036 organizations, while before 1989 there were only several hundred large, centralized organizations'.

These are not unimpressive numbers and have been taken as an indication that the intermediary sphere is not as thin as some critics would like to depict it. They provide some evidence for suggesting that 'social capital' (Putnam 1993) is greater in the region than might be initally be expected in view of the legacy of communism. Putnam (1993) argued that the existence of (horizontal) networks of civil associations benefits democracy in that it socializes partici-pants into the norms of reciprocity and trust, thus fostering cooperation for mutual benefit. The denser the networks, the more 'social capital' is created, which in turn improves the performance of institutions and the economy.

However, civil society cannot simply be measured in terms of the number of associational organizations in existence and there are reasons to treat the high level of associational organizations with some scepticism. A large major-ity of the associations operate in the field of recreation, sporting activities or hobbies. For example, around 70 per cent of all interest associations in Slovakia are either sport or gardening clubs; leisure and sport also account for about 50 per cent of Hungarian NGOs. Many organizations have parental links with the now disintegrated giant organizational complexes from the communist period and, moreover, they tend to be heavily dependent on state finances. This would not necessarily be a problem if they had any real participation in political decision making or if they made any meaningful contribution to the process of democratization. But, as Miszlivietz argues:

> a larger problem is presented by the artificial nature or pseudo-existence of many of the registered NGOs. Statistics do not speak about the direct influence by political parties and official authorities in the civil sector. Parties often create their own foundations officially dedicated to . . . human rights, education, woman or environmental issues, with the purpose of extending their influence . . . There are also many registered NGOs unable to fulfil their tasks because of the lack of skills and poor organizational qualities.
>
> (Miszlivietz 1997: 29)

The rising number of civil society organizations, therefore, should not obscure the fact that many are heavily dependent on the state and have little capacity for autonomous action. This is chiefly the result of the strength of the state in the emerging East and Central European democracies, which is maintained by the nature of the emerging party systems. Parties in the region have tended to operate as exclusively high politics actors focused on governmental and state-building tasks, rather than as as actors with grass-roots and representational responsabilities (Kopecky 1995; Agh 1996; and Bielasiak 1997). Ironically, it is the (ex)communist parties which may have the greatest claim to operating as a channel of local democracy, largely due to their organizational inheritances. Furthermore, although a great deal of activity is unpenetrated and unregulated by the state, for example unlicensed networks of child-carers or black economy associations, the texture and density of these social links has always been thin. It is also arguable that a great deal of this unlicensed activity reflects social atomization rather than tight networks, something we return to below.

Civil society may actually have been much weaker in the region than the dissidents believed. It was an effective weapon in the struggle against the communist regime in that it offered a platform which united the opposition, but it offered little in terms of a coherent strategy for democratization. Whatever sense of social belonging, community and identity existed before 1989 was primarily predicated on opposition to communism, framing civil society as an essentially defensive entity. It is not surprising that, viewed as the antithesis of the state, the programme of civil society could not be put into effect and did not survive the demise of communism.

The monolithic conception of civil society simply as opposition was specific to a particular historical era. At that time, in comparison with the need to defeat an all-encompassing state, all other issues could be categorized as being of secondary importance. Sectional demands and partisan politics were avoided in order to present an image of total opposition. For example, as early as 1981 Michnik wrote of the danger that sectional pay demands represented to Solidarity's cohesion. This stance was facilitated by the universalist and pre-political language in which the civil society project was expressed, which stressed the moral aspect of opposition and the unity of those on the side of 'good' against 'evil'. This anti-political conception of civil society was portrayed as a sphere of activity superior to the 'political' realm in both social and moral terms.

In opposition it was possible to avoid hard decisions and to present this as a high-minded concentration on the central issue of opposing the state. However, the collapse of communism meant that, at a stroke, both the source of unity and the touchstone of moral legitimacy had been removed. It also meant that the terminology of traditional politics and the reality of conflicting political interests made a rude re-entry to the stage.

From very early on in the negotiation processes with the former communist leadership, economic, industrial and territorial questions were put on the agenda, and the language of 'moral civil society' was simply not suited to the business of haggling for sectional privileges. Social and ethnic differences triumphed almost immediately in the post-communist period, with the result that 'politics' became a question of resolving sets of differing interests rather than moral imperatives.

With the benefit of hindsight, it is even possible to argue that the general schema of civil society against the state was a misleading one. Many of the dissidents had contrived to conflate civil society with opposition in general by identifying civil society as the antithesis of totalitarianism. This was civil society at its most inclusive, with the personal sphere feeding directly into it. An analogy frequently used was to imagine resistance as an iceberg: the tip of dissident activity may have been the only opposition visible to observers, but it was in an energizing and co-dependent relationship with the submerged anti-state resentment of the population at large. This was undoubtedly an overly simplistic interpretation.

At the same time, it was a conception of civil society that encouraged the presumption of leadership on the part of a self-selected alternative elite made up of dissidents and civil society theorists. Their assumption of a moral right to lead society was further strengthened by their hostility towards those who claimed legitimacy by belonging to institutions, and their tendency to frame legitimacy in entirely moral terms. This allowed relatively small groups of intellectuals in Hungary and Czechoslovakia to believe that their organizations were as significant as a mass movement like Solidarity in Poland. It has even been suggested, rather more cynically, that dissidents championed civil society so ferociously in order to claim the legitimacy which only representative or mass organizations can achieve.

Following this argument, rather than a conflict between state and society, therefore, East and Central Europe witnessed a competition between rival elites in the communist period, with the opposition forced into the language of civil society by the needs of the time. Looking back on events, Smolar (1996: 27) writes 'civil society, it turned out, had been a historical costume; its usefulness disappeared with the times that dictated its wearing'. Certainly, civil society was used in the East and Central European region to express an elitist project, with a strong flavour of visionary imagination and wishful thinking. It is even possible that, once the incumbent communist elite had been removed, the commitment of the former opposition to civil society diminished. Among the population at large, the level of support for the alternative sphere of society was always more assumed than real, a fact painfully highlighted in the new era.

The new democratic era was characterized by a massive exodus of the dissident elite from civil society into the state. The people who once proclaimed themselves the representatives of the 'parallel polis' became the representatives of the state. The extent to which the former dissidents and civil society activists in East and Central Europe swept into power in the post-revolutionary days, assuming either high state functions or moving into the emerging capitalist business sector, was striking. To be sure, this meant that the state apparatus liberalized and that, therefore, civil society was no longer threatened by state intervention. The new post-commnuist states tried to lay down a legal basis for civil society and for protecting private life from state intervention. This meant drafting extensive Bills of Rights to put legal constraints on the state, and passing basic laws on associations to regulate associational activity.

However, as Dryzek (1996: 482) argues, 'if the impetus for democratization begins in oppositional civil society rather than in the state . . . a degree of exclusion is desirable if civil society and so democracy itself are to flourish'. Yet after making a commitment to preserving civil society from the state, many dissidents and champions of the project rapidly opted for a different personal course. Rather than remaining outside the state, they tended to try and colonize it: civil society appeared as a stepping stone to more lucrative careers within the state. One pessimistic observer argued that this has been sympto-matic of the behaviour of many former dissident intellectuals and civil society activists, who have appropriated the term 'civil society' to refer to their own activities and associations. These often have little to do with the emergence of a truly autonomous self-organization of society (see Lomax 1997).

As a result, the nascent civil societies in the region became and largely remain leaderless. Combined with their own organizational weaknesses, this represented a significant blow to their development. As it turned out, not every former civil society activist was successful in high politics. Many left politics soon after the transition or were forced out of the office. Yet it is intriguing that little is heard today about the former opposition leaders in relation to any kind of organized associational activity, particularly in projects that might activate social groups outside the major cities of the region. Those who stayed within the state and its institutions, such as Havel in the Czech Republic, Mazowiecki in Poland, or Carnogursky in Slovakia, in the best of cases lead the struggle for civil society from above. Those who left politics have tended to return to a kind of moral dissent, confined to relatively closed intellectual circles, and are unwilling to take any sustained action on behalf of society at large. In this respect, Whitehead's warning (1997) on the consequences of social unevenness in associational life is particularly appropriate: although the civil society argument is pursued, often vigorously, by intellectuals, their limited sphere of action means that their impact is small.

It is therefore clear that civil society organizations still need to challenge the state in order to carve out better institutional-legal conditions for themselves, in spite of the improvements brought by the initial reforms. However, some of the difficulties with developing strong and automous civil societes in the region are rooted in their very lack of institutionalization. This is at least partly the consequence of the anti-political attitudes of the former anti-communist oppo-sition outlined above. In the immediate aftermath of the revolutions, and very much in line with their conception of anti-political politics, civil society activists expressed profound scepticism about traditional institutions and insti-tutional politics, including political parties and partisanship. It was assumed that society at large was equally sceptical of the public realm. Michnik's comment that 'to the vast majority of Poles, "Right" and "Left" are abstract dimensions from another epoch' (see Ash 1986: 45–52) seemed as appropriate to the new era as to the previous one.

As a result there was an urge to experiment and find the new forms of 'post-democratic' political organization and representation that had previously only existed in dissident texts. Amorphous mass movements were to be encouraged instead of political parties and pressure groups, and their organizers and founders strove to preserve their unity and apolitical nature. Even as the reform process unleashed conflicting demands, and the language of moral civil society was reaching its limits, there was a reluctance to make the institutional changes necessary to accommodate the new systems.

There was a tactical element to this: it was hoped that the organic unity that had helped to overthrow the old regime could be maintained in order to establish the legitimacy of the new one. However, the result was that the early pluralization of political life was to some extent put on hold in the name of organic unity which, perhaps ironically, backfired against some of the civil society activists. The experience of Civic Forum in Czechoslovakia provides a useful example. Attempting to maintain its organizational autonomy, the organization created a dual identity as both a political party and an independent mass movement. In order to do this, some of the leaders initially refused to centralize their party structure, making it impossible to impose any discipline and system of accountability and, in turn, creating a fissure between the central leadership in Prague and activists in the rest of the country. As a result, serious questions were raised over the competence of the dissident elite to lead the new state. Disgruntled dissidents within Civic Forum watched in dismay (and disarray) as new liberal radicals and technocrats led by Klaus seized power within the organization, transformed it into a centralized political party and, in the process, largely discredited the whole project of civil society. The law on non-profit organizations saw the light only in 1995, by which time Klaus' dominance had begun to wither, and a sustained campaign from both international and domestic NGOs began to make an impact upon the political establishment.

It seems, therefore, that the dissident fetishization of autonomous organizations was partly responsible for a number of problems in post-commmnuist East and Central Europe. Civil society was always conceived of in abstract terms. Despite Havel's conviction that that these organizations would operate as a 'rudimentary prefiguration' of a better society, this proved impossible to translate into reality. There was little to explain the exact dynamic between civil society organizations and the state; instead the trend was to decide upon a social goal and then assume an automatic link with 'civil society'. This was a result of the ambiguity which was felt towards political society in general and the state in particular. By concentrating upon autonomous networks of organizations the dissidents sought to avoid the social fragmentation which they associated with pluralist democracy. In so doing, they failed to recognize the importance of traditional institutional politics and lost the opportunity to create new rules in the post-communist period which might have strengthened the foundations of civil society itself. It is certainly more difficult to encourage major institutional changes now that ideological differences and conflict have become embedded in post-communist politics.

Clearly, though, not all the responsability for the weaknesses of civil society in the region lies with the errors of former dissidents and intellectual leaders nor even with the weak institutional foundations for the civil society project. There were alsoproblems at the mass level. Neither leadership nor established institutional frameworks are a substitute for a long standing traditions of autonomous collective action, which are largely absent in East and Central Europe. Generally weak under communism, autonomous social organizations went on to suffer major set backs as a result of the upheavals of transition. This has produced societies reluctant to engage in autonomous social activity.

Communist regimes taught people to enclose themselves in their private world as a way of rejecting the forced mobilization and participation of the time. They produced highly individualized and cynical societies, linked together only by the family relationships and close friendship, kinship ties, or black market relations, all of which were formed as a defence against the regime and its production inefficiencies. This, in essence, is Smolar's argument (1996: 37): 'civil society is being created in an unfavourable atmosphere of economic recession, withdrawal from public affairs, egotistic individualism, mistrust, and lack of legal culture. It is arising from expressions of autonomy that often are far removed from civility'

Paradoxically, contemporary East and Central European societies may now look even more atomized than before, for the old mentality of shadow society and public withdrawal have combined with the uncertainties and dislocations of post-communism. It is hoped that the liberal economic reforms, pursued vigorously in the region with the help of international financial institutions, may create conditions more favourable to the emergence of civil society. Private property, it is suggested, and greater liberties in the economic sphere will raise standards of living, thereby creating new middle classes and an affluent citizenry, who in turn will be more capable and willing to pursue their views and interests in the form of collective action. The reforms have indeed started to change social relations in the region and, in the long-term, they might prove conducive to such civil society developments. Nevertheless, the reforms have also introduced inequality into societies previously accustomed to egalitarianism, disturbed people's traditional roles and positions, and generated painful social and economic dislocations.

Although there is relatively little to prevent citizens from forming associative networks and publicly expressing their concerns, the flight to the private sphere and/or the re-inforcement of strong ethnic solidarities have been the most common response of people facing the chaos of the transformation. This is particularly the case for those (large) sectors of the population which have so far received no benefits from the emerging market structure. The middle class is thin and has been unable and unwilling to halt the tide to privatism because their concern is to penetrate political society or protect their own limited sectional interests through business and professional associations.

Conclusion: the role of the international community

The civil society project, or democratization through strengthening autonomous social organizations in East and Central Europe has enormous obstacles to overcome in the future. The expected resurgence of civil society faded rapidly in the aftermath of Communism and it became clear that East and Central European theorists of civil society had over-estimated its strength in the region. Their assumption that the civil society project had generated mass support was the result of equating opposition to communism with support for their project. As a result, the immediate period of post-communist flux came as a rude awakening. The hoped-for strong and dense intermediary sphere of organizations has so far failed to take root in East and Central European societies despite strong statistical indications to the contrary. As a result of a combination of cultural, socioeconomic and historical legacies, the conditions for building civil societies in the region remain structurally weak.

Nevertheless, a number of analysts have asserted the importance of social networks in strengthening democracy in the region. Attention is now being paid to the need to involve an alienated public in politics at the local and national level, to curb the corruption and clientelism increasing prevalent within business and political society, and to improve the current legal regulatory structure of state-society relations. In a general sense, this is partly because the recent literature on democratization has recognized that the establishment and consolidation of democracy requires more than an act of will and a set of particular governing institutions.

However, attempts to rebuild civil society cannot be based on the overly moralistic, idealistic and anti-institutional positions typical of the early 1990s. Intellectuals and newly emergent social groups must accept a positive engagement with associational *and* political life. Equally, for democratic consolidation to proceed, civil society should be understood as a complement to normal institutional politics, not as a replacement or as moral superior. It is also important that the strong state does not absorp or reduce the autonomy of what remains a fragmented and weak social sphere.

The international community has recently tried to carve out a role for itself in terms of supporting democratic consolidation through strengthening the intermediary sphere. International assistance is currently committed to developing a number of strategies for strengthening civil society in the region. If we assume that building new institutions of civil society requires leadership, skills and funds, then it follows that international support might have an important role to play.

Post-communist countries became recipients of western assistance almost in the same space of time as the Berlin Wall fell and, perhaps surprisingly, a large number of international organizations participated in efforts to promote democracy and markets. With the end of the bipolar international system, both supranational and national organizations have incorporated the goal of promoting democracy explicitly into their agendas. Financial assistance and integration into western institutions became politically conditional on adopting at least minimal procedural standards of democracy and basic human and minority rights. Although the precise application of these broad criteria turned out to be problematic in practice (as Slovakia, for example, learned through its exclusion from the first wave of accession to the EU), political conditionality has now set parameters for linking domestic political contexts to to international assistance.

Until recently, western assistance to the new democracies in the region has been ambigous in terms of its impact on civil society development. Quigley's (1997) pioneering study on democratic assistance in East and Central Europe provides a great deal of evidence about how Western European, North American and Japanese foundations responded to the changes in the region. The focus of international help has, by and large, been on re-building the institutions of the state, reforming bureaucracies, training parliamentarians, supporting political parties, and promoting markets. Less effort and money have been spent on promoting local democracy and horizontal links between associations and independent groups. Rose (1994: 29) argues that 'the West will probably need to shift more of its attention to small-scale institutions that resemble face-to-face primary groups or extended friendship networks'. Quigley's (1997) work indicaties that, although there has been some support for small-scale grass-roots projects such as *Atonomia* in Hungary, a critical mass of support from private foundations, large financial institutions and bilateral assistance programs has been directed towards supporting economic reforms. Only very recently have there been signs of a more concerted shift towards funding and assisting NGOs and civil society.

Of course, given the weakness of post-communist states, institutions and political society, the attention that the international community has paid to institution-building is understandable, Democratic consolidation *is* problematic without a functioning political society (Linz and Stepan 1996). But it would now make sense for international agencies to contribute towards strengthening the organizational capacity at the grass roots level of society and encouraging the participation of the emerging middle classes as a step towards democratic consolidation.

Notes

1 The exchange between the ex-Premier Vaclav Klaus and President Vaclav Havel in the Czech Republic is perhaps the best known example of this debate. Klaus, echoing the well-known arguments of Mancur Olson, equates civil society with the rise of new bureaucracies and particularistic (as opposed to general and aggregated) interests, and a threat to the smooth functioning of modern states and markets. Havel, on the other hand, believes in the positive effects of associational life in general, defending civil society as a means to strengthen people's participation in government. See Havel, Klaus and Pithart (1996).

2 The most widely shared definition, and the one which we also adopt here, conceives of civil society as an intermediary entity between the state and the social or private sphere, excluding individual and family life, business firms and profit making enterprises (Diamond 1994). See Linz and Stepan (1996), who distinguish between *civil society*, business (*economic society*) and political activities and organizations aiming to take control of the stae (*political society*).

3 The frequently cited piece of Polish graffiti Give us Democracy, not Politics reflects these sentiments very well.

6

INTERNATIONAL POLICIES TO PROMOTE AFRICAN DEMOCRATIZATION

Oda van Cranenburgh

Since the collapse of the Soviet Union and the end of the bipolar world system, virtually all western governments have incorporated the goal of promoting democracy into their policies toward developing countries. Multilateral institutions such as the United Nations (UN) and the Euorpean Union (EU) also began to support democratization and established new policy units to support it in developing and post-Communist countries. New policy instruments have been designed and country studies analyzing the state of democracy are regularly commissioned for international and governmental bodies across Europe. New research institutes have emerged dedicated to the promotion of democracy and non-governmental organizations (NGOs) aimed at furthering democracy are mushrooming; existing NGOs add the issue to their mission. At first glance, then, idealists might think that we have entered a new area in which the international community is united in pursuing lofty and shared goals, all of them contributing to the welfare of people in the so-called 'Third World'.

However, some pressing questions need to be asked which may disturb those idealists. Specifically, what kind of intended and unintended effects can we expect from policies to promote democracy in developing countries? What are the assumptions about democracy, implicit and explicit, that constitute the basis for these policies? Do donor governments take sufficiently into account the context into which they are attempting to promote democracy? And to what extent can democracy be influenced from outside?

While some policy makers are realistic and pragmatic in pursuing the goal of democracy, others appear to assume that democracy can be engineered mechanically from outside, and operate as if creating democracy merely requires implementing a 'tool box' of policies. The new industry of consultants and think tanks on democratization tackle the issue in a variety of different ways and there are few attempts to deal with it in a systematic fashion.

Meanwhile a range of normative judgements by European donor governments about the 'right' way to promote democracy abound. Few of these analyses and judgements make much distinction between the different kinds of policy measures aimed at the promotion of democracy.

This chapter therefore offers an analysis of the various kinds of donor policies which have been pursued with regard to African democratization and pays particular attention to the policies which the Dutch government has put in place. I will analyse the extent to which the different kinds of policy interventions work as they were designed to, and point to the unintended consequences and constraints which result from trying to implement them in Africa. An assessment of the policy instruments that have been deployed leads to the conclusion that, in view of their likely effects, policy makers urgently need to examine more explicitly the assumptions underlying their policies to promote democracy. In particular, policy goals should be more clearly specified and it should be recognized that the possibilities for rapid and immediate democratization, in Africa at least, are limited by a number of constraints. The analysis will also show that the policy instruments themselves need to be refined.[1]

International factors in democratization

Democratization processes are first and foremost the result of complex pressures and developments internal to countries. Nevertheless international factors have also received attention recently, especially in comparative studies of democratization. Redemocratization in Latin America during the 1980s was analyzed chiefly in terms of domestic factors such as elite pacts, but international factors such as defeat in war and the human rights policies of the US were also identified as significant (O'Donnell et al. 1986). Since 1990, weight has increasingly been attached to international factors.

Diamond et al. (1990: 31–4) attempt to identify systematically how international factors such as colonial rule, cultural diffusion and demonstration effects from abroad affect democratization. They argue that the most direct form of international impact occurs when democracy is imposed by foreign powers after a military victory, but they also identify an important role for international economic factors. Huntington (1991) examined five factors in the 'third wave' of democratization, all of which, to varying degrees, have an international dimension: the unprecedented economic growth of the 1960s; legitimacy problems linked to declining performance during the 1970s; doctrinal and policy transformation on the part of the Vatican and a new social and political role for national churches; changes in the policies of international actors, including Carter's human rights policies, the new interest of the EU in human rights, linked in part to Gorbachov's policy changes in the late 1980s; and, finally, snow-balling or diffusion effects.

93

In a general sense, international policies to promote democracy have also evolved in the context of an important shift in thinking within the global development community since the early 1980s. There is growing agreement about the relative importance of political factors in development. In this sense, the World Bank Report of 1981 marked a turning point when it identified failures of policy as a fundamental factor explaining the economic crisis in Africa. This marked the beginning of a trend for international donors to pay explicit attention to political and administrative aspects of development. Some eight years later, the World Bank defined the issue specifically as a problem of 'governance' (World Bank 1989). At first its concern was mainly with matters of 'good administration', largely conceived in a technical sense. Only later, was an important role in the debate on 'good governance' ascribed to issues such as transparency and accountability in government, suggesting a movement to broader political issues including democracy.

The current generation of international policies to promote democratization must be examined in particular in the context of an earlier concern for human rights, from which in some senses they flow. In terms of governmental interest in human rights, in the US at least, these policies date from the Carter administration in the 1970s. While there remains some disagreement as to the sincerity and consistency of the new human rights emphasis on the part of powerful countries such as the US, human rights have gained an increasing place in US foreign policies. Even in the 1970s, shaping western foreign policies to promote democracy was not completely without precedent. During the Cold War, the US incorporated democracy promotion as an explicit goal of its foreign policy towards a number of Third World states and the policy was given a legal basis in the Foreign Assistance Act of 1961. Pursued by different administrations in different ways, it gained most momentum with the creation of the National Endowment for Democracy in the early 1980s. At this time, however, the US was frequently criticized for using these policies and its international resources in its ideological and strategic struggle against the Eastern bloc. It was only after the collapse of the Soviet Union that they began to lose their heavy ideological connotation.

In terms of the literature on African democratization, international factors have featured prominently since 1989. Weight has been attached in varying degrees to the diffusion effects emanating out of Eastern Europe and subsequently from neighbouring countries on the African continent. Some studies have also explored the link between democratization and global economic policies of structural adjustment (Chazan *et al.* 1992: 315–16; Healey and Robinson 1992: 113–21). The policies of economic liberalization which have been assiduously promoted by international financial institutions through the 1980s have been perceived either as complementary to democratization or as a process undermining it. Pinkney (1992: 116) argues that in so far as economic and political liberalization *are* complementary, the link is in the attitudes of governments upon which African regimes are dependent. In other words, there is no necessary correlation between market liberalization and the introduction of democracy. Instead, heavily aid-dependent African countries find themselves directly confronted with the policies of bilateral donor governements, which increasingly link the giving of aid to the adoption of policies of democratization. The introduction of policies of democratization thus flow out of the economic and political dependence of African states.

The current policy consensus about the desirability of democracy must be seen in the context of a general convergence around the importance of African countries adopting a liberal macro-economic policy framework. International financial institutions press governments to adopt policies of economic adjustment. The current concern with political issues is then coupled with a consensus around the necessity of policies of economic liberalization and structural adjustment.

Such are the pressures from international financial institutions and donor governments in Africa that the capacity of states to conduct or design economic policies with any real autonomy has been almost completely eroded (see Healey and Robinson 1992: 91). Thus the global consensus about the importance of spreading democracy, conceptualized as a system to ensure that policies reflect the preferences of citizens (Dahl 1971), comes at a time when the room to manoeuvre for domestic policy makers in Africa has been considerably narrowed. This paradox, which of course undermines the chances for democracy at the national level, remains unresolved because the kind of democratic reforms undertaken in Africa today do not touch the policy making process itself. Instead, they are simply focused on the introduction of multi-party elections.

Policies to promote democracy in the 1990s

In Europe, explicit policies to promote democracy in developing countries were introduced in the wake of the collapse of the Soviet Union and the break-up of the bipolar world system. The strategic necessity for western European states to support 'friendly' authoritarian governments disappeared. France, for example, adopted policies to support democratization from the summer of 1990, and they were laid down by former President Mitterand's La Baulle speech.

Most European countries still lack a legal basis for their pro-democracy policies. However, the EU incorporated an explicit clause linking development aid to human rights and democracy in the Maastricht Treaty of 1991. The Fourth Lomé convention had already set a precedent in 1989 with the introduction of the clause allowing for the suspension of aid if human rights were violated in aid-recipient countries. In 1990, the Dutch government adopted policies linking aid to democracy in a government paper entitled A World of Difference which introduced the idea of a 'positive linkage strategy', aimed at supporting democratization processes.

In the years following, concrete measures were taken to support democratization processes. Emergency aid and human rights funds, for example, were provided for elections in regimes deemed to be in transition to democracy. Election observers were sent to countries undergoing so-called 'first-generation' elections. NGOs received increasing funds to engage in civic education or democratic promotion policies in developing countries. Media projects also received funding. Some political parties had been supporting 'sister' parties in Eastern Europe since 1989, although there was no general government programme aimed at assisting the creation of a multi-party system in aid-recipient countries in the Netherlands until 1992 when a programme to support political parties in South Africa was established. This channelled government funds through an all-party foundation to all South African political parties on a roughly proportional basis. The programme was favourably evaluated in 1996 and is being tentatively expanded to some other African countries.

As with human rights policies, it is useful to distinguish between negative and positive linkage policies which couple aid with democracy (see De Feyter *et al.* 1995; van Cranenburgh 1995). *Negative linkage*, or conditionality, implies that the volume or nature of the overall aid programme is dependent on performance with respect to human rights and democratization. It adds political conditions to previously established forms of economic conditionality which made economic aid dependent on the implementation of certain macro-economic policies. The new political conditionality of aid resembles in effect the 'the carrot and stick' approach. Aid allocation can be increased as a reward for progress in democratization. Conversely if the performance of the recipient country is judged to be deteriorating, aid can be suspended or the direction of policies (and aid) may be changed: for example, governments may switch to supporting projects directed at specific target groups or they may choose to channel aid through NGOs rather than through governments.

Positive linkage, on the other hand, means trying to further democratization itself without making aid specifically dependent upon the introduction of sets of changes. It does not link economic aid to democratization directly but aims to establish programmes to strengthen (the prospects for) democracy in the recipient country. The following types of policies typically constitute the positive linkage approach.

1   *Electoral assistance: financial and technical assistance to governments that have announced the introduction of multi-party elections.* Developing countries in transition to democracy often lack the funds and expertise to organize elections and external support is therefore useful. Electoral assistance from outside comes in many different forms and through different channels. As well as bilateral donor governments, multilateral institutions and international NGOs provide electoral assistance. The UN created the Division for Electoral Assistance in 1992, for example, and in 1994 a new public-private initiative resulted in the creation of the Institute for Democracy and Electoral Assistance located in Stockholm. Apart from multiateral and third sector organizations, there are also a myriad of private foundations of different ideological persuasions engaged in electoral assistance.

2 *Election observation and monitoring.* In order to prevent electoral abuse and corruption and to create confidence in the electoral process (in particular with the emerging opposition) international observers are sent to countries experiencing 'first generation' elections to assess whether they are free and fair. Representatives from governments implementing aid policies in the country, international organizations and NGOs are typically engaged in election observation.

3 *Support for voter education programnmes.* This is either carried out by national electoral commissions or by local or international NGOs. In recognition of the often high levels of illiteracy and the lack of experience with multi-party elections among the citizenry, donors wish to support programmes to educate citizens about their rights and duties in elections.

4 *Support for human rights groups and other NGOs aiming to strengthen democracy.* The idea behind these policies is that, ultimately, democracy depends on the development of civil society. Hence it is important to create counter-vailing organizations in society to balance the powers of the state .

5 *Support for the media.* Democracy, it is argued, can only flourish where a free and pluralistic press is present. In many developing and ex-authoritarian countries where one-party rule has been dominant, a free press has obviously been lacking. Support is therefore directed at establishing new initiatives to create a pluralistic media.

6 *Support for political parties.* Emerging opposition parties, often weak, new and inexperienced, frequently have problems making the transition from clandestinity and illegality. They may lack resources and have little experience in developing policy platforms. Donor governments and sister parties channel funds in a variety of ways to emerging political parties in transition countries. In the US, the party-linked foundations the National Democratic Institute (NDI) and the National Republican Institute (NRI) have long been involved in funding political parties; in Germany, party-linked foundations have supported sister parties in developing countries for decades; in the UK, the Westminster Foundation, representing all British political parties on its board, channels funds to parties in developing countries (see Carothers 1996; De Feyter *et al.* 1995).

Assessment of policies for democratization

The policies outlined above appear initially to be wide-ranging, but in fact almost all converge strongly around supporting the introduction of multi-party elections. The majority of western programmes to promote democracy in Africa involve basically electoral assistance and election observation. Support for voter education tends to be directly related to elections in practice and channelling funds to political parties stem from the belief that they are the central actors in elections and democratic politics. Implicit in this approach is a concept of democracy which places the holding of multi-party elections at the centre. This is a consequence of what has been called the 'minimal approach' (Huntington 1991) to democratization in the political science literature.

A strong emphasis on 'electoral democracy' brings with it several problems, however. First, while it is true that electoral democracy does at least give citizens the power to remove their leadership, there is often less political change than might be expected. The new politicians coming into office hardly ever transform the basis of local and national politics. They remain essentially reliant on personalistic and clientelistic mechanisms of internal control within their parties and their relationship with the electorate tends simply to reproduce that of the outgoing regime.

Second, in cases where respect for the rule of law and protection of civil rights are not guaranteed before the elections are held, elections may actually contribute to violence and violations of human rights. For example, the aid-recipient regime of Kenya was pressurized to hold elections during 1991–2, a time when the leadership was clearly bent on obstructing free competition and the general pre-conditions for fair and free elections, such as respect for human rights, were lacking (Geisler 1993).

Third, the emphasis on elections at all costs and as soon as possible is coupled with a relative neglect of issues related to the policy making process. The state remains untouched and unreformed with the introduction of 'democratization' policies. African parliaments in practice are not much involved in policy making and have little authority over the executive, while the role of interest groups throughout Africa is minimal. The political reforms which aid-recipient governments have to introduce as part of democratization hardly address the policy making process and contain few measures to force governments to consult interest groups from broader society (see Healey and Robinson 1992:89–90).

Most European institutions involved in the promotion of democracy in developing countries appear to be aware of these issues. The Dutch Ministry of Foreign Affairs, for example, recognized in the Budget memorandum for 1997 the limitations of elections as a strategy for achieving and consolidating democracy. However, this recognition does not seem to have resulted in any fundamental re-assessment of the effects, possibilities and constraints of operational policies, which still converge around the introduction and practice of multi-party elections, however flawed they are seen to be. Partly this is because there is a general assumption that these policies are good in themselves, even if they are not sufficient, or certainly that they can do no harm. Donor governments have a tendency to take at face value political reforms and processes which, on the surface, appear to introduce democracy in the European mould. Western governments and NGOs tend to see what they want to see in Africa, and to imagine that politics everywhere operates in the same way. They therefore assume that certain characteristics such as the introduction of multi-party competition actually reflect a process of democratization.

However, research in several African countries has revealed that the impact of electoralist policies is by no means unambiguously positive and that they do not necessarily produce the effects that are intended. Formal reforms mask substantive continuity in African politics. In some countries opposition parties have gained power as a result of elections but have continued to rule the country in the style of the former one-party regime (e.g. in Zambia after 1992). In other cases, the ruling party remained in power without much change in either leadership or policies (e.g. in Kenya after 1992). In Tanzania, formal political reforms centered around multi-party elections mask substantive continuity in the country's politics and have served to consolidate a dominant party's position (van Cranenburgh 1996). Clientelism and localism flourish as before, and corruption thrives. In some cases, political reforms have actually made things worse. Elections have stirred ethnic or religious rivalries in Kenya, and the Tanzanian elections of 1995 correlated directly with increases in human rights violations in Zanzibar.

In view of the context in which multi-party elections are being introduced in African countries, then, an emphasis on elections seems bound to produce limited and sometimes even harmful effects for democratization. Such policies implicitly rely on a 'minimalist approach' to democracy, equating it with regularly held multi-party elections. In fact, even those political scientists who adhere to a minimalist approach to democracy (Huntington 1991 for example) argue that there are some fundamental conditions which must be present for elections to be free and fair. These include, centrally, respect for civil and political rights. More broadly, democracy has to be embedded in a system where the rule of law prevails, and separation of powers or some checks and balances are guaranteed.

In many African countries currently adopting multi-party politics these pre-conditions in the field of human rights and the rule of law are not present. Elections in this context inevitably become instruments for manipulation by the state. They often provoke repression resulting in violation of civil rights, not only on the part of the ruling party but in many cases also by opposition parties. A political culture of tolerance is frequently lacking and parties often claim a specific territory as their exclusive domain. Thus it is not surprising that elections frequently produce results which are at odds with fundamental western democratic values.

Consequently, the first and most widely used instrument to promote democracy, financial or technical support for elections, must be viewed with some reservations about its actual impact on democratization. Financial support for elections when the fundamental pre-conditions for free and fair elections are not present is clearly counterproductive. Western governments and international agencies therefore need to make a careful assessment of when to support elections and when to refrain from doing so. In practice however, few governments engage in any systematic preliminary pre-election assessment as to whether the essential pre-conditions are in place before they offer electoral support.

Some western governments are even caught in the spell of experiments in 'African democracy' in the form of a no-party system (Uganda's 'movement system') or 'ethnic democracy' (Ethiopia). Few look systematically at whether, given the absence or predominantly ethnic definition of parties, the elections offer a real opportunity for the opposition. The decision to support elections appears to be influenced by broader political and diplomatic concerns, or even by the fact that governments have previously expressed approval of a particular country's macro-economic policies. These issues appear to take precedence over a serious assessment of the relationship betwen the elections and democracy and to determine whether the electoral process should be supported.

As a result, western governments are finding themselves supporting elections which are far below the minimum standards of 'free and fair'. Sending international observers to witness the elections, a policy which has been adopted as an additional guarantee, does not solve the problem. The ability of international observers to assess whether the elections meet international norms is compromised by several inter-related factors. First, they are present for only a small part of the electoral cycle. Despite recent attempts to achieve a better coverage of the electoral process, most governments send full-scale observation teams only around polling day. Second, the observers lack a clear mandate for action and have no clear criteria for judging the process. Third, partly because of the absence of criteria, there is a tendency for observer reports to be generally positive, whatever actually happens. Political and diplomatic concerns enter in the process of making a judgement on elections and observers tend not to want to rock the boat. Moreover, they are not able to address wider institutional and cultural factors. These are judged to be outside the scope of election monitoring, although in practice they are the most influential factors shaping the conduct and outcome of the electoral process.

One institutional issue of particular concern in Africa is the electoral system which many ex-British colonies inherited from their former rulers. Former British, and indeed some former French colonies, use majoritarian election systems based on the single member district system. This strengthens the strong localist tendency of African political parties and reinforces a 'winner take all' mentality in the political system. The allocation of seats in parliament concentrates power in the hands of larger parties. Parties appealing to ethnic groups concentrated in a specific region tend to capture the seats within the region. Where ethnic groups are concentrated regionally, the electoral system results in the coexistence of a series of regional 'one-party systems' (in Kenya and Malawi for example). If regions contain minority groups, they almost inevitably have difficulty in obtaining representation. Minority representation depends on whether they are geographically concentrated in particular electoral districts. Drawing the electoral boundaries therefore becomes a weapon in the elections, but it remains outside the attention of international election observers.

Lijphart (1977) warned that in the context of heterogeneous, and divided societies, majoritarian electoral system can actually undermine national stability.[2] Apart from instability, however, it can also generate two other possibilities, neither of which is conducive to democratization. In some African countries emerging from one party rule, a majoritarian electoral system is likely to result in a *de facto* one-party-dominant party-system which allows opposition parties only a marginal role in the political system; alternatively, it might result in the country being divided into regional one-party systems, making national government difficult and marginalizing minorities.

Given this context, the idea of supporting African political parties presents a number of complications. It needs to be acknowledged that African political parties are not like their western counterparts. They are primarily based on primordial ties such as ethnicity or locality and they tend to lack a clear policy platform or ideological orientation. Thus it is difficult for western parties to identify African parties as 'natural partners'. Relying primarily on personalistic and clientelist ties they lack linkages to specific societal interest groups, and are incapable of articulating and aggregating interests, a function normally ascribed to political parties in western countries. In fact, African parties appear more like 'political machines', vehicles to mobilize votes in return for specific benefits. The 'bosses', while nominally committed to protecting clients, are primarily interested in furthering their personal power. In this context, it is highly questionable whether supporting political parties is an effective way to promote democracy. Western political parties, donor governments may well become enmeshed in political processes revolving around factionalism and power politics rather than democratization.

Some African countries pose even more fundamental problems for western actors wishing to support democratization from outside. All western policies presume the existence of a viable central state. In some African countries, this is a mistaken assumption. In the former Zaire, for example, the state was a fictive entity before armed rebellion against Mobutu began. The basic infrastructure and services associated with any state were absent, civil servants and army personnel went unpaid, and loyalty to the leadership claiming to represent the state was meaningless. Yet the international community was pressing for multi-party elections in 1997, a process which at that stage was almost certainly bound to consolidate the authoritarian though ineffective rule of President Mobutu. The removal of Mobutu from office has not necessarily strengthened the chances for democratization because the problems besetting the country lie in the operation of the state itself, not in who is formally running it.

Although few states have collapsed to the same extent as Zaire, Chazan *et al.* (1992) describe the general picture in the region as one of 'silent crisis' which chips away at state power from below. Populations have found survival strategies which imply circumventing the state through informal or illegal markets, local associations or religion. Democratic reforms have been introduced in the context of a decaying state power, exacerbated by the financial crisis forcing governments to dismantle the basic infrastructure of the state and the most essential social services. These policies of retrenchment have removed any basis for loyalty to the state. At the same time, three decades of independence have failed to create a sense of nationhood. Instead ethnic or religious groups emerge on the political scene, and politicians mobilize their constituencies around these social divisions. Politics thus becomes a zero-sum game and the general societal conditions necessary to make even formal democracy work are largely absent in African countries.

Going beyond a minimal approach to democracy, a more substantive or material approach to democracy centres around the question why competition is meaningful to citizens at all; what kind of choices are offered to citizens by the democratic system? As well as many procedural requirements for 'polyarchy', Dahl (1971) included the requirement that policy must depend on the preferences of citizens. In other words, along with extending participation to all citizens, democracy requires a substantial degree of liberalization: the opportunity to conduct opposition. Conditions allowing this are frequently absent. Moreover, most African political parties have neither a policy programme nor the capacity to formulate one, and, since they tend to be factions around a single individual, they lack linkages to civil associations. African parties are loose networks based on patronage and, often, corruption. Financial support from abroad to parties in these circumstances can hardly contribute to democratization. Also absent are other institutional mechanisms, such as advisory structures, which would allow the preferences of citizens to play a larger role in the policy process.

Even where interest groups exist, governments do not consult with them on any regular basis (Healey and Robinson 1992). In many African countries organized interest groups are so weak that they cannot force their way into politics. Where associations do flourish, they are characterized by localism and frequently operate in isolation from the state, not as a forum for engagement with it. As Ake (1991) has argued, they do not form the building blocks for democracy. For that reason, many authors speak of the weakness of African civil societies.

Neither do the mushrooming NGOs in Africa, which are heavily supported by foreign donors, necessarily function as agents of democratization (Fowler 1993). Some of them are internally undemocratic, led by personalistic leaders, and without any clear local constituency; moreover, they are forced to be responsive to financial donors' demands rather than to local constituents. The idea that supporting NGOs helps to strengthen civil society cannot be taken as the key to democratization in Africa.

While the influence of domestic interest groups is generally weak in African politics, the role of bilateral and multilateral donors in national policy making is great. Instead of policies emerging out of the interaction of politicians with organized domestic interests, they tend to result from the interaction of the national elite with international actors representing donors. National elites do ensure a minimal base of domestic support, but this is done primarily through patronage.[3] Thus national politicians act as brokers between international financial institutions and donor governments on the one hand, and local patrons upon whom their domestic power base rests on the other. Personalist and clientelist politics form one of the most important and omnipresent constraints on democracy in Africa.

Conclusion

As should be evident from the arguments presented above, multi-party elections in the context of weak or failing states, in the absence of the rule of law or respect for human rights, and with a relatively weak civic community and civil society, are unlikely to be able to generate substantial progress toward democracy. Democratization policies revolving around multiparty elections are misdirected because they assume that formal reforms reflecting western democratic institutions will produce democracy in the African context. The western experience was coupled with the development of a relatively strong central state, the rule of law and gradual developments toward the protection of civil rights. In that context, political parties came to act as a linkage mechanism between civil society and the state. Multi-party elections represented a significant step towards democracy due to these broader developments.

The implications of this perspective for policies to promote democracy is that governments need to engage more deeply with the *context* in which democratization takes place and policy goals must be made more specific. Policies must be oriented not to the creation of institutions which represented significant markers of democracy in the west, i.e. multi-party elections, but to the substance which made these institutions work in the west: a viable state and a strong civil society. The implications of this analytical approach is that 'good governance' is much more relevant to democracy than the mere holding of multi-party elections.

Healey and Robinson (1992: 163–4) defined governance as 'the use of legitimate authority exercised in the application of government power and in the management of public affairs.' This concept is useful in that it focuses on institutional arrangements in the interaction between government and citizens, for example in the policy making process.

In line with specifying more precisely what the goals of western policies are, concrete policy instruments must be adjusted to reflect them, although it must also be recognized that not all issues can be influenced from outside. Western policy instruments can contribute to creating the rule of law in Africa, to the establishment of civil and political rights and to reforming the policy making process. Examples of concrete measures which might help include support for programmes of legal reform, exchange programmes, and the training of the judiciary or the police. Programmes such as these do currently exist under new initiatives aimed at 'good governance', but they need to be upgraded and viewed as the essential elements of a policies to promote democracy.

Present donor approaches to democracy and good governance, however, contribute little to reforming the policy making process in Africa. Indeed, the practice of development aid actually hinders efforts to make the policy process more responsive to domestic constituencies. Policy making in aid-dependent countries is heavily influenced by donors and the formulation and implementation of development programmes and projects represent a heavy burden, especially on weak governments. Donors can help to make the policy process more responsive to domestic groups only by decreasing their own prominent role. Of course this approach requires a degree of agreement between donor and recipient countries. Where donor governments agree with the general thrust of policies in aid-recipient countries, they should refrain from detailed involvement in programme or project formulation and implementation. They could instead ask recipient governments to design institutional mechanisms that would increase the voice of domestic groups in policy making. Experiences could be shared on the merits of various schemes of interest group involvement through international interaction, advisory structures and other consultative mechanisms. Where donors and recipient countries disagree fundamentally on the overall policy framework, it would be wiser for the West not to engage in an official development aid relationship at all.[4]

With respect to civil society, the role of outside donors is necessarily limited. A strong civil society by definition depends primarily on domestic constituencies. The main role for the international community is to help remove obstacles to the development of a strong civil society, rather than to imagine that donors can directly strengthen it through external support. Donor governments can do some things: they can stimulate partnerships or twinning agreements between professional groups (lawyers, parliamentarians, police, civil servants) in order to promote professionalism and strength, but their role is inherently circumscribed. More viable political parties in particular can only develop out of a stronger civil society and through social demands that parties change. The idea that direct support to African political parties as they function at present is an instrument to further democracy assumes, mistakenly, that they are actually 'agents of democracy' or can be made to function as such.

In sum, increased emphasis on the concept of governance would avoid the bias toward merely formal changes such as multiparty elections in the formulation of current policies for democracy. This in turn would imply an attempt to ensure that pre-conditions for democracy – civil and political rights, the rule of law and reform of the policy making process – are present before elections are held. But while this approach has the merit that democracy would be built on firmer foundations that it presently is in Africa, it has the defect, from the perspective of western governments, that donors would have to understand that creating democracies is a gradual and time-consuming process. Many seem unwilling to recognise this.

Notes

1 The kind of analysis attempted here may be understood as policy evaluation 'ex ante', i.e. an attempt to analyse the (potential) effects of policy measures to be undertaken, since there are no systematic research findings about actual effects as yet (see Blommestein et al. 1984: 173–6). Seen as part of a rational approach to policy evaluation, it is directed at the consistency of policy goals and instruments applied.

2 For alternative systems suited in the context of divided societies see Lijphart (1977), and for an application to Uganda see G. Hyden (1994).

3 For the prevalence of personalist and patronage politics see also Sandbrook 1988, Chazan 1992, Healey and Robinson 1992.

4 My argument flows from a now widely held view that the success of development aid depends in large part on good policies of the recipient government. See also World Bank 1997.

7

MILITARY INTERVENTION AS THE TRANSNATIONALIZATION OF DEMOCRATIZATION

The case of West Africa

Francois Prikic

The recent politics of democratization in Sub-Saharan Africa have been determined by three intertwined sets of events: the end of the Cold War, the rise of regional powers, and the intensification of internal – often ethnic – conflicts. At the same time, Europe and the US have tended to withdraw from peripheral regions which are no longer relevant to their primary interests. This has led to their reliance on regional hegemons – local states – to keep law and order in their areas of influence (Chase, Hill and Kennedy 1996). These developments are taking place at a time when the UN's capacity to manage peace keeping missions in Africa is also shrinking (Kennedy and Rusett 1995; Carlsson 1995; Mendez 1995). As a result, regional powers are now more able to intervene in transborder politics than before 1990. They do so primarily to defend or extend their own interests, but find it necessary to mask their interventions under the guise of humanitarian or peace-keeping operations. In other words, regional hegemons need to secure international support for their interventions.

In the particular case of West Africa Nigeria, the local hegemon, decided to intervene in the Liberian conflict and later in Sierra Leone because the government determined that national interests were at stake in both countries. The style of the intervention was very different from the European gun-boat policy in the 19th century, however. Nigeria needed the international community's backing and thus found itself promoting, introducing or defending democracy in both states. At the same time, Nigerian efforts at keeping law and order in the sub-region reinforced the position of the military dictatorship at home and thus created a paradoxical situation: a military intervention from outside took place in both Liberia and Sierra Leone which was positive for at least formal democratization in both states while it had adverse effects on the democratization process in Nigeria itself. This gave rise to a peculiar situation in which the international community was actively supporting Nigeria's efforts abroad at the same time as it was condemning the Nigerian government for its lack of commitment to democratization at home.

This chapter thus analyses the effects on democratization of the current trend toward military intervention by regional states in conflict situations in peripheral areas. It reveals the complexities and difficulties of supporting democratization from outside. It is organized in three parts: first, I discuss Nigeria's West African policy, explain the reasons for its interventions in Liberia and describe how the intervention was presented internationally in order to gain support; second, the chapter looks at the paradox of a non-democratic state intervening in a neighbouring country to promote democracy and the negative effect of the intervention in Liberia on democratization in Nigeria; finally it analyses the positive effects of the Nigerian intervention in both Liberia and Sierra Leone on the establishment of formal democracy in these two states.

Nigeria's West African policy

Nigeria, with a population in excess of 100 million, important resources, especially petroleum, and a large economy, can claim to be the unchallenged regional power in West Africa (Ihonvbere 1991). As one analyst points out, 'every Nigerian Government since independence has come to assume for the country the natural role of regional leader' (Akinrinade 1992: 50). It is not surprising then that the West African sub-region lies at the heart of Nigeria's foreign and defence policy (Nwokedi 1985; Ekoko and Vogt 1990; Ate and Akinterinwa 1992). As a result, Presidents Mohammed and Obasanjo created a concentric foreign policy which his successors have maintained as a key strategy. Their immediate successor, General Buhari, explained it as follows, 'a pattern of concentric circles is discernible in our attitude and response to foreign policy issues within the African continent and the world at large. At the epicentre of these circles are the national political and economic interest of the Federal Republic of Nigeria, which are inextricably tied up with the security, stability, and economic and social well being of our immediate neighbours' (Yoroms 1993: 85). These neighbours form the first of a series of circles. In the words of former Foreign Minister Joe Garba (1987: 40) 'Nigeria's neighbours are a matter of colonial heritage and making friends out of her neighbours has been and will continue to be a major preoccupation of Nigeria's foreign policy'. President Babangida, who came to power in 1985, took up this idea and vowed to privilege the 'ring countries' since 'crisis or conflicts [in these countries] would inevitably have adverse spillover effects on the peace and tranquility of our country' (Yoroms 1993: 85).

It was logical, therefore, to expect that the events in Liberia after December 1989 would be followed with attention in Nigeria. Even though it is not an immediate neighbour, Liberia is clearly part of the first circle of Nigerian interests. As such, the unstable situation in the country was intereprered in Lagos as a potential threat to Nigerian security. Initially the conflict itself was deemed less dangerous, however, than the fact that Nigeria's ally, President Samuel Doe, was under threat from an internal rebellion. President Babangida and most of his peers in the subregion knew that Charles Taylor's National Patriotic Front of Liberia (NPFL) had the backing of Libya, and that among his troops were some non-Liberian opposition groups, especially from Sierra Leone, the Gambia and possibly even from Nigeria itself.

Lagos concluded, therefore, that the situation in Liberia signified the possiblity of a major destabilization of West Africa and this set in motion Nigeria's response. It was fuelled by the fear that an NPFL victory over Doe in Liberia would convince other insurgents or would-be liberators in Nigeria and elsewhere that a civilian-led uprising could bring down military dictatorships elswhere (Sesay 1995). Indeed, the Nigerian media also picked up this idea: in 1994 a Lagos-based newspaper predicted that 'Charles Taylor has shown the way; it is only an uprising of the people that can purge Africa of military dictatorship, corruption and under-development' (*The Guardian*, Lagos 16 February 1994).

As a result, the Nigerian military judged that their own fate depended on their ability to control the situation in Liberia. President Babangida's aim, despite claims that that the intervention was on humanitarian grounds, was less to stop the fighting in Liberia than to prevent at all costs a NPFL victory which might lead to other insurrections in the sub-region. In his view, the crisis affected the 'peace and security of the West African sub-region, indeed the African continent as a whole' (Ofori 1991: 140). The objective was to crush the NPFL in Liberia before the problem got out of hand (Adeleke 1995). To gain the support of the international community, however, he had to rule out any option which would look like a unilateral intervention in Liberia's internal matters. To this end, he created a two-pronged strategy: involving other countries in the military intervention and introducing the notion of supporting the democratization of Liberia as justification for the operation. Behind these official reasons lay the goal of managing the crisis in such a way as would benefit the military regime in Nigeria.

The Economic Community of West African States (ECOWAS), an organization grouping all sixteen West African states, was used as a cover for the operation. Babangida requested the formation of a five-member Standing Mediation Committee (SMC) during the May 1990 annual summit of the organization, officially with the purpose of settling the crisis peacefully within the sub-region (Adisa 1994). This committee was controlled by Nigeria. It shaped a peace plan for Liberia on the basis of the Community's 1981 Protocol on Mutual Assistance on Defence with two main components: the creation of a West African peace keeping force, labelled ECOMOG, and the formation of a neutral interim Governement, called the Interim Government of National Unity (IGNU).

Behind the appearance of a genuine regional effort at restoring peace in war-torn Liberia, this plan corresponded perfectly to Nigeria's objective.

ECOMOG's mission was to separate the warring parties and implement a cease-fire, but in effect it was designed to prevent the NPFL from taking over the presidential palace where Samuel Doe and his last troops were besieged. At the political level, the IGNU, formed under the aegis of the SMC in Banjul by a dozen Liberians, was to thwart Taylor's pretensions at representing the country even though he then controlled all but the centre of the capital, Monrovia.

In order to avoid any dissent, all decisions were taken by the SMC as opposed to the whole Community. Furthermore, the Committee, instead of mediating between the parties, presented the provisions of this peace plan to them and then adopted and started to implement it, despite the opposition of both interested parties. President Doe opposed the plan and claimed that no interim President could head Liberia since he was still the incumbent President. The NPFL vowed to fight against any peace-keeping troops that threatened to deprive them of the fruits of victory.

ECOMOG's methods prompted strong criticism from other ECOWAS member-states who argued that the Community had no right to intervene in the internal affairs of Liberia and that the SMC was not the appropriate body to form a regional peace-keeping force (Kufuor 1993, Ofodile 1994, Mindua 1995, N'Diaye 1996). ECOWAS thus had to convene its first ever extraordinary summit in November 1990 to settle the legal questions raised by the SMC decisions. The summit was left with no alternative but to endorse the SMC since the interim goverment had already been formed and ECOMOG forces were by then deployed in Liberia. From then on, Nigeria managed to implement its own policy in Liberia with the backing of the regional organization. Other members of the regional peace-keeping forces were two of its close allies, the Gambia and Sierra Leone – both with a token contingent – Ghana, which appeared to participate out of genuine concern for the civilian population in Liberia (Aning 1996, Prikic 1998), and Guinea, also prompted by the desire to prevent a NPFL victory (Gbanabome 1992).

The second aspect of the Nigerian strategy was aimed at gaining the support of the international community. This was achieved by introducing the concept of democratization. As far as Nigeria was concerned, promoting democracy within the region was simply a strategy to defend its own interests. Nonetheless subsequent developments in Liberia reveal that opportunities can sometimes be created for democratization through external intervention. Such interference in the internal politics of other states, especially by middle or regional powers, now has to be shaped in accordance with the goals of the international community as otherwise it is unlikely to get the backing it needs. Nigeria's intervention in Liberia received the support of the UN as well as that of the Organization of African Unity and other regional bodies. The UN even participated actively in the intervention alongside ECOWAS and ECOMOG from 1993 onwards, both at the political level, with UN sponsored peace-talks and the appointment of a Secretary-General Special Representative for Liberia, and at the military level, with the deployment of a UN Observer Mission in Liberia (UNOMIL). The irony of Nigeria pretending to restore democracy in Liberia even at the same time that Babangida's regime was subject to international condemnation for human rights abuses and a systematic delaying of the promised democratic transition could not escape notice. At the heart of this paradox is the question of whether regional organizations are adequate as instruments to enhance democracy when they reflect the aspirations only of the most powerful local state (MacFarlane and Weiss 1994). In the specific case of West Africa, the question was also how successful and deep democratization could be when it was introduced from outside for cynical motives by a foreign administration opposed to democratization within its own borders and when the Liberian state had to all intents and purposes collapsed (Zartman 1995).

The paradox of the Nigerian intervention

During the initial row within ECOWAS over the SMC decisions, some observers were quick to point out the irony of military dictators pretending to fight for democracy, not in their own but in a neighbouring country. For example, *The Washington Post* published an article entitled 'Authoritarian Africans Take Up Democratic Mission' (Amoo 1993: 26; Sesay 1995: 8). ECOMOG's leadership, made up of Ghanaian Flight Lieutenant Jerry Rawlings, Guinean Colonel Lansana Contè as well as Nigerian General Babangida had all came to power through coups, in 1981, 1984 and 1985. Major General Joseph Momoh in Sierra Leone became President after being designated by his predecessor, Siaka Stevens; he is also a former head of the Sierra Leone Armed Forces. President Dawda Jawara in the Gambia, the only civilian of the five heads of state participating in ECOMOG, had come to power on Independence and had not relinquished it since. At the time of the intervention, he had been in office for 25 years. Nigeria, more than any other ECOMOG country, exemplified the paradox of non-democratic states vowing to promote democracy abroad. Whereas the leaders of the other ECOMOG states had managed to avoid drawing attention to the lack of democracy within their own borders, the Nigerian leadership has antagonized the international community to such an extent that it has been facing sanctions for the past five years. Thus, at the same time that the Nigerian leadership was investing financial and human resources in the promotion of democracy in Liberia with the support of the international community, it was under pressure for its blatant human rights abuses and refusal to push the dmeocracy agenda at home.

In fact, since Independence in 1960, Nigeria has been ruled by civilians during only two periods and for a total of less than ten years. The last elected head of State, Shehu Shagari, was overthrown in 1983 by Major-General Buhari. Almost all the military leaders have promised to return to the barracks after completing a programme of transition. Only two such programmes were even partially implemented – a six-year programme by General Gowon in 1970, abandoned in 1974, and a four-year programme by General Mohammed in 1975.

General Mohammed's programme was completed by General Obasanjo who succeeded him after his death in a failed coup attempt and it led to the inauguration of an elected civilian President in October 1979 (Odinkalu 1996). General Babangida's own five-year transition programme, detailed in Decree No. 19 of 1987, was thus nothing new in Nigerian politics. The repeated delays in its implementation as well as obvious government manipulations of its conditions – General Babangida decided in 1989, for example, that the thirteen newly formed political parties did not qualify for recognition and created instead the only two parties authorized to contest the elections – were also a familiar feature: that of a military ruler reluctant to relinquish power. On 12 June 1993 presidential elections finally took place, but General Babangida went on to annul them ten days later when counting was still underway and announced that the transition process was officially terminated. General Abacha, who succeeded him in November 1993, had a very similar approach to the return to civilian rule: he also announced a transition programme in October 1995 but kept changing the terms under which the elections would be held (Human Rights Watch/Africa 1997). Had he not died suddenly in June 1998, the programme might have been implemented, but probably only because he had already assured himself of victory since all five of the registered political parties – including four 'opposition' parties – had already chosen him as their candidate.

The two Nigerian leaders, therefore, who pressed for a democratic outcome to the Liberian crisis, Generals Babangida and Abacha, had a track record only of opposing or manipulating democratic elections at home. Both had brought Nigeria into disrepute internationally and sanctions were imposed on Nigeria as a result. In 1993, the first batch of sanctions followed the annulment of the June elections and General Abacha's coup in November. Two years later, more sanctions were imposed on Nigeria after the execution of nine Ogoni leaders, an ethnic group opposed to the government on a variety of matters ranging from minority rights to environmental pollution in the Niger Delta. These included human rights activist and writer Ken Saro-Wiwa.

In both instances, the most damaging sanctions were imposed by the European Union (EU) and the US. EU sanctions included visa restrictions for the military in 1993 and for all civilians in the government in 1995, an embargo on all military equipment, a severe reduction in governmental development assistance and the expulsion of all military personnel attached to Nigerian embassies in Europe, as well as withdrawal of all European military personnel attached to embassies in Nigeria (Council of the European Union 1995a and 1995b). Furthermore in November 1996 the European Parliament adopted a resolution in favour of an oil embargo. The US also stopped all military assistance to Nigeria in 1993, extended in 1995 to cover the repair of military equipment and the sale of spare parts, and, like the EU, imposed severe restrictions on visas for all military and civilians linked with the government. One of the more damaging of the US actions was its decision to identify and criticize the Abacha administration for a lack of commitment in the international fight against drug trafficking in 1994. As a result, Nigeria was deprived of most US assistance and Washington voted against granting financial assistance to Nigeria in every international body.

The most symbolic action taken against Nigeria was its suspension from the Commonwealth in 1995 for a period of two years, due to Nigeria's disrespect for the provisions of the 1991 Harare Declaration, a document compelling all signatories to adopt a democratic form of government and respect human rights. In October 1997, at the Edinburgh Summit, the progress made by General Abacha's administration in these two directions were considered insufficient and the suspension was extended for another year (Prikic 1997).

The paradox of the situation thus lies in the fact that the Nigerian military intervention in Liberia was in utter contradiction to the perpetuation of dictatorship in Nigeria, a policy to which the military were still completely committed. The Liberian intervention, carried out with international approval, actually served to prop up the Nigerian dictatorship, giving Babangida and Abacha the opportunity to reinforce their grip on power and to delay the transition programme in Nigeria.

The operation had a number of advantages for the dictatorship. It consolidated Babangida's regime mainly because it proved to be an efficient way to control threats from within the Armed Forces, the only source of a possible threat to his hold on office. Up to 5,000 Nigerian troops were deployed in Liberia between 1990 and 1993. This pleased the Nigerian military-industrial lobby, a very powerful pressure group with no particular loyalty to Babangida unless he served their interests. ECOMOG operations were also a good way to keep officers who were a potential threat to the regime out of Nigeria. That was the case with General Dogonyaro, for example, ECOMOG Field Commander in 1990–91 and a member of the powerful 'Langtang Mafia'. Babangida had recently dismissed another influential 'Langtang', General Bali, from the Ministry of Defence and thus had reason to fear a reaction from the group. Furthermore the intervention in Liberia was an opportunity to form seasoned troops with an experience in both fighting insurgencies and keeping law and order in urban areas. The attempted coup against Babangida in April 1990 showed just how important it was to keep the troops loyal to the regime in a state of readiness to face internal challenges.

Finally, ECOMOG troops were in a position to gain substantial profits from their tour of duty in Liberia, thus making up for unattractive wages – a maximum of $5 a day – and high risks. As a consequence, the intervention created a core of officers and troops indebted to General Babangida for the wealth they acquired while in Liberia, with the result that they were more likely to remain faithful in case of a coup. So widespread was the looting, in fact, by the Nigerian 'peacekeepers' and so extensive their involvement in all kinds of illegal trafficking that Liberians claimed that ECOMOG really stood for 'Every Commodity Or Moveable Object Gone' (Africa Watch 1993).

In sum, the main effect of the intervention in Liberia on the political situation in Nigeria was that the regime used it as an excuse to remain in power. The Armed Forces argued that it was necessary for them to remain in power for as long as it took to resolve the Liberian intervention because national interests were at stake and a civilian regime could not be trusted to carry the intervention through to the end. Partly, of course, their fear was that a civilian administration might obtain a military or political victory in Liberia, thereby putting the Armed Forces to shame. Since an early end to the conflict was not something they could entirely control, they suggested that meanwhile the promised elections be delayed. This was the view the regime chose to disseminate from as early as 1991, that is before General Babangida announced the decision to postpone the elections originally planned for October 1992 until June 1993.

This view was even supported by groups outside the Armed Forces: a respected Nigerian academic explained that 'it is definitely not in Nigeria's interest for the troops deployed to Liberia to remain there beyond 1992. Apart from the foreign policy complications which such a procedure would bring about, as the newly elected civilians would lack foreknowledge of the strategic calculations that attend the deployment of the force and might unwittingly commit expensive blunders by taking measures which they consider to be politically expedient, the civilians would find it extremely difficult to deal with battle-tested troops returning from Liberia who are used to receiving their orders from their military superiors . . . It is therefore important for them to be brought home and re-oriented under a military government' (Vogt 1991: 118–119). In February 1991 the editorial of a Nigerian daily also considered that it was 'crucial for the government to resolve our involvement in Liberia before its stated tenure expires. It would be clearly against the grain to pass an heirloom such as this to any incoming civilian government in 1992' (*The Guardian*, Lagos 25 February 1991). There can be little doubt, therefore, that the invasion served to justify stalling or even preventing the democratization process in Nigeria itself.

The invasion and democratization in Liberia and Sierra Leone

Despite its negative impact on Nigerian politics, however, the invasion was positive for at least formal democratization, that is the holding of elections and the return to power of civilian leaders, in Liberia and later in Sierra Leone. The Nigerian authorities were dependent on international approval to carry though their policies; the holding of elections in Liberia and Sierra Leone was the only way that international support could be obtained. They also hoped that the intervention could be used to reassure the international community of the Nigerian government's democratic credentials, despite the internal dictatorship, and thus soften the sanctions.

Three positive effects of the intervention on democracy can be identified in the cases of Liberia and Sierra Leone. First, Nigeria used the introduction of democratic procedures to manage the crisis and thereby introduced at least the idea of democratization as a potential outcome into the political debate in Liberia. Second, Nigeria imposed the holding of elections, thereby ensuring that post-war Liberia would have at least some of the trappings of democracy. And finally Nigeria found itself, almost by chance, fighting against a military junta and in favour of the introduction of democratic procedures in Sierra Leone. The policy of supporting democratization externally thus spread to a second country.

Liberia

The legal basis for the intervention in Liberia, as well as the methods used, were in fact highly questionable in terms of international law: as a result, Nigeria and the SMC resorted to the introduction of democratic principles and practices in an effort to secure international legitimacy. Their objective was to try to gain support in the UN and with the US government, which tradition-ally had a close interest in Liberia. Apart from serving Nigeria's interests, however, this had the unexpected advantage of making a breach in the Liberian system through which the internal groups which had for years been arguing for the introduction of some form of democracy in politics could step.

At the Banjul meeting of August 1990, the SMC decided that the head of the interim government should be a civilian independent from all warring parties (ECOWAS 1990). That was intended to make the accord more acceptable to all factions since none would have exclusive control over the new administration. It also excluded all those individuals who had been involved with Doe's dictator-ship. As it turned out, the new head of the interim government was a university professor of political science who had been an activist in pro-democracy organi-zations since the 1970s. Most of the members of the government he formed were, like himself, individuals known for their opposition to past dictatorships: a mixture of student leaders and political activists from various pre-war opposi-tion parties and pressure groups, most of them returning from exile.

In 1993, when a new peace plan replaced the IGNU with a Liberian National Transitional Government (LNTG) led by a Council of State, the same principle was used. Even though the Council of State included factional lead-ers, seats were also allocated to the ex-IGNU, representing the 'unarmed masses' (ECOWAS 1993: art. 14). Council members elected a civilian from IGNU as Chair of the Council instead of a faction representative. Therefore, when a second LNTG was formed, in 1994, this time with faction leaders themselves in the Council of State, two seats were again allocated to the 'unarmed civilians'. Their representatives in the Council were 'prominent Liberians', one of which ended up, once again, Chair of the Council (ECOWAS 1994: art. 14). Despite further minor changes to the Council, the 'unarmed civilians' retained represenation, itself a major achievement in Liberian politics, and, as a result of internal elections and a general consensus among the parties, they were also able to keep the Chair of the Council of State. The net effect of these decisions was that, despite the relative inefficiency of the collegial leader-ship created through the LNTG, Liberia was ruled, for the first time, by pro-democracy activists including a woman.

Once the invasion was underway, neither Nigeria nor the SMC were able to impose leaders on the Liberian people. The political situation in Liberia developed a momentum of its own. Heads of the interim administration were chosen and at times elected by Liberians themselves, although the elections were not fully democratic. For examle, Professor Amos Sawyer, who led IGNU from the onset in 1990, was elected by a small group of Liberians gathered by the SMC in Banjul. Within the first and second Council of State, Council members elected the Chair. Finally, after subsequent changes in the organiza-tion of this Council in 1995, instead of internal elections, it was decided that one of the civilians in the Council would also be automatically the acting President (ECOWAS 1995: art. 14). Lastly, as a demonstration of some tentative moves towards more democratization inside Liberia, a national conference was organized, in imitiation in some respects to those in Francophone Africa (see Nwajiaku 1994). This gathered together delegates from two factions, six pre-war political parties and fourteen interest groups empowered to choose the type of government they wanted, and to elect their leader (Republic of Liberia 1991). The effects of this conference were limited in scope since the NPFL delegation walked out. As a consequence, the government which emerged was very much the same as the one formed in Banjul with Amos Sawyer still at its head. Nevertheless, this type of conference where delegates from the civil society are empowered to decide on their leadership was something new in Liberia politics and an indication of change, though far from western ideas of democracy.

Thus the peace plan which was shaped to fill the power vacuum in Liberia ultimately turned an operation designed to protect Nigerian interests into an endorsement of democratic procedures in Liberia. The objective was to introduce elements attractive to the international community so that, considered as a whole, all aspects of the peace plan, including the more dubious ones and ECOMOG excesses, would win the backing of other, more powerful states such as the US, and international organizations. The other major aspect of the SMC's strategy was therefore to assert that its efforts would culminate in the organiza-tion of presidential and general elections in Liberia, to mark the end to the conflict and to determine the leadership of the country. This was enshrined in all the proposed peace plans, from Banjul in 1990 to Abuja, six years later.

In this way, the proposals of the SMC fell in line with the policies the international community was promoting in the rest of the continent, including Nigeria. As such, the idea of democratization was used to allay the international community's suspicions that the Nigerian leadership was opposed to democracy and thus possibly soften the hard line taken by Europe, the US and the Commonwealth. It was even thought that the fact that Nigeria was assuming financial and human costs in pursuing democracy in Liberia might be taken as an indication of the leadership's commitment to regional democracy.

No statistics have been published of the exact costs of the intervention. These figures are sensitive and have not been released because they might provoke criticism in view of the poverty of the country, the economic crisis and the austerity programmes that the government has pursued. However, it is likely that ECOMOG operations in Liberia cost over US $6 billion, most of it spent by Nigeria, the only country able to sustain this kind of military operation financially. In human terms, the intervention cost ECOMOG around 2,000 dead and many more wounded. Since Nigeria provided some 75 or 80 per cent of the force, it suffered most of these losses.

Nigeria's strategy in trying to persuade the international community of its democratic credentials was similar to that of other autocratic regimes in the sub-region. Both Lansana Contè in Guinea and Jerry Rawlings in Ghana, for example, organized presidential elections which they went on to win, mainly in order to gain international approval. The elections were basically about appeasing international opinion without losing the Presidency or introducing any meaningful democracy and became known in West Africa as 'gun powered democracy'. But whereas other dictatorships were introducing cosmetic changes at home, the Nigerian leadership was trying to indicate its commitment to democracy abroad. The military intervention in Liberia thus became indirectly a way for the military to remain in power since it provided, in their mind, a clear enough indication of their faith in democracy.

Whatever its impact inside Nigeria, however, the effect of the policy was undoubtledly positive for Liberia. A step was taken towards democratization, although the process remains fragile and incomplete. After almost eight years of civil war, elections were held on 19 July 1997 under conditions all international observers present in Liberia judged satisfactory. A total of thirteen parties presented candidates; Charles Taylor received slightly over 75 per cent of the vote while the two runners-up ended up respectively with less than 10 and less than 5 per cent. Elections for the Parliament held the same day also gave an absolute majority to Charles Taylor's party, the National Patriotic Party (NPP). The NPP won twenty-one seats out of twenty-six in the Senate and forty-nine out of sixty-four in the Assembly, the remaining fifteen seats being shared by five other political parties. Taylor's overwhelming victory was, however, less a result of his popularity than of a widespread fear that, if defeated, he would rebel against the government. Taylor was invested on 2 August 1997 in Monrovia in the presence of eight heads of state, including General Abacha, the first ever elected president in the history of Liberia.

Sierra Leone

The rebellion which started in Sierra Leone in 1991 was an offshoot of the NPFL uprising in Liberia. As such, President Babangida decided to meet President Momoh's request for military assistance. Within a few weeks 1,200 Nigerian troops were deployed in Sierra Leone, which was strategically important because Freetown was the main rear-base for ECOMOG operations in Liberia. In this case, therefore, it was much less easy for Nigeria to pretend that the intervention was taking place in order to push democratic principles on to the agenda.

However, when civilian rule *was* introduced in Sierra Leone and President Ahmad Kabbah elected in March 1996, Nigeria saw it as an opportunity to further its attempts at gaining abroad the international credit it was losing at home. From the perspective of General Abacha, demonstrating his determination to protect an elected leader might increase his standing internationally while at the same time defending Nigeria's own interests. This was important as the second round of sanctions had just been imposed on Nigeria and Abacha was aware of the regime's unpopularity abroad. A defence pact between Nigeria and Sierra Leone was rushed through in March and a few days later the Sierra Leonean rebel leader, Foday Sankoh, was arrested upon his arrival in Abuja where he came to attend peace talks at the invitation of President Abacha.

The situation changed, however, on 25 May 1997 when Commandant Johnny Paul Koroma of the Sierra Leone Armed Forces staged a successful coup against President Kabbah. This gave Abacha the opportunity to reject the coup, oppose the new military junta and declare Nigeria's resolve to protect democracy throughout the sub-region. His idea, as ever, was to appease the international community. In a situation even more paradoxical than that of Liberia, General Abacha, who himself came to power through a coup, was fighting in Sierra Leone against a military-led uprising in favour of a civilian President. As a result, the very day of Koromah's coup, Nigeria flew 800 more troops to Sierra Leone and further reinforcements arrived there two days later. From the beginning of June onwards, Nigerian troops engaged Koromah's troops in and around the capital city of Freetown while the Nigerian Air Force and Navy started strafing Sierra Leonean positions, killing hundreds of civilians in the process. By July 1996, some 4,000 Nigerian soldiers were deployed in Sierra Leone, officially as part of ECOMOG forces.

Nigeria's policy in Sierra Leone was relatively successful. Criticisms were voiced about Nigerian actions and especially of the massive bombings of Freetown, and concern was expressed by the UN and the EU that Nigeria was using ECOMOG as a cover for its own interests. Nevertheless, the international community also condemned the coup and supported Nigerian efforts at bringing down the new regime in favour of President Kabbah. The UN for example helped General Abacha to defeat the junta by imposing an embargo on arms and fuel to Sierra Leone in October 1997, a few weeks after two Security Council resolutions had expressed UN support for ECOMOG objectives in Sierra Leone. The combined effect of Nigerian military actions and international pressure finally forced the junta out of Freetown in mid-February 1998. By March, President Kabbah had returned. The Nigerian intervention in Sierra Leone thus became the first ever military intervention directed against a successful military coup in West Africa.

Conclusion

Nigeria's interventions in Liberia and Sierra Leone raise two questions from the perspective of democratization. First, what are the effects of external military intervention on the politics of democratization inside countries where the state is collapsing due to armed rebellion? And second, to what degree can regional hegemons such as Nigeria defend their own dictatorship internally by advancing democratization elsewhere and sealing off their own regimes from international criticisms?

In terms of the first question, it appears from the West African case that intervention can, pardoxically, have a positive effect, at least in pushing for a transition to civilian rule. How far democratization, meaning the development of long-term democratic social and political practices, is placed on the agenda, is of course entirely different. With relation to the second question, what is at issue is whether the military dictatorship in Nigeria benefited by appeasing the international community through supporting democratization in the region, but not introducing it domestically. The answer is that the policy was a partial success. Sanctions were not lifted against Nigeria and international pressure for reform was kept up. However, the policy also produced some benefits for Nigeria's military leaders. In July 1996 for example, few days before a Organization of African Unity summit, President Mandela of South Africa, who was in favour of increased sanctions against Nigeria, admitted he had received delegations from West African States and from the UN reminding him that Nigeria was keeping law and order in Liberia and Sierra Leone and asking him to reconsider his position (Human Rights Watch/Africa 1997: 43).

This reveals the profoundly ambiguous position the international community has found itself in with relation to global democratization. It is no longer possible to control the activities of regional hegemons and the invasions of Liberia and Sierra Leone could not be prevented. Neither could they be completely controlled. As a result, pro-democracy international actors found themselves pursuing contradictory policies. Nigeria's intervention in West Africa also indicate just how easy it is for dictators to clothe themselves in the language of democratization while at the same time thwarting democratic movements at home. The case of Nigeria is therefore profoundly disturbing. It reveals the limitations of international policies in support of democracy as well as the possibility that the democratization agenda itself can be manipulated to suit the interests of entrenched authoritarian elites committed to keeping themselves in office at all costs.

8

EUROPEAN NGOs AND DEMOCRATIZATION IN LATIN AMERICA

Policy networks and transnational
ethical networks

Jean Grugel

Developmental non-governmental organizations (NGOs) are an important vehicle for transmitting support for democratization from the North to the South, in this case from Europe to Latin America.[1] At the same time, Latin American NGOs are seen as a vital component of the fabric of civil societies and a means to deepen participation in the restricted or limited democracies which have developed since the 1980s (MacDonald 1997; Pearce 1997a; Serbin 1997). Consequently a recognition of their role forms an essential part of 'second wave' democratization studies, which is shifting attention away from transition and a preoccupation with institution building and constitutional change towards analysing the ways in which an active civil society contributes to creating 'substantive democracy' and the consolidation of stable democracies over time. This is stimulating a new research agenda around the global and regional activities of NGOs, the transnational relationships in which NGOs participate, and state-NGO relationships in terms of implementing the new aid agenda of good governance, democratization and reform of the state.

Political conditionality that links aid to improvements in political systems – the introduction of some form of democracy and evidence of an increased respect for human rights – has increased the prominence of NGOs in delivering European aid to the developing and post-Communist world. NGOs are a central pillar of the 'New Policy Agenda' of aid in the post-Cold War (Robinson 1993). While Northern NGOs have rarely been consulted in drafting programmes of political conditionality, they 'are looked to as vehicles for channeling political aid to promote empowerment, civic education and domestic reform'; they are seen by official donors as having 'the capacity to enrich civil society by supporting a range of programmes aimed at empowering poor and disadvantaged groups in countries where they are deprived of basic freedoms' (Robinson 1995: 360, 367). Trends towards governance in a number of European countries, leading to policies of privatization and encouraging private sector actors to assume responsibilities that were once seen as the state's exclusive preserve, have magnified this tendency. Hence NGOs have become attractive to official European donors and the 1990s aid regime has been marked by an increased readiness on the part of states to incorporate NGOs into aid delivery.

The legitimacy of European NGOs as agents of overseas development does not stem from their relationship with government and the supposed efficiency of their operations. Their role has traditionally been legitimized by the fact that they can claim to represent the desires of society at large for a better, more just world. Historically, they have generally articulated a vision of development and democracy which is redistributive, egalitarian and based on moral, not market, imperatives. In contrast to European states, their partners in the developing world have always been other NGOs, grassroots organizations, religious and local communities. They have therefore been able to claim that NGO-delivered aid is close to the poor and the disadvantaged, and uncontaminated by corrupt, authoritarian or personalist governments in the South. As European NGOs are brought into deeper relationships with states and become instruments for delivering state-funded aid, the priorities of which have been determined by state actors, they are drawn into more complex and potentially discordant relationships than in the past. Since they strive at the same time to retain links with both their own civil societies and Southern-based local groups and NGOs, European NGOs now have three overlapping responsibilities: to states, to European civil societies, and to non-government groups and organizations in the South. There is considerable dispute, within the academic world and among the NGOs themselves, about how this affects their role in supporting democratization in the South and the kind of projects they encourage (see Chapter 3).

All of this complicates the search for an appropriate theoretical framework in which to analyse the activities of European NGOs and assess their contribution to democratization. This chapter will first propose a framework for analysing European NGO activities before describing aspects of their role in promoting democracy in Latin America. It will then go on to outline briefly the increasing tendency in European cooperation to promote NGOs as agents of decentralized cooperation. It will also consider the central role assigned in European aid to cooperation between civil societies as a means to deepening democracy in societies after transition. The third part of the chapter consists of a detailed discussion of the role in Latin America of NGOs from one EU member state in the UK.

Researching European NGOs: coopted, independent or networking?

Conceptualizing the NGO role in international politics is not a straightforward task. The role of development NGOs in the international order is in a process of profound change and the nature of the transformation is hotly contested. Is the prominence of international NGOs an expression of global citizenship and an indication of the emergence of a global civil society or is it a symptom of new mechanisms through which to diffuse popular demands and structure them in ways that do not challenge the existing order?

The 'association revolution' (Salmon 1993: 1) detected in the 1980s has been heralded as the emergence of a new grassroots movement reforming and renewing the left (Escobar and Alvarez 1992). But scepticism has also been expressed, gathering strength particularly by the middle of the 1990s, about the capacity, and even the desire, of NGOs to effect substantive global or even local change. Despite the increased interest in their role in the international arena, empirically-grounded research is a comparatively recent phenomenon. Much of the literature on the international role of NGOs has been generated at the theoretical level and concentrates more specifically on the extent to which a global civil society is emerging (Colas 1997; Shaw 1994). Many of the empirical studies have been carried out by the NGOs themselves, although a more critical and academic literature, focused especially on the changing role of Southern-based NGOs, is now emerging (Bratton 1990; Fowler 1991; Jones 1992; Parry Williams 1992; Ndegwa 1996; Pearce 1997a; MacDonald 1997).

Research into both Northern and Southern NGOs points to their participation in increasingly dense sets of responsibilities and relationships. The debate on their new role turns essentially on two issues: the relationship between NGOs and states; and the position of NGOs in a supposedly globalized world order where new forms of governance which by-pass states are rapidly emerging (Gordenker and Weiss 1996; Princen and Finger 1994). Both perspectives contain important insights into changes at the international and state level in terms of managing global issues such as development, democratization and the environment. The first, concentrates on the deepening dependence of the voluntary sector as a whole on states and sees NGOs as 'sovereignty-bound' actors, with their main responsibilities and relationships inside the nation state in which they have arisen. The second conceptualizes them as 'sovereignty-free organizations' capable of exercising an independent role in world politics (Rosenau 1990).

I want to argue here that a network approach can prove a fruitful way of conceptualizing the multiple relationships in which development NGOs now operate. It has greater flexibility than either an exclusively state–NGO perspective, which has given rise to what I characterize as the 'cooptation' approach, or a perspective which concentrates on identifying the new prominence of NGOs as agents of global governance. Focusing of the multiple activities of NGOs over time and space – their roles inside states as well as their transnationalized interactions – allows us to see the range of relationships in which most development NGOs operate.

In other words, NGOs are not simply either partners or agents of the state or participants in a global associational revolution. Tracing the relationships in which they participate captures the different roles they play. This chapter looks at two of those roles: it identifies the network which is pulling European development NGOs into closer relationships with European states, and the emerging network of non-state actors which draws those NGOs into closer contract with their Southern counterparts over key issues relating to development and democracy. Identifying these two separate networks is a way of illustrating the conflictual and at times contradictory role that European developmental NGOs play in democratization in the South. There is in fact a third relationship into which they are being drawn, one between development and non-development NGOs, a network that stretches across national-based voluntary sectors. There is not the space here to enter into detail about this network and only brief mention will be made of it.

A network approach has been used to describe some aspects of NGO activity in the past, in particular advocacy. Sikkink (1993; 1996) has deployed such an approach to human rights groups very effectively, arguing that a network is the most appropriate term to describe the international activities of NGOs, foundations and churches. This is characterized by 'informal, non-hierarchical links...the concept of a network does not imply high levels of coordination among groups. Rather groups . . . must share values and participate in a dense flow of information and services' (Sikkink 1996: 61). Information flows through the network informally, through conversations, shared conference attendance and personal connections. The kind of network Sikkink is describing, however, coheres around a single issue: it is an issue network. It is generally loosely structured, access is relatively open and power relations within the network are more or less symmetrical. More recently, the term 'associative network' has been used to describe relationships between social movements and popular organizations in the Americas, including some trans-border relationships (Chalmers et al. 1997; Cook 1997).

Neither the NGO–state relationship nor the North-South NGO–NGO network which I am identifying here can properly be described as an issue or even associative network. The term does not fit the European state–NGO relationship for at least three reasons. First, access to the state throughout Europe remains relatively closed and only some NGOs are invited to cooperate. Second, there is the question of resources. Members of an issue network have different resources but these do not necessarily translate into relationships of structured inequality; most European NGOs have a relationship of clear financial dependence on the state. Third, the network does not rest on shared principles and goals but rather on pragmatic cooperation in certain policy areas, although it is possible that regular and sustained contact and the sharing of ideas will lead to greater consensus on points of principle. It is therefore better described as a policy network.

An issue network is not the appropriate term either for the transnational network which is emerging between NGOs located in different countries. Issue networks focus on concrete themes (human rights or environmental degradation for example) and bring together a set of actors from state, non-state and suprastate levels. However, NGOs are increasingly cooperating in horizontal relationships in a range of activities such as the exchange of information, agenda setting and project-based and advocacy activities. This network is loosely structured, open to all NGOs regardless of their size and the resources they command and, above all, coheres around a set of shared values and principles. It reflects a rhetorical and principled commitment to citizenship and democracy inside internationally active NGOs. The concept of *co-development* is now used by a number of NGOs to bridge citizenship and democracy and forms the moral bedrock of the network's activities. It is, therefore, a transnational ethical network. It is somewhat closer to the 'associative networks' of Chalmers *et al.* and Cook, although their term lacks the specifically transnational dimension which characterizes North-South NGO interactions. States are excluded from this network and its chief role is to share information and ideas between NGOs and to diffuse and reassert values between participants.

To what extent is membership of both networks compatible? Or to put it another way, how does membership of the policy network affect the work carried out through the transnational ethical network, and vice-versa? This is particularly important in terms of the role NGOs play in democratization. A number of commentators have suggested that membership of a policy network with governments diminishes the commitment of NGOs to radical global change. Hulme and Edwards sum up this perspective:

> the contribution of NGOs to development is under threat. Increased organization, scale and influence for NGOs can only be valued when it contributes to the achievement of developmental goals. If expansion and recognition mean diverting an agency from its mission, then there may be a higher price to pay. While the empirical evidence shows that the influences of the New Policy Agenda on NGOs are many and various, we concur with Smillie (1995) that the 'alms bazaar' of which NGOs are now a part increases the likelihood that they are becoming the implementors of donor policies . . . As NGOs get closer to donors they become more like donors . . . donor approaches to beneficiary participation remain instrumentalist . . . this is incompatible with the proclaimed vision of the vast majority of NGOs who conceptualize participation as a means to empower the poor and the disadvantaged, not simply to achieve short-term goals.
>
> (Hulme and Edwards 1997: 7–8)

My empirical research on UK development NGOs was designed to test Hulme and Edwards' (1996; 1997) assumption that membership of the policy network diminishes the commitment to people-centred development and participative democratization. Following intensive interviews with UK-based development NGOs, I argue instead that membership of the transnational ethical network can sometimes act to counter-balance pressures from government and allow at least

124

some NGOs to maintain their commitment to more radical visions of global change than European state agencies envisage. Balancing the two sets of commitments, however, is not easy and NGOs struggle to do so.

European pro-democracy cooperation in Latin America: the importance of 'civil society'

Latin America is not an especially significant target for European development cooperation in terms of the volume of aid disbursed. The region accounts for only about 10 per cent of total EU aid. Within the EU only Spain, a relatively small and new donor, makes Latin America a priority within its national aid programme. British bilateral aid to Latin America is worth around £25 million, only 8.5 per cent of the total aid budget. In some EU countries, indeed, co-operation with Latin America is being squeezed in order to finance the strategically important relationship with Eastern and Central Europe. Since Latin America has never been regarded as vital to European foreign policies, there seemed little need to use aid there to forment relationships of dependency on European governments, as occurred in other parts of the developing world. At the same time, the development needs of Latin America are regarded as less than those of other areas of the South, in particular sub-Saharan Africa.

Nevertheless, solid relationships have been built up between European and Latin American non-state actors, such as political parties, churches and unions, as well as NGOs, since the 1970s (Grugel 1996). Exile and immigration have played their part in developing these relationships. They were cemented in the struggles in the 1980s against the authoritarian and military governments of the time and in favour of political pluralism, tolerance and respect for human rights in the region. Largely as a result of the activities of non-state actors, European cooperation with Latin America, both at the level of EU member states and in Brussels, is now institutionally embedded in the aid regime. For some NGOs, Latin America is their principal area of activity; for others it represents a significant financial commitment over a number of years. Furthermore, in countries such as the UK where Latin America is a low priority for the state, NGO-based cooperation remains important. For Save the Children for example, the area represents £2.5 million out of a total budget of £66 million, still a substantial figure. Within Latin America, European aid (that is, the sum of member states bilateral aid, plus aid dispersed by the EU) is around 53 per cent of the total volume of aid that Latin America receives.

Latin America has become an important region for monitoring the effects of decentralized aid, or aid dispersed through civil societies, because the rich associational life in the region provides European NGOs with a choice of partners as well as appearing to offer some genuine prospects for building democracy through strengthening and empowering civil society. Both the aid coordinating agency of the OECD, the Committee for Aid and Development (CAD) and the EU have drawn attention to the importance of decentralized cooperation in the 1990s. The EU Commission guidelines of aid to Latin America noted in 1995 that:

> recent years have been marked by the democratic transition of Latin America. The Union has been particularly active in promoting the rule of law and the participation of civil society in the development of a culture of human rights . . . though government institutions remain key partners in the recipient countries, decentralized cooperation has led to a diversification of partners via the establishment of networks drawn from civil society.
>
> (European Commission 1995b: 7)

This has increased the relative importance of NGOs in European aid provision. They are seen as the principal vehicle through which to channel decentralized aid, as well as serving to legitimate aid donations domestically. It is estimated that the EU co-financed 1,467 aid projects in conjunction with European NGOs between 1992 and 1995, disbursing around 80,193,666 ECUs to them for their work in Latin America (Freres 1998: 415). As a result, they were thrust into the vanguard of official European aid, deepening their relationships with Southern NGOs as strengthening local civil societies became an official European development priority. Hence both the policy networks linking NGOs with states and the transnationalized ethical interactions bringing together Northern and Southern NGOs are, at least in theory, strengthened by the new focus and mode of delivery of European aid.

The contemporary emphasis of European aid on civil society represents to some degree a continuation of the kind of projects European NGOs have been developing in Latin America over a number of years. European NGOs began to operate decentralized cooperation through local partners in Latin America in the early 1980s. The current belief that democracy requires a strong and active civil society is therefore in line with aspects of the NGO perspective on democratization. Most European NGOs operating in Latin America would see contributing to social and economic democratization as a *sine qua non* of both development and political democracy since they tend to identify the persistence of authoritarian political practices and cultures as the source of social injustice and exclusion and the chief obstacle to development in the region (Grugel 1999).

This should not be taken to imply, however, that NGOs and official European donors have come to share the same vision of democracy and democratization. In particular, there is a gulf between how NGOs use the term 'civil society' and its meaning for official European donors. In Latin America, it has assumed significations of '*lo popular*'; civil society is seen as chiefly composed of those excluded from the formal political system (Pearce 1997b). Supporting democratization through empowering civil society suggests, therefore, a radical project of redistribution of power. Hence the notion of 'civil society', as it is used in Latin America, carries with it far fewer associations of liberalism than in Europe.

Official European donors see strengthening civil society in Latin America as a means to bring about a set of social changes which compliment the development of the market and liberal-oriented development. NGOs, in contrast, have tended to share the view of their Latin American partners that there is no essential link between the market and democracy. Thus while strengthening civil society is perfectly compatible with the emphasis on liberal economic reform for official EU donors, for many NGOs and their Latin American counterparts, the two represent opposing projects. The majority of European NGOs reject the view that political democracy and economic redistribution can and should be conceptually differentiated. The boundaries between the political and the socio-economic spheres are thereby blurred and the meaning of democracy itself takes on a socio-economic dimension within NGO discourse.

The result is that there can be a very real gap between the goals of funders and NGOs' aspirations. This gap is one source of the tension generated within development NGOs as they are drawn into policy networks yet remain committed to, and indeed wish to strengthen, the transnational ethical networks as a coalition for global change. For some NGOs, this is sufficient reason to be suspicious of the new climate of NGO-centred aid.[2]

UK NGOs: the policy network

These tensions are well illustrated in the case of UK development NGOs and their operations in Latin America.[3] British NGOs remain financially much more independent of government than most of their European counterparts. Even for OXFAM, the largest of the UK development NGOs and the one which benefits most from government funding, official donations accounted for only 24 per cent of the organization's income in 1992. Nevertheless, a number of NGOs have been brought into a much closer relationship with the state since the beginning of the 1990s. This relationship is not only financial. It includes regular dialogue between the NGOs and the state. Many NGOs, especially the large ones such as OXFAM, Christian Aid, Save the Children and WATER-WORLD, are perceived by the state as having a range of professional skills and resources which the government wishes to employ for the the overseas development programme.

The new relationship began with the restructuring of the state in the 1980s. A series of reforms were introduced which changed the parameters of state activity and introduced the principle of privatization of public services. This has involved the devolution of what were previously seen as public responsibilities to private agencies or the voluntary sector. Over 50 per cent of the public sector had been privatized by 1991 (Marsh 1991:463; Rhodes 1994). Inevitably, privatization crept into the provision of development aid. The boundaries are slowly being dissolved between official development cooperation, administered through the Department for International Development (DFID), and cooperation through NGOs, financed either totally or in part through the state.

In 1993 the British Overseas NGOs for Development (BOND) was formed, half the funds of which came from the Overseas Development Administration (ODA, now the DFID). BOND's remit was to bring together the NGO community, to provide the state with a formal partner for dialogue and to encourage NGOs to access public funding. Describing the new situation between the state and the NGOs, an official responsible for aid administration commented:

> In the past, there were clear distinctions between assistance through NGOs and regular programmes which were government-to-government. This situation is now complex. The ODA [now DFID] accepts that involvement with NGOs is growing in importance and a necessary part of our . . . programmes.
>
> (interview with the author, July 1996)

According to official figures, more than £185 million was transferred to NGOs in 1994/5. Government funding to NGOs flows through a variety of channels, including block grants, a Joint Funding Scheme (JFS), emergency aid and programmes of technical collaboration. Only four large NGOs benefit from block grants: Save the Children, Christian Aid, OXFAM and CAFOD. In 1994–5, these were worth nearly £3 million, of which OFXAM received just over half. The JFS, whereby DFID matches NGO funding in development projects run by NGOs, was allocated a budget of £35 million in 1996–7. This scheme is open to all NGOs, large and small. NGO receipts from the state increased more than three times in real terms between 1983 and 1994 (Maxwell 1996: 117). More than 200 British NGOs now receive public funding, although the largest receive the lion's share of public money. The low priority given to Latin America is reflected in the fact that projects there took up only 3 per cent of the total JFS funds in 1995/6.

This partial privatization of the aid budget has dramatically altered the relationships between the state and the NGOs and has led to the formation of a policy network linking the state with (some) NGOs. This poses a set of dilemmas, prominent among which is the danger of cooptation (Edwards and Hulme 1996: 961). It is clear that, even in the relatively short time that the network has existed, it has transformed the NGO universe in the UK. However, it is too simple to argue that all NGOs are, or are in danger of becoming, coopted by the opportunities for increased funding and dialogue with official donors. First, only some organizations are able and encouraged to enter into dialogue with the state, although all development NGOs can become members of BOND. Indeed, a number of representatives of smaller organizations have criticized BOND (interviews with the author, June–July 1996) for over representing the big NGOs whose skills and resources the state hopes to harness.[4] What separates OXFAM, CAFOD, Christian Aid, WATERWORLD and Save the Children from, for example, CODA, WOMANKIND, and the

CUSICHACA TRUST, organizations with development and democratization programmes in Latin America but without influence over the state, is the size of their operations, their bureaucratic sophistication, their technical capacity and the range of international contacts they possess. OXFAM, Christian Aid, etc. have the capacity to perform important tasks that the state wishes to devolve to the private sector. To do so effectively, it must consult with those agencies.

One result of the formation of the policy network is to deepen divisions within the British NGO universe. The smaller organizations are fearful that they will be marginalized and that a hegemonic project of what constitutes development and democratization will be constructed emphasizing efficiency over redistribution. Representatives repeated their fears that the large NGOs are converting development issues into an industry, and one which is very profitable for them (interviews with the author, June–July 1996). Some also expressed the fear that close relations with the government inevitably distances the NGOs from civil society and closes them off from 'the pluralism of British civil society, which is its strength, not its efficiency in market terms' (NGO representative, interview with the author, July 1996).

The state does not, as yet, intervene in any detailed way in the kind of projects UK NGOs carry out. Fears of cooptation, at least in a direct way, would therefore appear to be exaggerated. The state depends on large NGOs to administer and even to shape policy. It lays down guidelines for the kind of cooperation it would like them to pursue but what those guidelines mean is determined largely by the organizations implementing them – the NGOs themselves. Hence the ODA decided in 1995–1996 that support for good government and the liberalization of markets were important elements of policies to support Latin American democratization. The large NGOs with block grants determined what this might mean in-house, after the grants were made. Block grant funds in Latin America were used in this period to create a black newspaper, to fund projects on empowering the landless and shanty-town dwellers, to run workshops on empowering women, and to develop non-formal educational strategies: projects with little connection or relevance for market-oriented development strategies.

Even JFS funds, in which the projects are evaluated before funds are assigned, showed no evidence of ideological policing. Despite the guidelines, JFS-funded projects in Latin America between 1994–1996 included supporting solidarity groups in Colombia, setting up a black woman's cultural centre in Brazil, organic gardening centres in Argentina and Uruguay, a herbal medicine centre, a mental health and drug rehabilitation programme in Peru, and the creation of a halfway house for female beggars and prostitutes in Brazil. Clearly, British official guidelines on development are elastic and the NGOs still retain the key function of deciding how to interpret them on the ground.

This freedom over projects, however, does not preclude the very real possibility that the NGOs in the network *will* be influenced by 'official' thinking about development and democracy. It is possible that they may come to accept the links made by official donors between democracy, the market and liberal economic reform. Regular and sustained contact with state representatives, the opportunities of influencing state policy, the lack of clear alternatives to the New Policy Agenda, all make it likely that some NGO officials will be brought round to accepting official recipes for development. While it is also possible that the NGOs will exercise some influence over key figures within DFID, it is unlikely that this would correct the current bias within the institution associating economic liberalism with democracy. There is also a danger, high-lighted by some NGO representatives, that these NGOs will be negatively associated with unpopular government policies and lose legitimacy within their own civil societies. Equally, if they are too close to government, they may be viewed with suspicion by their Latin American counterparts (although on the other hand, with access to large volumes of official funding they may actually appear more attractive and stable funders).

It is too early to say with any certainty what the effects of the new policy network in development may be. It has certainly increased the divisions within British NGOs between those who see development and democracy in Latin America as undermined by neoliberalism and those who see the two as compatible. But even for those in receipt of relatively substantial and regular funding from government, there is a clear reluctance to allow the government to determine the content of projects pursued in the name of 'democracy', as witnessed by the description above of the kind of projects which are being funded. At the same time, NGOs are trying to use their links with Southern counterparts to strengthen their own commitment to 'substantive democracy'. For British NGOs, I argue, this is one of the main roles the ethical network plays.

The ethical network

Scepticism has been expressed, both within academia and among NGOs themselves, about the possibility of building relationships of equality between Northern and Southern NGOs. Most Latin American NGOs depend upon external funding, generally from Northern NGOs, though increasingly also from official funding agencies such as the EU and even the World Bank, not only to implement programmes but even to carry out their basic administrative activities and pay salaries. Given this financial dependence, to what extent is it valid to speak of European and Latin American NGOs and social movements participat-ing in a network of shared values, morals and principles and having a mutual commitment to reducing inequality, as I propose to do here?

A growing number of NGOs claim to promote relationships of equality and partnership with their Latin American counterparts. This is dismissed by one Salvadoran NGO, as, at best, a pipe dream because 'the idea of partnership supposes a degree of autonomy of the two parts. This is hardly ever seen in practice because the nucleus of the relationship is based on the channeling of funds one way, towards the Southern counterpart' (PRISMA 1994). I want to argue here that, although the relationship between European and Latin American NGOs is structurally unequal in funding terms, an important number of European NGOs have a genuine and deeply-held commitment to creating relationships of equality and respect with their Latin American counterparts, and reject the idea that financial dependence is the totality of their relationship.

The network with Latin American NGOs not only serves to channel financial resources southwards; it fulfills the function of allowing Northern NGOs to commit themselves to creating a better world. It has a moral role to play in developing Northern NGOs' consciousness. It represents an ideal type of the kind of North-South relationships most NGOs wish to promote. For these reasons, I am terming it an 'ethical network'. It reaffirms the importance of a moral, non-marketized approach to development and democracy.

Development NGOs have always forged relationships beyond national frontiers, whether with Southern states, Southern community organizations, churches or foundations. The impact of the globalization debate within the NGO world and the increasing importance of NGOs in the delivery of services have meant the conscious adoption of a global logic and an affirmation of the significance of transborder contacts in their activities. This has made European NGOs more aware of the importance of developing relationships with their counterparts which go beyond simply funding programmes, and there is now a conscious commitment to building ties between NGOs across the North–South frontier.

The ethical network fulfills a number of important functions for European NGOs and they devote a considerable amount of time and resources to it. The network is loose and NGOs find incorporation easy. In the first instance, it is useful for finding counterparts or partners for programmes. But its central importance lies beyond this. Actors in the network engage in sharing information about development and in creating strategies for putting development and democracy issues onto the agenda of states and multilateral agencies. It is a way to alert other NGOs to the need for mobilization around a particularly urgent issue. It reinforces the traditional values of solidarity and morality within the NGO world. Membership of this network implies sharing a world view. It is built upon shared beliefs in the principle of co-development, in the values of partnership and in the importance of democracy and citizenship. The participants share a conviction that NGOs have a particular responsibility in terms of representing civil society and of promoting participative development. It emphasizes accountability and the democratization of social relationships.

Partly in order to implement the principles around which the ethical network coheres, UK NGOs have moved towards adopting the principle of co-development as the touchstone for their operations in Latin America. At its simplest, this means implementing a pattern of cooperation which depends essentially on supporting projects by Latin American counterparts. It is an attempt to break with the idea of cooperation as something externally-funded, externally-designed and carried out by 'experts' from the North. The ideas is to collapse the North–South dichotomy which dominated development practice until the 1980s. But co-development means more than devolving to Latin American organizations the responsibility for the design and implementation of projects. It is a new philosophy of development. In interviews with UK NGO representatives, three facets of co-development could be identified:

- *Co-development understood as skills, assets or learning which individuals acquire from their contacts with others in the network.* These skills are then applied to the promotion of democratic practices in the country in which they work. Individuals who work in UK NGOs therefore see themselves as learning as much as those who work in Latin American ones. One organizer in the UK argued that working with Latin American NGOs was important for him in learning how to 'respond to the cynicism which can sometimes be found in the UK around the possibilities of political change and to show what can be achieved by small popular organizations' (interview, June 1996).
- *Co-development meaning the strengthening of organizations dedicated to change, the NGOs themselves.* This comes about through the joint activities of the network, exchanging information, mutual support and personal relationships, thereby contributing to building movements within societies in favour of change.
- *Co-development as a fundamental part of democratization.* This is a strategy in its own right to effect global change and promote global citizenship, a pattern for future relationships. The task of promoting democratization thus becomes a global responsibility, the co-responsibility of all members of the network. This third perspective is the most strategic interpretation of co-development and fits those NGOs which have a long term goal of promoting new, non-market relationships of citizenship. It represents an ideal, not a working model, of North-South relationships.

Despite this idealism, the need to balance ethical commitments to other NGOs with the demands placed upon them by states and the EU, coupled with the real limitations in resources, means that the task of NGOs is not an easy one. European NGOs can easily find that their role in promoting democratization and equitable development more limited and, even, more contradictory than they had hoped. We can see more clearly the kind of tensions this generates in European organizations by looking at how the relationship between UK and Latin American NGOs works in practice.

UK NGOs in Latin America

Any importance UK NGOs might claim for themselves in Latin America lies not in the volume of aid disbursed but in the kind of democratization and North-South relationships they promote. They should not therefore be judged in terms of the size of their contribution, but by how far they are able to put co-development into practice as a strategy for supporting democratization. This section first gives examples of the kind of projects in which UK NGOs are engaged. It then looks at how UK and Latin American NGOs relate to each other, using examples from project evaluation.

Using contacts generated and sustained through the transnational NGO network, a number of UK NGOs are engaged in small scale projects which contribute to democratization through promoting the economic and political participation of the poor, the marginalized and the excluded in the societies in which they live. A good example of this kind of project is an initiative which involves two small UK NGOs, CODA and WOMANKIND, and a Nicaraguan collective of women builders, the Maria Jose Talavera Collective in Condega. The collective, which was formed by eight members in 1987, erects small houses and makes concrete blocks to be used in the construction industry .It was formed to solve the problems the members were faced with: high levels of unemployment, making it difficult to find jobs; the exclusion of women from formal sector employment; a sexist work culture which prevents male employers taking on female labourers; and their need, as poor women with families, to provide for themselves and their dependents. Supporting the collective promotes democratization by giving these women rights through their incorporation into the workforce as well as helping to alleviate their poverty. In 1992 CODA organized courses for the members to train as electricians and thereby enlarge the scale of their activities, and WOMANKIND organized a series of courses on health and safety in the workplace in 1994. The collective has since expanded and created employment options for other women in Condega and cooperation between the three organizations continues.

A different example of the kind of work UK NGOs carry out in Latin America has to do with the effects of war. Some UK NGOs, in collaboration with Latin American partners, are lobbying states and the UN to promote a final resolution of the dirty wars in Latin America in the 1980s. For those involved, this means more than bringing to trial those members of the Armed Forces or death squads responsible for human rights abuses and disappearances. Even more emphasis is given to finding out the fate of the disappeared, tracing victims of the wars and creating a social climate in which the families of victims are accorded respect and recognition of their losses. British NGOs, most notably Save the Children, are involved in lobbying for the clarification of the fate of the disappeared in Central America and support a local NGO in El Salvador, PRO-BUSQUEDA, in trying to trace children who disappeared during the wars. Save the Children also cooperates with the Olaf Palme Foundation, the University of Central America in San Salvador and the *Instituto de Promocion Humana* (INPRHU) in Nicaragua in developing programmes to rehabilitate children traumatized by violence. NGOs are also pressing Central American governments to incorporate a charter of children's rights into the constitution. Some European states, notably Spain, Italy, France and Sweden, have indicated their willingness to participate in pressing for solutions to these problems, evidence of very successful lobbying by the NGOs.

Collaboration between UK and Latin American NGOs has, in a few cases, led to a snowballing of projects. One example is how Save the Children has been drawn into promoting an AIDS education network in Latin America. The charity identified Aids education and prevention as a priority in its work in Latin America in the early 1990s. It then made contact with the Peruvian *Instituto de Educacion y Salud* (IES) and together they produced a textbook for use in schools in Peru to educate children about AIDS. Contact was then made with a Cuban NGO and the three organizations are working on a similar text for use in Cuba. Meanwhile, Save the Children has brought in another British NGO for advice and assistance. Although the UK Aids Consortium had no overseas experience or contacts, it is now working with Save the Children and two Brazilian NGOs, the *Grupo de Apoio em Prevencao da Aids* (GAPA) and the *Asociacao Brasilera Interdisplinar da Aids* (ABIA). As a result, a South American Aids Consortium was set up in 1995 which is seeking funding for a joint European-Latin American study of Aids prevention.

In all these projects, UK NGOs claim to be committed to building relationships of equality with their Latin American counterparts, in spite of the financial ties which place Latin American NGOs in a position of dependence upon them. Co-development and building ethical relationships combine as a transformative project for global change which begins by restructuring relationships between Northern and Southern NGOs. Commitment to these ideals cannot eliminate the material, structural and financial inequalities which confer on UK NGOs resources that Latin American ones lack. It means however, that UK and Latin American NGOs try to overcome these inequalities and create a sub-world in which hierarchy is less important and can be challenged.

This has changed the ways in which UK NGO-funded projects are evaluated. Evaluation of projects was traditionally seen as the job of the 'authority' or the 'expert' and was the responsibility of the financial 'owner' of the project. Evaluation was about financial accountability and value for money from the donor's perspective. Many UK-funded projects are now evaluated from the perspective of what they have contributed to development and democratization in Latin America. The evaluators now tend to come from Latin America, normally another NGO which has had no relationship with the project. Evaluation is no longer the job of the funder.

This has increased the costs of the projects and has to some degree bureaucratized the process of assessment but it has also placed the two sides of the relationship, the UK and Latin American NGO, on more equal footings. At the same time, it contributes towards diffusing power and responsibility among NGOs. Living Earth Foundation (UK) and *Tierra Viva* (Venezuela), who used a third Latin American NGO to assess their joint operations, describe the advantages of this form of assessment in the following way:

The strategy of working with an external evaluation body was . . . to accompany and support the identification of important elements for the development of projects. To highlight aspects which needed to be reworked or redefined in terms of projects. To maintain an objective vision of the development of the project . . . The external evaluation contributed to the process of continuous evaluation, highlighting certain elements and facilitating strategies to correct aspects which had not been picked up by the *Tierra Viva* team, for example reinforcing the diagnosis element of the training and development of thematic units

(*Environmental Education Project of the Lake Valencia Basin, November 1991–December 1995*, Final Report, p.29)

The projects and the evaluation described above are all examples of successful collaboration between UK and Latin American NGOs. The UK NGOs interviewed were unanimous in arguing that co-development enables them to design and carry out more effective, and more democratic, projects than in earlier periods. Some even claim that they have directly transformed the kind of cooperation they practice as a result of the critiques they have received from Southern counterparts. ACTIONAID, for example, has recently reviewed its child-centred activities as a result of dialogue with Southern NGOs, moving away from sponsorship programmes towards a series of activities which reflect the complexity of family roles, income distribution within families and the gendered activities of children and other family members. This has been possible only because ACTIONAID has learned from listening to Southern NGOs and abandoned its role as the 'expert'.

Conclusion: European NGOs' contribution to democratization

This chapter began by emphasizing the importance assigned to European and Latin American NGOs in the academic literature, by donors and even by NGOs themselves in building democracy in Latin America. It has ended by suggesting that the contributions of European NGOs can be positive, using the example of UK projects. But their role is also limited and circumscribed due to a number of reasons.

First, although these projects aim at democratization through strengthening civil societies, there are limitations on how far this can be done from outside. UK NGOs will eventually withdraw from the projects they support. This frequently leads to the collapse of the initiatives they have funded and sometimes to the disintegration of the Latin American NGO, which depended on external funding to survive. Any strengthening of the fabric of Latin American civil societies through promoting local NGO activity is frequently only temporary. UK NGOs are aware of these problems, as my interviews with their workers revealed, but are unable to tackle them.

Second, projects such as those described above are at best a fragile way to deepen democracy because they depend upon individuals transforming their immediate environment; they do not challenge the privileges embedded in the state or the international order. Gains in citizenship are not necessarily maintained beyond the life of the project and rarely challenge the system of social and political privilege which has been identified as the root cause of the lack of democracy in Latin America. These kind of citizenship gains are easily reversed.

Third, these projects do not challenge, in any direct sense, the neoliberal model of development. Most UK NGOs would see this as the biggest obstacle to promoting substantive democratization in Latin America. They fail to challenge neoliberalism not because they have become compromised through accepting money from the state and participating in a policy network with the state, as the cooptation approach suggests. Rather they are not influential enough to mount an effective opposition to it. Their role remains essentially one of mopping up the worst consequences of underdevelopment and exploitation, although now they do this in collaboration and through local organizations. UK NGOs remain committed to substantive democratization in principle and to changing the global order; they believe that participative development and strengthening civil societies are the keys building solid, stable and just democracies. But these tasks are enormous and they lack the resources to mount a major challenge to orthodox views on development and democracy.

This is not to suggest that they are unimportant. Conveying solidarity, working to construct idealistic visions of democracy and a transformed global order and moving towards partnership and equality with similar and like-minded social groups in the South are undoubtedly important steps towards building better societies and a fairer global order. It is important, however, to deflate the current assumption that NGOs, especially foreign-based NGOs, constitute one of the main vehicles through which substantive democracy can be built in Latin America.

Northern NGOs blame themselves for taking money from governments – and governments for using them – rather than being prepared to acknowledge their essential limitations. Latin American NGOs, by contrast, tend to argue that their European counterparts are, at best, naive in believing that they can contruct relationships of equality over the North-South divide. This reflects, ultimately, a zero-sum conception of North-South relations which presumes that there can be no common meeting ground between individuals in the South with those of the North and suggests that the task of constructuing democracy is, by implication, exclusively a local one. In my view, neither of these readings of the limitations of NGO activity is correct. I have tried to show that UK NGOs remain free at least to implement important aspects of policies as they wish, despite their increased reliance on government funding. At the same time, they are genuinely committed to building relationships of equality and co-development.

The essence of the problem is that NGOs cannot work miracles, and this is what they are increasingly being expected to do. They cannot overcome through good will or even good practice the undemocratic pattern of social and political relations and productive practices in Latin America which is rooted in historically and culturally embedded power structures. My conclusion is therefore similar to that of Pearce (1997a), writing on Latin American NGOs. She drew upon the 1993 United National Human Development Report to express both support and scepticism for the work of NGOs and to reflect upon the ambiguous role they play in contemporary democratization: 'In eradicating poverty and providing social services, NGOs are unlikely ever to play more than a complementary role . . . their importance lies in making the point that poverty can be tackled rather tackling it to any large extent' (UNDP 1993: 98–9, in Pearce 1997a: 274).

Notes

I would like to thank the members of the ECPR panel *Democratization and the Changing Global Order*, 25th ECPR Joint Sessions, Bern, February 27–March 4, 1997, for their commnents on an earlier draft of this paper; Lucy Taylor, Petr Kopecky, Christian Freres, Jenny Pearce, Martin Smith and Tony Payne for discussing some of the ideas in this chapter and commenting on an earlier draft.

1 Except where it is stated otherwise, all the NGOs referred to in this chapter are NGOs engaged in promoting development overseas, whether they are described as 'development NGOs' or simply 'NGOs'.

2 For one UK NGO representative, the new NGO-friendly official aid regime was problematic because it lacked 'a meaningful interpretation of development' and 'promoted a culture of new managerialism' within NGOs. Projects were funded by official donors if the 'recipe' for filling in the forms was followed; making grant applications requires using a 'logical framework' rather than making a genuine contribution to development, according to the interviewee. He made this point despite his own organization's ability to win a number of substantial grants from the EU. Hence NGOs ran risks of becoming organizations which aim to gather in resources through project applications to the EU and national governments rather than trying to promote egalitarian forms of development. While few NGO representatives interviewed expressed this view as categorically, it was clearly a worry for a number of NGOs, especially those which emerged from the 'solidarity' movements of the 1970s and 1980s.

3 Much of the information in this section is drawn from interviews caried out with representatives of UK NGOs in 1996, as part of an EU-financed research project on European Civil Societies' Development Cooperation in Latin America. I would like to thank Christian Freres of AIETI, Madrid, for his assistance as project coordinator and the the European Commission (DG 1) for financing the research.

4 The UK NGO world is extraordinarily diverse. Development NGOs vary in size from two or three members to multinational organizations such as OXFAM. Their origins, principles and goals also vary.

9

MARKET FORCES AND MORAL IMPERATIVES

The professionalization of social activism in Latin America

Lucy Taylor

Many of those who seek to understand the consolidation of democracy point to the importance of civil society in creating a bedrock of opinion and a foundation of relationships which enhance the democratic ethos. Key to civil society are two sets of agents: social movements (issue-related campaigning groups) and non-governmental organizations (professional organizations with a social agenda). Both of these contribute to the construction of civil society's fabric and influence the issues and demands expressed within society. The role of non-governmental organizations (NGOs) has become of particular importance with the expansion of the global trend to use them as agents in the implementation of government policy; this trend is common not only in western nations but also in the newly democratizing countries of Latin America.

This chapter explores these themes by drawing on the experiences of NGOs in two Latin American countries, Chile and Argentina. First, it discusses the nature and characteristics of neoliberal democracy and argues that civil society and NGOs play a crucial role in making this form of democracy both workable and acceptable in poor countries. Second, it examines the development of NGO activity with particular reference to Chile and argues that much of the funding which once went directly from international bodies to the NGOs is now diverted through central government.

The chapter goes on to look at the implications, both material and political, of this and suggests that the categories of social movement, NGO and state agency have become increasingly blurred as relationships between them have adapted to the new political environment. The 'natural affinity' between social movement and NGO is becoming increasingly strained as more professionalized relationships take root.

At the same time the supposed 'natural antagonism' between civil society and state agency begins to breakdown; they are coming to share an increasingly dense and complex network of relationships which link personal contacts, funding opportunities and shared political goals. These developments are discussed mainly in relation to the Argentine experience. The chapter concludes that government, NGO and social activist alike must recognize the diversity of opinion which is generated in democracy and the changing roles and political positions as potential strengths rather than an indication of dangerous division, thereby acknowledging that pluralism is essential to a successful democratic project.[1]

The role of NGOs in government and society

Neoliberalism is well established in Chile, as it was the focus of the authoritarian government's economic and political programme from the mid-1970s onwards. In Argentina, structural adjustment and liberalization came later and are less deeply embedded, having been first systematically implemented by President Menem in 1989. Both countries are engaged in the creation and consolidation of a specifically neoliberal democracy in which development projects at the local, social level take precedence over national, political solutions, and in which NGOs are privileged because they are regarded as private entities with a social foundation.

The advent of neoliberal economic strategies has also ushered in neoliberal understandings of democracy (Grugel 1998). A neoliberal democracy can be characterized by its strong emphasis on civil rights, particularly those relating to contract which allow individuals engaging in the market to have confidence in the transactions which take place. The ascendancy of the economic over the political sphere as the privileged arena through which ideas, preferences and needs are expressed implies that political rights also decline in importance. The sovereignty of the consumer, expressed through participation in market exchange, is privileged and so becomes a far more effective means of wielding influence than participation in political debate.

The formal mechanisms of democracy, such as elections, accountability, the procedures of policy formulation and the practicalities of policy implementation, retain democratic forms. However, the shift of participation away from the political to the economic arena diminishes the importance of such formal elements for daily life and allows political elitism to flourish. Citizens come to understand their problems not in terms of structures and ideologies but in terms of practical issues and tangible, visible obstacles. They therefore try to solve their problems not by engaging in intellectual debate, joining ideological political parties or seeking to change the world but by organizing self-help groups, lobbying local government and seeking to change their own little universe.

In this way, shifting citizens' perspectives away from the national and political spheres and towards the local and social arenas also implies an enhanced role for civil society, the 'private' element of democracy. It is in the context of such trends in participation that professional private organizations have become key actors in society and the polity at the same time as neo-liberal concepts of the state have enhanced their potential incidence in both.

The role of NGOs has been altered dramatically by the advent and development of neoliberal concepts of the state. Essentially, the role of the state in contemporary politics has been much reduced and private organizations, broadly defined, have become the favoured agencies of interaction with society. These explicitly *non*-governmental entities, of varying types, form relationships which are based on the workings of the market and respond primarily to its dynamics, allocating resources and channelling activities in response to impulses expressed through supply and demand (Haggard and Kaufmann 1992; Smith, Acuña and Gamarra 1994). This dynamic contrasts with previous understandings of the role of the state in which ideology and political objectives were the primary motive force behind policy decisions and in which the state played a key role as both formulator and implementor of policy objectives.

Such trends follow global patterns in that they can be observed in action in almost any part of the world. This is in part due to the imposition or spread of a global 'norm' upon the actions and policies of domestic governments, a norm which has frequently been adopted in Latin America as a result of constraints and pressures imposed by international financial institutions such as the International Monetary Fund (IMF) and World Bank (Bresser Pereira 1993). However, trends towards market deregulation and privatization can also be identified with international understandings of 'best practice' which emanate from US and European thought and policy.

What is particularly persuasive about these 'understandings' is that while they are very political proposals, their wider dissemination is founded upon a 'treatment' which portrays them as being the accepted wisdom; privatization becomes the common sense option. Indeed, once a critical mass of international opinion seems to be backing neoliberalism, then proponents of privatization can go on to claim that it *does* reflect the accepted wisdom and that it *is* the sensible policy option. The claim that neoliberalism has become the orthodox development solution is of course reinforced by the dearth of examples of other policy approaches which have achieved a measure of success. Any governments attempting to buck the neoliberal economic norm must also work against trends in the flow of capital, investment and credit which sustain the whirlpool of global financial markets, and which are underpinned by the logic of neoliberal deregulation. Such an air of inevitability is perhaps depressing for those broadly 'on the left', but it is essential that we recognise that governments, especially in countries that are debt-ridden or dependent, have little option but to work with the grain of international constraints.

Latin American governments, and indeed those in all newly democratizing countries, have therefore had little option but to accept neoliberalism. Equipped with policy advisors, renegotiated debt schedules and a sharp knife, they begin to cut into public services, to free markets, to allow the 'invisible hand' to work its magic. However, the voting public is seldom willing to endure the concomitant hardship without comment and governments run the risk of losing popularity very quickly. Political leaders therefore become caught between, on the one hand, the demands of the international financial community, backed up by a global neoliberalism, which are based on an economic imperative and, on the other, the political imperative of the need to retain popular support (Maravall 1994; Przeworski 1995). What is of primary importance to the domestic politician (dominance at the ballot box) is in some cases jeopardized by the primary concern of the international financial community (economic orthodoxy).

Moreover, with the retreat of the state from many areas of social life, governments have lost much of their influence over the socio-economic sphere. For example, structural adjustment often creates lower standards of living for the poorer classes, at least in the short term. If governments are to retain support they must offer a political response to impoverishment and adopt anti-poverty measures; they must be seen to be 'doing something' to tackle the issue and 'to care'. Otherwise, important sectors of the electorate will come to regard governmental indifference as 'callous' and 'immoral'. Yet the minimal state severely curtails the ability of governments to respond to contentious issues such as poverty; they can neither devote substantial public resources to tackling it, given the trend towards low levels of public expenditure, nor can they justify state interference in the lives of individuals since individual liberty is pre-eminent in such neoliberal democracies. One way in which governments can square this circle is to utilize non-governmental agencies as vehicles through which politically motivated policies can be enacted (Taylor 1998).

NGOs come to occupy a privileged position in neoliberal democracies for several reasons. First, they are regarded as compatible with the neoliberal trend towards a minimal state in that they are private organizations tendering in a competitive arena for funds with which to develop their projects. As such, they are seen as having the virtues of the market, primarily efficiency and responsiveness to the 'consumers' of their programmes who exercise power and express preference through the laws of supply and demand. Second, they are regarded as intrinsically virtuous by those who seek to engage in ethical development projects. They generally target the most impoverished sectors of the population or those who are marginalized from the dominant dynamic of growth (such as women, ethnic minorities or indigenous peoples) and they stress empowerment and participatory practices. The key to their success lies in their perceived credibility as agents of change in the eyes of all concerned: governments, international agencies and those they serve directly at the grassroots. In the cases of Chile and Argentina, and indeed in many other newly democratized countries, their credibility at the base is enhanced by their active participation in the anti-authoritarian struggles in the past, when they were viewed as progressive agents for the dissemination of democracy and rights.

Neoliberalism does not necessarily imply a passive and atomized society engaged in selfish individualism; to be successful, the neoliberal polity must beware of unbridled individual competition which tends to fragment society, to create conflicts and internalized problems, and leads to bitterness on the part of those who fail. It must counter the tendencies towards atomization by fostering a 'privatized' social arena which encourages cooperation and social responsibility, which operates for the benefit of all and which is able to forge links between citizens and create a coherent and cohesive society (Berger and Neuhaus 1993).

This form of democracy highlights the individual yet locates her within society, emphasizing her social role, rather than privileging her position within the polity and underlining her political role. Indeed, in an age of increasingly complex and elitist politics and an ideological context which presents no real alternatve to liberal democracy, the political sphere offers few opportunities for the citizen to enact change, and consequently a socialized understanding of participation has a great deal more resonance.

In this socialized arena, NGOs can implement policies in a localized and responsive manner and can credibly act as channels for the expression of grievances and needs, as well as being the vehicles for solving problems of government. This use of NGOs as service deliverers strengthens the trend for focus of participation to shift away from political activity and the conflict of ideologies towards local and social initiatives. It goes with emphasis on private and 'practical' social organizations which concentrate on delivering material improvement of individual lives through collective action, for example, the building of a community centre or the creation of a children's playground.

The kind of activities these organizations undertake privileges civil society as the agent of social change and the improvement of individual lives through community development (Diamond 1994). By encouraging civil society, a neoliberal democracy enhances its position in two ways. First, an active civil society plays a social role as in all democracies: it teaches and encourages forms of conduct which enhance democratic values in public behaviour, such as listening to and respecting the views of others, negotiating and reaching a consensus, organization and delegation, upholding rights and taking responsibilities seriously in relation to the community and its project. Second, increasing the social power and capability of civil society demonstrates that it is society and not the state which is best able to solve people's problems. It thereby justifies the presence of a minimal state and encourages citizens to search for solutions at the local level and among themselves. While the former contributes to the consolidation of democracy, the latter outlines and reinforces the neoliberal form which that democracy will take (Taylor 1998).

Social movements, NGOs and democratization

During the dictatorships in Chile and Argentina, social movements, local NGOs and international NGOs created networks of activism which directly challenged the authoritarian governments and their policies. NGOs and social movements were best established in Chile, where they were also more numerous and more active (Oxhorn 1991; Campero 1987).[2] Broadly, under the dictatorship, there were three kinds of social movement: human rights organizations, women's groups, and shanty town organizations. NGOs typically focused on campaigning and awareness-raising, emergency relief and project development, and sometimes also academic analysis.

The following example provides an illustration of how social organization operated under Chilean military rule. A typical shantytown would have a soup kitchen, an *ad hoc* organization which had developed out of necessity. Its structure was organic and horizontal and it had no official accounts or formally demarcated areas of responsibility. It would be funded at first by those who came to eat and later also perhaps by a western solidarity group. Such funding often came about though contacts forged by Chileans in exile or through links made between western political activists who came to Chile on formal delegations (linked to trade unions, for example) mediated by political support groups in the West. More informal personal encounters might also play a role, as in the case of Europeans or Americans who came to Chile with the aim of undermining the military regime. These international links were a crucial element in the work of social movements and grassroots groups such as the soup kitchens from the mid-1980s onwards. What brought together such disparate individuals was that they shared an explicitly political commitment to oust the military regime.

The women who ran the soup kitchen would meet to discuss not only their project, but also the political situation in general and strategies for dissent, such as participation in a demonstration (Valdés and Weinstein 1993; Valenzuela 1995). The group would form part of a wider network of dissent, linking with community human rights groups, health groups, theatre groups and so on. Working for women's emancipation as well as democracy was often an important element of such activities. This was often one of the reasons why the western solidarity movement would support soup kitchens since in doing so they were helping women, both in a material sense and as part of a wider political agenda. The group of women would commonly be approached by a local feminist organization which would teach skills that women could use to earn money and would also run consciousness-raising workshops.[3]

In contrast to the soup kitchen, these local NGOs would often have a semi-permanent staff – paid or voluntary – and were formally structured and organized. In turn, they were often supported by external funding, which might come from a sister feminist organization in Europe or the US, or they might be the beneficiaries of aid channelled from western governments or the European Union. Thus an intricate network of contacts was built up both horizontally (among shanty town organizations or within the community of national NGOs) and vertically (local, national and international links). International contacts of this kind were integral not only to the more formal NGOs but also to grassroots political movements in the West and Chile.

The relationship between NGOs and social movements was largely unproblematic during the mid-to late 1980s as both were united in their aim of removing General Pinochet from power. Indeed, NGOs became a central element in the issue-led social movements and in the broader pro-democracy movement. They could often be seen marching alongside the more *ad hoc* movements during demonstrations and participating in the plethora of umbrella groups which sought to coordinate dissent within civil society. Both were encouraged and assisted by the efforts of their international partners, the solidarity groups and the western NGOs, which sought to raise awareness of, for example, human rights abuses, and to keep the issue on the international agenda of the western media and western governments.

With the transition to democracy, social movements in Chile have undergone a dramatic decline in importance. This can be attributed, at least in part, to the improvements in standards of living which many Chileans (the principal exceptions being the very poor) have experienced. It is also a result of a sense of political exhaustion after prolonged struggle, mixed with relief that finally people can get on with their own lives and hand responsibility for the country's fortunes to elected authorities (Taylor 1995). In turn, this has tended to reduce western activism. Western solidarity groups have frequently turned their attention to more immediate crises such as Bosnia or Sudan. However, while the solidarity activists in the West are losing some of their interest in Chile, which no longer serves as a focus for campaigns, the work of professionalized local NGOs has blossomed and they have become a more important social and political force than before.

It is interesting that the nature of the work undertaken by Chilean NGOs today is broadly the same as during the military regime, reflecting their twin tasks of encouraging 'good citizenship' and teaching economic skills to individuals. Under the dictatorship, 'good citizenship' took the form of actively pursuing democratic practices within the organizations and upholding the values of democracy (justice, equality and freedom) in the campaigns (Garretón 1989). As such, the NGOs helped to sustain a democratic practice and ethos within an overarching culture of authoritarianism. The NGOs had begun by teaching skills to individuals and the poor, their second task under the dictatorship, in response to the hardship generated by neoliberal restructuring. In addition, and alongside shanty town movements, NGOs played a role in organizing groups within given localities to solve the everyday, practical problems faced by residents of poor communities. Perhaps surprisingly, nothing much has changed with democracy. NGOs still practice participatory methodologies which involve an active engagement with the local communities and encourage participation. They also teach civic education, which commonly involves raising awareness about citizenship rights and the responsibilities of the police or municipality, and many organize workshops in 'leadership training' which aim to empower local or community representatives.[4]

There is one striking difference, however, between the activities of NGOs during authoritarian and democratic rule. During the dictatorship, Chilean NGOs were engaged in active denunciation of the military regime and its tactics of authoritarian rule and physical repression; their stance was overtly political. Similarly, they taught survival strategies whilst at the same time denouncing the economic policy to which they responded. Now, with the democratic governments, this element of political opposition has been substantially eroded. Whereas before, they attacked the incumbent government and neoliberalism and placed themselves outside the system, now many are acting in tandem with the state and are firmly incorporated within the system. During the dictatorship, one of the slogans of the women's movement was 'democracy in the country and in the home' which sought to show that the personal was political. For many NGOs this has changed, almost without their noticing, to become 'neoliberalism in the country and in the home', thus indicating that the personal is economic too.

To sum up, the strategy of encouraging a strong yet depoliticized civil society has been adopted in contemporary Chile. Whether this strategy was selected by design or by default it is hard to say, but certainly it is aligned to the dominant economic and political dynamic. As we shall see, the government has enlisted the help of the professional agents of civil society, the NGOs, in providing the finance and expertise to oil the workings of civil society and to act as the private sector conduit for social investment. The Argentine experience differs, in that the country is still in the throes of adjustment and has yet to reap any substantial rewards from the neoliberal project beyond currency stability. However, similar relationships are beginning to emerge between the state and human rights and women's issue NGOs. It would be logical to assume that this will deepen and that NGOs will become, as in Chile, one of the key avenues of policy implementation.[5] The relationship between NGOs, social movements and the state has certainly changed considerably with democratization and the introduction of neoliberalism. Not only have NGOs become more distanced from the grassroots movements but many have also developed intimate links with the state. At the same time the role of state organizations has also undergone a qualitative change. These shifts are related to the process of democratization itself and also to the changing role of the state and its altered relationship with society.

Changing relationships between NGOs and grassroots movements

As I argued above, the coming of democracy has changed the relationship between local NGOs and the grassroots movements in both Chile and Argentina. There had always been substantial differences in their roles and goals. The grassroots groups were more combative and felt a greater emotional commitment to the anti-military movement due to their direct experience of repression and poverty. The NGOs approached the issues from a more professionalized

145

position. It was they who 'taught' and the movements who 'learned' many of the skills and the analysis of patriarchy and political oppression. Also, while many of the grassroots activists came from the lower classes, the majority of workers in the NGOs were university-educated and middle class.

During the dictatorships, then, a form of power relationship developed between the educators and the recipients of 'knowledge', but this was largely counteracted by the force of political commitment among the social movements and their courage, determination and ability to mobilize which won the undoubted respect of the NGOs. Each had a role to play in the wider anti-military movement and valued the efforts of the other. Once the military were ousted, though, the common cause which had united NGOs and grassroots groups disappeared, and while vestiges of the former equality have survived, hierarchy has become a more marked feature of their relationship.

With the general decline in political activity, the grassroots organizations withered and lost much of their power and energy. The NGOs, however, maintained their commitment to projects in the shanty towns and to 'vulnerable' groups such as women and youth, and continued to be active as educators and agents of empowerment. Nevertheless, without the political focus, the relationship between agency and beneficiary has become more formalized and less reciprocal, and is increasingly translated as professional/client, teacher/pupil, problem solver/problem bearer, social worker/social victim. A concomitant distance between NGO and grassroots group has emerged which has been encouraged by a newly legitimized rhetoric emanating from government which focuses on personal development and the acquisition of applicable skills as a means of fostering the economic development of the individual and of the nation (Taylor 1998).

The element of continuity has contributed to the success of the various projects in a range of ways. First, these organizations had the skilled personnel, the premises and the technology which allowed them to start programmes immediately or to continue successful projects already established; there would be no lead-in time, and no delays. Second, they had wide experience of running similar courses and had developed forms and styles of instruction which were attuned to their potential clients. Third, they had a wide range of contacts within the target communities and enjoyed established networks onto which the government schemes could be grafted. Finally, they carried with them the trust of the people and the political credibility which accrued from their anti-regime activities; their credentials as progressive organizations were established and would lend credibility to the government-funded projects (Taylor 1996).

Chile provides an example of a polity in which the neoliberal project is well advanced and indicates a possible future course for neoliberal democracies seeking to create a sustainable economic and political regime through investment in civil society. The government does not just verbally encourage this form of NGO activity; it has shown itself very willing to finance projects, largely through the auspices of the Fund for Solidarity and Social Investment

(FOSIS), which was set up in 1990 under the slogan 'Investing with the People' (Ministerio de Planificación y Cooperación, 1992).

FOSIS aims to target state funding to the poorer sectors of the population, using intermediate organizations as the vehicles of development. These include technical colleges, municipalities, community organizations and, most especially, NGOs. During the period 1990–93 FOSIS financed 5,102 projects of three basic types. The first of these, Investment in Production and Training for Work, accounted for 64.5 per cent of the total funding. Its projects included the development of family allotments, well digging, reforestation projects and the buying of agricultural machinery, as well as training programmes geared towards self-employment in fields such as car mechanics, hairdressing, baking and plumbing. The second, Housing Improvements and Community Infrastructure, received 21.2 per cent of the funding for that period and included projects related to sanitation, street lighting and the building of community centres and sports fields. Finally, Training and Education accounted for 14.3 per cent of the projects funded by FOSIS, investing in the training of community healthworkers, workshops on leadership skills, after school clubs and pensioners' clubs. NGOs undertook 37.1 per cent of the projects, of which three-quarters were within the area of Investment in Production and Training for Work (FOSIS 1994).

The use of NGOs as agents of personal development is nothing new; as we have seen they performed this role throughout the 1980s with substantial success. What has changed, however, is the source of funding and the growing relationship between Chilean NGOs and the state. Whereas funding previously came from external entities and was distributed directly to the local NGO, much of it is now channelled from western governmental development agencies, from large international NGOs and from international organizations to the national government. The government then distributes it via FOSIS to NGOs working at the local level (Director of Educatión, interview March 1993; FOSIS 1994).

The reasons behind this shift are not clear, but it is likely that as the new Chilean government is perceived as a democratic regime by a wide range of international actors it is therefore included in the category of 'good' governments which are regarded as trustworthy in their dealings with their citizens. While it was possible to justify the by-passing of delinquent regimes such as Pinochet's by pointing to the blatant lack of human rights or representative political practices, there was no reason to continue to 'interfere' in domestic politics by funding groups outside the control of the government. Moreover, now that mechanisms of accountability had been reinstated in Chile, channelling funding through national government also implied that the representatives of the citizenry could and should decide where and how such money should be spent. This was clearly a more democratic and 'trustworthy' way to invest in Chile's political and economic development.

The diversion of international aid through the national government has a number of repercussions. Not least is the sudden lack of contact between local

NGOs and external funding advisors from international agencies which has eroded of some of the links between domestic NGOs and external agencies. There is a trend away from internationalization, away from a globalizing perspective and towards a 'domestication' of Chilean NGOs.

Domestication in this case implies that finances increasingly come through the national government, and that the government now has available to it a valuable tool to control the type of projects being pursued and the type of NGO which might grow or shrink or fail. While there is no direct evidence that such a political selection process is underway, the structural potential for such manipulation of the funding system is evidently present.

It should come as no surprise that politicians seek to further their own careers, the fortunes of their party or the greater prosperity of the country through the manipulation of project funding. Such activities are widespread and very well established. What demands attention is the prevalent idea that social investment is not political, that the rigorous application of the laws of supply and demand means that politicians cannot interfere or nominate favourite projects, and that because NGOs are undertaking the work, truth and righteousness will prevail over corruption. Clearly, political bias comes as part and parcel of government funding, yet politicians proclaim its absence.

Such changes in funding have also had an impact on the NGOs themselves. Whereas previously funds might set up and maintain an NGO for a number of years, the grants now only allow for running costs in terms of the proposed project, excluding overheads. Funding now more typically covers a shorter time span (six months to a year). These trends make it more difficult for NGOs to plan ahead as they are unsure of their budgets, even in the short term, their employment needs and indeed their existence in the near future. Short term grants also have an impact on the character of the projects undertaken by the NGOs. While they may be compatible with programmes which seek to achieve short term concrete objectives, they cannot be used to tackle deeper problems. A shift has occurred towards funding projects that address more superficial and easily achievable goals, rather than engaging with more profound issues which defy 'quick-fix' solutions. This short-termism leads to financial insecurity on the part of the organizations and curtails the possiblity of developing projects over the long term.

Although the competition for NGO project funding was always serious, it is now more intense than ever and a new spirit of market competitiveness infuses Chilean NGOs, placing professionalism at a premium. The competition for project finance is intense and presentations require a high level of expertise, knowledge of the funding system and access to desk-top technology in order to gain success. The climate of insecurity and competition among NGOs, of which FOSIS is an integral part, implants ideas of cost-effectiveness and marketing which displace the political convictions which dominated NGO work during the dictatorship. In the process, the solutions offered by NGOs have also been depoliticized to become compatible with wider political trends.

For example, whereas previously training for work was often aimed at women, linked to economic survival and related to the rejection of neoliberal policies, current initiatives target young men, training them in long-term skills and promote functional not political goals.

These shifts towards professionalism and supposedly ideologically-neutral projects should be understood not only in relation to the dominance of the neoliberal economic development project, but also in terms of the decline in grassroots political activism which is related to the advent of representative democratic government. These factors are two sides of the same coin: the decline in political activism has allowed the expansion of government-sponsored initiatives and both have contributed to the depoliticization of social issues and NGO activities. Having said this, there are a substantial number of NGOs which continue to function independently of FOSIS and the government, and which pursue projects directly designed to politicize, to mobilize against neoliberal concepts of democracy and development, or to raise awareness of issues such as patriarchy or structural poverty. There is also anecdotal evidence to suggest that some project proposals submitted to FOSIS might adopt the current jargon merely as a cynical move to gain funding.

Nevertheless, the role of Chilean NGOs has both expanded and changed significantly with democratization. During the dictatorship they implemented policies directly counter to the authoritarian regime, which were funded from outside the country; they were in this sense 'subversive' and as such they were overtly political. Now they are vehicles for policy implementation funded by the incumbent government; they are the implementors of 'cooptive' projects and they are integral to anchoring a particular concept of development in society while appearing to play a non-political role. They have grown and expanded with the consolidation of democracy. They have directly contributed to the success achieved by the Chilean government in its aim to tackle poverty. Their aptness and sensitivity have ensured that most of the projects have been a success and this has reflected upon the government, ensuring its re-election in 1993 and continued good standing in opinion polls. More profoundly, the stability, prosperity and material improvement in people's lives has assisted in the consolidation of democracy by proving that democratic governments too can run a clean and prosperous economy and that they can be responsive to the needs of those they represent.

NGOs and state agencies

With the advent of democracy, NGOs and grassroots movements no longer stand in opposition to the state. Instead a complex relationship has developed of interaction, mutual dependence and guarded conflict. This changing relationship is based partly on the greater dependence of NGOs on the state for funding. Links are also particularly strong in relation to the new state entities which were set up with democratization to look at human rights issues and the position of women.

In both Chile and Argentina, the democratic governments created commissions to investigate human rights violations by the military. These developed into post-transition state agencies, designed to investigate denunciations and to develop human rights programmes in the future (in Chile the Corporation of Reparation and Reconciliation; in Argentina the Subsecretariat of Human and Social Rights). These entities are staffed by former human rights activists (typically lawyers involved in human rights' defence) and they have brought with them an experience of political combat and personal commitment which is uncommon in other state agencies. Public servants in these agencies already had strong links to the grassroots movements and NGOs through their personal involvement and contacts and, due to the emotive nature of the issue, these contacts could not easily be severed. Indeed, many of those involved in human rights have clear political and personal motives which guide their actions and programmes. They were active in the era of demonstrations in favour of investigating human rights abuses and tended to see the creation of state agencies for human rights as another way to ensure that 'never again' should state violence, murder or disappearance befall a Chilean or Argentine citizen.

Similarly, the governments of both countries set up state entities to respond to calls for national action on women's issues (in Chile, SERNAM the National Service for Women and the Family; in Argentina, the National Women's Institute). The creation of these institutes had been a central demand of the women's movements which had been very prominent during the struggle for democracy, and feminist activists (as well as female politicians) in both countries have become involved in the new state women's agencies. The aim of the women who took up posts in these state entities was to further the cause of the women's movement, broadly understood, by raising awareness of women's position in a patriarchal society and by incorporating women into the formal political and economic realm.

Clearly, people expected that norms and behaviour in the state agencies dealing with women's issues and human rights would be entirely different to those of civil servants from other ministries and directorates. This encouraged the sense that the state agencies were in fact simply super-NGOs. At the root of the confusion and ambiguity surrounding the new state agencies lies the partial relocation of the issue (human rights or the position of women) from the social arena and the social movement to the political arena and the state. This tended to inject party politics into the issues and encouraged a 'pragmatic' approach to them. It created tensions between the desire of governments to 'solve' the problems and the continuing demands for a moral, ethical and intransigent approach which had given each of these issues its identity.

This contradiction is perhaps most keenly felt by the employees of the state agencies. The structural position of the institution, which demands loyalty to the incumbent government, is hard to reconcile with their emotional ties to the issue and the grassroots movement. For example, in interviews with employees of the Argentine Sub-secretariat of Human Rights it became clear that many had experienced a crisis of conscience when President Menem granted a pardon to the leaders of the *junta* who had been imprisoned for involvement in human rights violations. They were forced to balance the heart-felt ideals of the movement with the pragmatic demands of political expediency, within an institutional context which regards their activities as peripheral 'extras' and a financial context of public spending austerity.

This awkward position is exacerbated by the pattern of policy implementation which sees NGOs and grassroots groups as simply government vehicles into society. They provide links to the grassroots, but also channel communication from the base towards the state, which leaves the government open to criticism of its programmes or insufficient funding. On the other hand, the general decline in social movement activity and public mobilizations in the informal political arena places greater pressures on state organizations to 'lead' the social movements. Movement activists criticize the state agencies for not being radical enough and at times claim that the agencies rather than the social movement should take responsibility for putting issues on the public agenda.

This trend is resisted by the agency workers, as one employee of the Argentine National Women's Institute explains in reference to the issue of abortion:

> it is important to make priorities and to defend our institutional space. There is no sense in taking risks when there is no social movement . . . if there were marches in the streets then it would make sense to put ourselves out front. It is not the role of the state to put itself in the vanguard when sufficient forces are not present in civil society.
> (Project Director, *Instituto Nacional de la Mujer*,
> Buenos Aires interview, 1 July 1994)

The agencies are also subject to intense criticism from NGOs and women's groups at the base precisely because they are part of the government machine which has overseen the introduction of neoliberal reforms with the attendant hardship they bring for the poor and the marginalized:

> If we do things well, they react against it because this goes to the credit of the government which the majority of feminists are against, and if we do it badly, we do it badly. It almost as if they prefer us to do things badly, because this is easier to cope with in party political terms.
> (Ibid.)

The root of these ambiguous responses to the state agency lies in its position straddling civil society and state. Its identity comes out of the social movement but its (relative) power is structual and lies in its penetration of the state.

Within this uneasy relationship lies a degree of mutual dependency. For the NGOs and grassroots groups, this dependency takes the form of financial assistance, in relation to the 'tendering out' of projects, and also political assistance. An example of the latter is given by the Grandmothers of the Plaza de Mayo who are engaged in the search for their disappeared grandchildren, as one activist explains: 'we get a lot of help in the Subsecretariat . . . we have people who will help us to present our work where we couldn't gain access, or they may be able to obtain documents because they are from within' (activist, Grandmothers of the Plaza de Mayo, Buenos Aires interview, 21 June 1994). Conversely, the pressure applied outside the institutional arena is vital for the state agencies. It strengthens them within the institutional hierarchy and allows them to apply pressure for increased (or sustained) budgets and enhances (or maintains) their status within the governmental machine. One human rights activist explains the nature of this relationship, speaking of the then Director of the Argentine Human Rights Subsecretariat, Alicia Pierini: 'If she feels our pressure, she must respond and she needs our support in order to apply pressure herself within the government. She needs our support, because if we don't support her, she doesn't exist' (Activist, Association of the Detained-Disappeared and Political Prisioners, Buenos Aires interview, 21 June 1994).

In sum, the relationship between NGO and state agency is complex and riddled with tensions and contradictions. At the heart of this ambiguity is the blurred boundary between civil organization (social movement and/or NGO) and state agency, and the multiple identities of those who work in the new state entities, who are often party members, institutional employees and former activists in the social movements. This creates a pattern of contacts and affiliations, both formal and affective, which may coincide but which often conflict.

The situation is exacerbated where the issues themselves have become, in part, a state responsibility, complicated by the intrusion of party politics and negotiated solutions which this implies. Confusion abounds as to the points and strategies which each element of the broad campaign should promote and in relation to who is responsible for what in the pursuit of common goals. In part, though, this cross-fertilization is also the greatest asset of these broad women's and human rights 'movements', in that a real relationship exists between state and civil society, fostering dialogue, responsive policies and a campaign which functions within both arenas.

Conclusion

We have seen that the role of NGOs has been expanded and enhanced during the transition to neoliberal democracy. This is more advanced in Chile, where the neoliberal project was introduced in 1975. Just as Chile provided an early blue-print in Latin America for neoliberalism, so perhaps it gives us a foretaste of how other polities might consolidate this project through an enhanced civil society mediated by NGOs.

It was argued at the beginning that NGOs can assist in the consolidation of governments and democracy itself. An essential feature of a democratic government is representation, usually 'measured' in terms of its responsiveness to demands from the citizenry. In a neoliberal system NGOs can mediate and bring substantial improvements to the lives of the people. If they succeed, not only do they improve the standing of the incumbent government, they also prove that democracy 'works' in that it provides a mechanism to articulate and satisfy demands. NGOs provide another essential feature which embeds government and democracy alike in that they are associated with progressive policies and with an ethical attitude to political and economic change. They are perceived as moral agencies staffed by committed individuals acting in the best interests of those who they wish to help; more often than not this is true. Finally, NGOs both exercise and encourage democratic relationships which help to embed the values of a democratic ethos in the fabric of civil society.

It is interesting that, along with the advent of liberal democracy, we can also note that the renaissance of democratic government has been a focus for NGO activity and that individual governments have become conduits of international funding for NGO projects. In this way, however, international funding sources allow national governments to appear to be investing in their populace or tackling their worst problems, whereas actually the finance frequently comes from outside the nation state. That is, external funding for social projects allows the perceived role of the state to be adapted from one of provider (associated with welfare benefits) to an image as concerned facilitator of social advance (helping people to help themselves). In fact, however, it might be more accurate to say that the state acts as a central allocator of external funding at the level of the nation state.

In the complex world of the non-governmental sector, there is obviously a strong sense that boundaries are being blurred, between the international organization and the national, between NGO and social movement, state bureaucratism and political activism. The incorporation of NGOs and former NGO workers into the state machine, either directly through employment in state agencies or indirectly through project tendering and finance, has led to ambiguities in terms of the boundaries between civil society, NGO and state. This has led, on the one hand, to confusion concerning the relative roles and responsibilities of each sector, and, on the other, to the development of antagonisms and conflicts which were much less visible during the dictatorships.

Partly this is due to incorporation, a process which, it could be argued, shows that government is acting with sensitivity and is following good democratic practice. It is also, though, due to the ending of an era during which the players on the political scene were easily categorized as being 'good' or 'evil', 'with us' or 'against us'. The social movements are understandably bewildered by the dissolution of such dichotomies. They have maintained their staunch positions but the NGOs and the state have changed; politics and policy have been injected into the issues and taken them over, making them subject to negotiations and to the strictures of public spending. A new kind of civil society has taken root, one which strives for social, not political, goals and which seeks tangible personal or community benefits, rather than holistic, societal goods of a less material nature.

The combative and intransigent campaigns of the social movements clash with the dominant discourse of negotiation and compromise. They are portrayed as being a danger to the consolidation of democracy, when only a few years ago they were heralded as its champion.

Some interpret these changes as capitulation to the military and/or to neoliberalism, but it would be wrong to claim that NGOs are no more than Trojan horses bringing neoliberalism into the social sphere and facilitating its colonization; they are often outspoken about government policies and few have adopted any more than the rhetoric of neoliberal self-help. However, we should also beware of going too far the other way, of claiming that NGOs are the Trojan horses of the 'left', infiltrating the state and utilizing its funds to promote moves against neoliberalism. In the complex world of state/NGO relations under democracy, their projects are altered by the nature of the policies being implemented and the acceptance by NGOs of negotiated compromises and short term goals.

NGOs are neither gorgons nor paragons; rather they have the aspect of Janus, looking both to the civil society and the formal arenas of state, to the past and to the future. While undoubtedly their projects, particularly training for the self-employed, secure neoliberalism's anchorage, they also project democratic values into society and help to create the structures of civil society which encourage organization and participation. They have an impact on state policies through the nature of the projects which they propose and the personal links between state and NGO employees. And, in the human rights and women's issue agencies, social movements can also influence the nature of the projects and the means of policy implementation formulated by the state.

The days of 'us' and 'them' are gone, replaced by a complex network of old and new connections within and between the movements, NGOs, international donors and state agencies. Each seeks to preserve its own integrity yet each needs the other in order to survive. What continues to link those who work on the same issue is the common sense of purpose, in broad terms, and the common past they share. It is this emotional experience and its ethical element which unites social movement, NGO and state agency and it is upon this foundation which each must build, recognising and accepting each other's limitations and building multiple alliances which emphasize commonalities instead of differences. Within this relationship is the capacity for mutual destruction but also the capacity for mutual reinforcement, and it is towards the latter that each must strive if the goals of meaningful human rights and substantial advances for women are to be achieved.

Notes

1 This paper is based on research carried out in Chile and Argentina during the academic year 1993/4 as fieldwork for doctoral studies. The assertions made in this paper relate to findings based on extensive interviews and research.

2 This description is also based on accounts of this period taken from interviews with activists in women's organizations in the shanty towns (Casa de la Mujer – Huamachuco, Centro de Apoyo y Formación de la Mujer – La Granja, Centro de Promoción de la Mujer – Tierra Nuestra).

3 Examples of 'feminist' organizations working in the shanty towns include: Colectivo El Telar, Casa Sofia, DOMOS Centro de Desarollo de la Mujer, MEMCH Movimiento Pro-emancipación de la Mujer Chilena).

4 Examples include: ECO – Educación y Comunicación; KAIROS – Centro de Desarollo Popular; PIRET- Taller de Promoción e Intercambio de Recursos Educacionales y Tecnológicos.

5 Examples of Argentine human rights NGOs include Asamblea Permanente de los Derechos Humanos, Conciencia, Poder Ciudadano, Servicio de Paz y Justicia; women's NGOs include Centro de Estúdios de la Mujer, Fundación para Estúdio y Investigación de la Mujer, Lugar de Mujer.

CONCLUSION

Towards an understanding of transnational and non-state actors in global democratization

Jean Grugel

Democratization has been understood throughout this book as the 'creation, extension and practice of social citizenship through a particular national territory' (page 11), as well as the building of democratic institutions and the formal establishment of a democratic framework for government. Contemporary, or 'third wave', democratizations have been placed in a global context in which the transnational dimension has become increasingly significant, though difficult to measure in any quantitative sense. In fact, the tendency of the book has been to assert that it is no longer meaningful to separate domestic from international factors as the boundaries between 'the external' and 'the internal' are increasingly blurred.

At the same time, democratization itself is now recognized as a complex, open-ended social process for which there are no quick-fix recipes. Introducing democracy in countries with an authoritarian, populist or militaristic legacy requires substantive social and cultural changes and supportive international policies as well as a transformation of governing institutions.

Several of the chapters point to deeply rooted structural practices within regions or states which constitute formidable obstacles to building democracies, despite all the external inducements which work in favour of its introduction, and indeed sometimes despite the desires of elites and citizens alike. Many of these obstacles, it is argued, can only be overcome through social activism over time. Hence our attention is directed towards analyzing the role of civil society organizations, such as non-governmental organizations (NGOs) and social movements, in creating and embedding democracies. These organizations operate in an increasingly transnationalized environment which fixes their ideas about what democracy should be and affects their practice.

The theoretical chapters in this book (Part One) stressed different aspects of the growing importance of transnational and non-state actors in understanding the processes of democratization. Chapter One, 'Contextualizing Democratization: the Changing Significance of Transnational Factors and Non-State Actors', drew attention to the importance of civil society actors and the regional context for understanding the degree to which democratization succeeds. It argued that democratizations constitute different experiences in different states and regions. The chapter also raised the question of whether international activism on the part of social groups constituted the emergence of an 'international civil society' committed to the spread of global democracy. Finally, it noted the uneven development of civil society in the three regions under discussion in the book and the differing impact this has on democratization.

Chapter Two, 'International Factors in Processes of Political Democratization: Towards a Theoretical Integration', pointed to the importance of globalization, understood not as an explanation of change but as a context variable, in shaping actors' behaviour in democratization and the need to incorporate transnational processes more fully into explanations of democratization. It stressed the theoretical weaknesses of the two dominant theoretical approaches in democratization studies, the modernization school of analysis and the agency perspective, especially because of their failure to incorporate the transnational dimension in any significant way. It drew attention to the importance of the international system, not merely as a set of constraining or facilitating institutions, but also as an arena for supplying ideas about how to construct democracy at all stages of democratization, liberalization, transition and consolidation.

Chapter Three, 'European Actors in Global Change: The Role of European Civil Societies in Democratization', pointed to the need to examine how civil society actors from the developed world may contribute to democratization in developing countries. It was therefore concerned with the transnational activities of civil society actors. Using examples of cooperation between civil society organizations and NGOs from within EU member states and Latin America, the chapter stressed the potential contribution civil society actors can make in two areas: first, establishing mechanisms for a more equitable distribution of income, which it argued was a basis for meaningful participation in society; and second, pressurizing states to permit the incorporation and access of new groups into the political system. The chapter stressed the importance of 'distributing democracy' across society and looked at ways that civil society organizations from the developed world could contribute to this task.

The book assumes a number of factors will affect countries experiencing democratization. These include the growing importance of civil society actors in domestic and international politics; processes of globalization which reduce the room for manoeuvre on the part of nation states; the dependence of many of the states-in-transition on international approval; and changes in the nature and modes of delivery of aid and international cooperation. Since democratization is multi-layered and multi-dimensional, it is difficult to attribute causality to any one actor. How, therefore, can the roles of transnational and non-state actors in democratization be more exactly determined? It is easy enough to assert that the transnational dimension is important and that non state actors must now be counted as *central* to the processes of building democracy, especially when it is understood as the creation of democratic citizenship; but we need to make more precise claims. The empirical chapters of the book, while recognizing the rich diversity of the case studies on East and Central Europe, Africa and Latin America, admit six generalizations about democratization. The remainder of this chapter will consider each of these in turn.

Democracy should be understood as the creation of social citizenship, not merely as the introduction of formally democratic institutions

All the empirical chapters indicate the inadequacy of a minimal definition of democracy which confines it to the arena of 'high politics' without reference to the lives of ordinary people or to state-society relationships. It is significant that civil society and transnational actors increasingly use the notion of substantive democracy in designing their strategies as a way of strengthening democratic consolidation. This is well documented throughout this book and raises the question of what precisely the social and civil components of democracy are.

We have argued here that democracy implies the development of cultures of tolerance and respect. As a form of government, it must be accountable, representative and consensual; democracy rests on the acceptance and support of the citizenry. This has frequently been interpreted to mean that democratic states must spread entitlements and economic rights through society. But democracy also means the extension of citizenship rights, including the right for people to have an input into decisions that affect them. Freres refers to this as 'distributing democracy'. It takes time to bring this about; it also requires resources. Hence building democracy is a long term project of creating the conditions for the introduction of a range of social and citizenship entitlements and enabling the state to carry them through and guarantee their existence.

Democratization is the result of the interaction between domestic groups, actors external to the state-in-transition and the global environment

It was once presumed that democratization was essentially a domestic affair. Only under particular circumstances such as extreme dependence, uncertainty or defeat in war would external actors (usually conceived of exclusively as states) be able to influence and shape transition and consolidation. The globalization of the international economic order, the interconnectedness between social groups, the

159

collapse of bipolarity and the subsequent difficulty of constructing alternatives to capitalism and democracy, and an interest in transferring examples of best practice across nation states, all mean that transnational actors now exercise a constant influence in what were previously perceived as the internal affairs of states. At the same time, what is meant by the term 'external actors' has undergone a significant change. Once used to refer to states – or in the case of states in the developing world which suffered from extreme economic and financial dependence, international agencies such as the World Bank – it is now used to cover a variety of state and non-state actors. It is recognised that the channels through which external influences flow are diffuse and multiple; the coercive transfer of democracy is no longer seen as the only way external actors can shape democratization.

Nevertheless, external actors can still, under particular circumstances, impose their criteria of democracy over those of domestic groups. Equally, such criteria can be used and manipulated by domestic groups to impose a kind of pseudo-democratization in which power is not in fact extended beyond the authoritarian groups of the previous regime. Van Cranenburgh, in Chapter Six, demonstrates how international observers representing western governments have defined clean elections as the most important determinant of democracy, with enormous implications for western aid policies and for how democracy is understood inside African states. In Chapter Seven, Prikic shows how a powerful regional state can impose its will on neighbouring states with ambiguous consequences for democratization in the area.

Pridham, in Chapter Four, also points out how external actors have tried to impose norms for democratization. In this case, his example is the conditionality imposed by the EU in Eastern and Central Europe, and the role European political parties play in trying to mould their counterparts in post-communist societies. Pridham's term 'conditionality' is similar to Van Cranenburgh's notion of positive linkages for democracy. In both cases, powerful actors specify conditions under which material aid or political opportunities are granted. Nevertheless, external actors appear more powerful in the case of African democratizations than in East and Central Europe. This points to the fact that the relationship between external actors and domestic groups is contingent on the position of the country experiencing democracy within the global order.

Of the three regions analyzed in the book, Latin America would appear at first sight to have experienced least direct external imposition. This is partly because the emphasis of the book has been on European initiatives; direct coercive action on Latin America has traditionally been exercised by US state or non-state actors. It is also a reflection of the fact that democratization has been underway in Latin America since the early 1980s and the direct impact of external actors on Latin American democratizations was greatest during the first stages of transition. Nevertheless, outside influences do still play a significant role in Latin American democracies. In much of the region, the influence is greatest in terms of diffusing values about democracy, economic progress and the importance of the market among Latin America elites.

In Chapter Eight, Grugel points to another set of influences: the role of European NGOs. These played a part in forming networks of non-state actors to press Latin American states towards adopting policies of social, economic and cultural democratization. They have also assumed a new role in persuading European governments to incorporate support for democratization as part of their aid policies. For the most part, these groups have tried to challenge the idea that democratization can be separated from social and economic reform and the search for equitable development. They therefore constitute a very different, and counterposing, set of influences to those emanating from international and US state institutions.

To sum up, the linkages between the domestic and external context are important for understanding how transnational and non-state actors behave, the kind of democratization project underway and how successfully it is implemented. The relationship is not one-way and transnational actors are not always able to determine the rules of democratization. They frequently have to accommodate the preferences and interests of domestic groups or of other external actors.

Transnational influences appear initially most powerful where the central state is weak, but the African example suggests this is not entirely so. External influences are strong in determining what democracy means in Africa, but are actually limited in their ability to control democratizations.

This points to the centrality of domestic actors and institutions; external actors, whether political parties, states or NGOs or supranational bodies like the EU, always need conduits inside states in order to implement their strategies. As a result, domestic actors, especially if they are not attached to the state, can use their relationships with actors outside the nation state to increase their own legitimacy and influence as well as to assure themselves of advice and funding. This gives domestic actors more autonomy than has sometimes been assumed. Taylor, in Chapter Nine, offers clear evidence of this. She demonstrates that Latin American NGOs do not carry out the bidding of international agencies. They are, in anything, far more responsive to pressure from domestic states. Prikic's findings, in Chapter Seven, point in a similar direction, in that the dynamic of politics in West Africa is regional, local and national as much as it is driven by international imperatives. This chapter also reveals the impossibility of non-regional actors managing or controlling political processes and democratization in Africa.

The presence of an active and dynamic civil society is necessary for the consolidation of democracy

Kopecky's work in particular, in Chapter Five, reveals that the fragility of the democracy in East and Central Europe lies in the weakness of civil society organizations and the failure of the state to nurture civil society. Taylor's research on social movements and NGOs in Chile and Argentina also points to the dangers civil society organizations face from strong states, although it must be recognized that the tradition of social organization outside the state is much deeper in Latin America than in post-communist Europe. It would appear, therefore, that one of the most positive roles international NGOs can play in democratization is supporting and legitmizing domestic social organizations. This is the central importance, of the deepening connections, documented here by Pridham and Grugel and theorized by Freres, between western social/civil organizations, such as parties or NGOs, and their counterparts in countries experiencing democratization. This research draws, on the one hand, on the more general tendency within international relations to highlight the growing trend towards social activism across national borders and, on the other, on the development of civil society theory which insists on the importance of the lives of ordinary people for understanding the quality of democracy.

Nevertheless, the book also warns against over-optimistic readings of the capabilities of civil society. Kopecky points out how intellectuals in Eastern and Central Europe tended to exaggerate the size and significance of local civil societies, with damaging consequences for the democratization project in the region. While recognising that a restricted or weak civil society will always pose problems for democratic consolidation, there are dangers in taking too voluntaristic an approach to analyses of civil society. A dense network of social relations based on trust, respect, tolerance and cooperation cannot come into existence simply through the desire to create it. Neither can it be established easily as a result of state policies; state-nurtured organizations will always be in danger of cooptation.

External donors have recently begun to stress the importance of civil society for democratization. A number of chapters indicated the impact of the shift in EU aid policies towards funding decentralized cooperation, aid through civil society actors. This creates dangers as well as opportunities for local civil society organizations. As local NGOs become the preferred partners of aid agencies, the resources at their disposal increase, enabling them to become important domestic actors. The same is true of political parties, as Pridham argues. But it also creates channels of accountability to actors outside the state; maintaining a good relationship with their international backers becomes essential for their survival. This can diminish their effectiveness domestically and even mean that they are perceived as the agents of external groups. In the worst of cases, it can provoke an nationalist backlash.

To sum up, we can say that *civil society is central to building democracy*. However, two points should be borne in mind. First, where civil society is weak, dense social networks cannot spring up overnight. Second, while transnational actors can be supportive of local civil society organizations, they cannot create an autonomous and dynamic civil society sphere from outside. We have here a possible explanation for why some democratizations succeed and others fail, an important question in democratization studies.

162

Transnational actors can play a positive role in democratization; but they can also play a negative one

Much of the literature assumes that transnational activity is good for democratization. Transnational actors themselves generally want to play a supportive role. But, as van Cranenburgh and Prikic point out most forcefully, actions by transnational agents can have unintended consequences. They can encourage powerful domestic groups to adopt the language of democracy while ignoring its substance. They can distort domestic politics by forcing it to mimic external patterns of organization. Therefore transnational actors, especially states and international institutions, should be cautious about the nature and extent of their interventions in domestic politics. They need to recognise that their contribution may not always be positive and that their recipes for democratization, based on western experiences, are not always appropriate.

Democratization is a qualitatively different experience in different states and regions

The examples this book brings together show striking differences in the causes of regimes change, the relationship between state, market and society, the transnational dimension, and even how democracy is normatively understood. The relative importance of different domestic actors, their relationship to each other and to outside forces, the degree to which individual and collective rights are respected, also vary. Globalization is sometimes presumed to be pulling the world together so that patterns of government are essentially the same everywhere and causing economic, social and cultural trends to move in the same direction. There is also a tendency to link all 'third wave' democratizations together. Nevertheless, the differences between democratization projects become evident on deeper analysis. This is especially marked when the focus of research into democratization is the relationship between the state and its citizens, rather than the formal institutions of governments or the holding of elections.

This results in a paradox: not all democratizations lead to democracy. The term 'democratization' has been coined to describe contemporary regime change because policy makers and academics alike presumed that the end of the Cold War, the evident failure of dictatorships of all ideological persuasions and the widespread demands for political change in the 1980s would inaugurate an era of democracy for all. This assumption has proved to be false but 'democratization' has nevertheless ineluctably entered the language of the social sciences. The term now suggests only a change of regime from forms of authoritarian government, with the potential, and perhaps the aim, of bringing about a more representative and democratic society; it does not imply that this is necessarily the outcome. The definition of democracy that we have worked with in this book, the 'creation, extension and practice of social citizenship through a particular national territory', cannot be presumed to be an automatic outcome of the collapse of dictatorships nor the result of the holding of elections.

This brings us to an important theoretical point. The dominance of the agency perspective on democratization since the 1980s led to the presumption that democracy could be introduced successfully anywhere. However, although democracy is now perceived as the only acceptable form of political domination in the international system, a variety of structural factors – including the lack of legitimacy of the central state, the weaknesses of civil society and the difficulties of implementing social and economic reform – obstruct its introduction or its consolidation. This raises the question whether it is possible to have global democracy. In other words, it confirms the structuralist assumption that democracy, to be successful and stable, requires certain preconditions. Despite a number of problems, democratizations are, generally speaking, relatively more successful in most (not all) of Latin America and East and Central Europe than in sub-Saharan Africa. This may be because of the strength of social organizations, influenced by the cultural and political legacy of previous democratic interludes in Latin America and parts of East and Central Europe or by the proximity of democratic neighbours. Whatever the explanation, it points to the importance of context, history and structure in determining the success of democratization projects.

Europe has an important role to play in building democracies

A striking feature of some of the chapters in the book is the importance assigned within Europe, including the EU, states, parties and NGOs, to building democracies globally. This can be attributed in part to geopolitics. European concerns with security in East and Central Europe have led European actors to offer inducements to post-Communist states to move closer to the western camp in terms of security, politics and economic organization. European interest in spreading democracy is also the result of its post-imperial ties and responsibilities. This accounts for the interest of European actors in African democratizations. Perhaps surprisingly, European actors also play a significant role in Latin American democratization, a region where European interest is motivated neither by security concerns nor post-imperial responsibilities. It therefore indicates a ideological commitment to building democracies within Europe that has sometimes been understated and one which this book has, we hope, helped to correct.

BIBLIOGRAPHY

Adeleke, A. (1995) 'The Politics and Diplomacy of Peacekeeping in West Africa: The ECOWAS Operation in Liberia', *The Journal of Modern African Studies*, 33 (4).

Adisa, J. (1994) 'Nigeria in ECOMOG: Political Undercurrents and the Burden of Community Spirit', *Small Wars and Insurgencies*, 5 (1).

Africa Watch (1991) *Waging War to Keep the Peace: The ECOMOG Intervention and Human Rights*, 5 (3) June.

Agenda 2000 (1997) *The Opinions of the European Commission on the Applications for Accession*, Brussels: European Commission.

Ágh, A. (1996a) 'The Europeanization of the ECE Business Interest Associations: The Models in Western Europe and the European Union', in Atilla, Á. and Ilonszki, G. (eds), *Parliaments and Organized Interests: The Second Steps*, Budapest: Hungarian Center for Democracy Studies Foundation.

—— (1996b) 'The End of the Beginning: The Partial Consolidation of East Central European Parties and Party Systems', *Budapest Papers on Democratic Transition No.156*, Budapest: University of Economics.

Ake, C. (1991) 'Rethinking African Democracy', *Journal of Democracy*, 2 (1).

Akinrinade, O. (1992) 'From Hostility to Accomodation: Nigeria's West African Policy, 1984-1990', *Nigerian Journal of International Affairs*, 18 (1).

Almond, G. A. (1989) 'Review Article: The International-National Connection', *British Journal of Political Science* 19.

Altvater, E. and B. Mahnkopf (1996) *Grenzen der Globalisierung. Ökonomie, Ökologie und Politik in der Weltgesellschaft*, Münster: Westfälisches Dampfboot.

Amoo, S. G. (1993) 'ECOWAS in Liberia: The Challenges and Prospects for African Peacekeeping', paper presented at the Defence Intelligence College, Alconbury, Royal Air Force Base, Cambridge, 6-7 May.

Anderson, L. (1997) Transitions to Democracy: A Special Issue in Memory of Dankwart A. Rustow (Introduction), *Comparative Politics* 29.

Aning, E. K. (1996) 'Ghana, ECOWAS and The Liberian Crisis: An Analysis of Ghana's Role in Liberia', *Liberian Studies Journal*, 21 (2).

Arat, Z. F. (1988) 'Democracy and Economic Development. Modernization Theory Revisited', *Comparative Politics* 21 (1).

—— (1991) *Democracy and Human Rights in Developing Countries*, Boulder, Colorado: Lynne Reinner.

Arato, A. (1993) 'Interpreting 1989', *Social Research*, 60 (3). .

Ash, T. G. (1986) 'Does Central Europe Exist?', *New York Review of Books*, October 1986.

Ate, B. E., and Akinterinwa, B. (eds) (1992) *Nigeria and its Immediate Neighbours: Constraints and Prospects of Subregional Security in the 1990s*, Lagos: NIIA and Pumark Nigeria Ltd.

Baloyra, E. A. (1987a) 'Conclusion: Toward a Framework for the Study of Democratic Consolidation', in Baloyra, E. A. (ed.), *Comparing New Democracies, Transition and Consolidation in Mediterranean Europe and the Southern Cone*, Boulder, Colorado: Westview Press.

—— (1987b) 'Democratic Transition in Comparative Perspective' in Baloyra, E. A. (ed.), *Comparing New Democracies, Transition and Consolidation in Mediterranean Europe and the Southern Cone*, Boulder, Colorado: Westview Press.

Barkan, J. (1997) 'Can Established Democracies Nurture Democracy Abroad?', in Hadenius, A. (ed.), *Democracy's Victory and Crisis*. Cambridge: Cambridge University Press .

Begroting voor Ministerie van Buitenlandse Zaken (1997) (Budget for the Ministry of Foreign Affairs 1997) The Hague.

Berger, P. and Neuhaus R. J. (1993) 'Potenciar el Ciudadano: el Rol de las Estructuras Intermedias en las Politicas Públicas' *Estúdios Públicos* 49, Summer.

Bernhard, M. (1993) 'Civil Society and Democratic Transition in East Central Europe', *Political Science Quarterly*, 108 (2).

Bernhard, M. (1994) 'Riding the Next Wave: Recent Books on Democratization', *Studies in Comparative International Development* 29 (1).

Bielasiak, J. (1997) 'Substance and Process in the Development of Party Systems in East Central Europe', *Journal of Communist and Postcommunist Studies*, 30 (1).

Bierkart, K. (1994) *La Cooperación No-Gubernamental Europea hacia Centroamérica: La Experiencia de los Ochenta y las Tendencias de los Noventa*. San Salvador: PRISMA.

—— (1995) 'European NGOs and Democratisation in Central America: Assessing Performance in the Light of Changing Priorities', in Edwards, M. and Hulme, D. (eds), *Non-governmental Organisations—Performance and Accountability. Beyond the Magic Bullet*, London: Earthscan.

—— (1996) 'Strengthening Intermediary Roles in Civil Society: Experiences from Central América', (mimeo).

Bollen, K. A. (1991) 'Political Democracy: Conceptual and Measurement Traps', in Inkeles, A. (ed.), *On Measuring Democracy. Its Consequences and Concomitants*, New Brunswick: Transaction Publishers.

—— (1993) 'Liberal Democracy: Validity and Method Factors in Cross-National Measures', *American Journal of Political Science* 37 (4).

Bombarolo, F. (1995) 'La Revalorización de las Organizaciones de la Sociedad Civil (OSC): ¿Hacia un Nuevo Modelo de Desarrollo?', *Pobreza Urbana y Desarrollo* (Buenos Aires, FICONG), Año 4, N° 10, agosto.

Bos, E. (1994) 'Die Rolle von Eliten und kollektiven Akteuren in Transition-sprozessen', in Merkel, W. (ed), *Systemwechsel 1: Theorien, Ansätze und Konzepte der Transitionsforschung*, Opladen: Leske and Budrich.

Bratton, M. (1990) 'Nongovernmental Organisations in Africa: Can they Influence Public Policy', *Development and Change* 21.

Bresser Pereira, L. C. (1993) 'Economic Reforms and Economic Growth: Efficiency and Politics in Latin America', in Bresser Pereira, L., Maravall, J. M. and Przeworski, A., *Economic Reforms in New Democracies: a Social-Democratic Approach* Cambridge: Cambridge University Press.

Brysk, A. (1993) 'From Above and Below. Social Movements, The International System and Human Rights in Argentina', *Comparative Political Studies* 26 (3) October.

Burkhart, R. E. and Lewis-Beck, M. S. (1994) 'Comparative Democracy: The Economic Development Thesis', *American Political Science Review* 88 (4).

Burton, M., Gunther, R. and Higley, J. (1992a) 'Elites and Democratic Consolidation in Latin America and Southern Europe: an Overview', in Higley, J. and Gunther, R. (eds), *Elites and Democratic Consolidation in Latin America and Southern Europe*, Cambridge: Cambridge University Press.

—— (1992b) 'Introduction: Elite Transformation and Democratic Regimes', in Higley, J. and Gunther, R. (eds), *Elites and Democratic Consolidation in Latin America and Southern Europe*, Cambridge: Cambridge University Press.

Butora, M., Kostalova, K., Demes, P., and Butorova, Z. (1997) 'Nonprofit Sector and Volunteerism in Slovakia', in Butora, M. and Huncik, P. (eds), *Global Report on Slovakia. Comprehensive Analysis from 1995 and Trends from 1996*, Bratislava: Sandor Marai Foundation.

Campero, G. (1987) 'Organizaciones de Pobladores Bajo el Regimen Militar', *Proposiciones* 14.

Cardoso, F. H. and Faletto, E. (1979) *Dependency and Development in Latin America*, Berkeley, California: University of California Press.

Carlsson, I. (1995) 'The U.N. at 50: A Time to Reform', *Foreign Policy*, 100.

Carothers, T. (1996) *Assessing Democracy Assistance: the Case of Romania*, Washington: Carnegie Endowment.

Chalmers, D. (1997) '¿Qué Tienen las Organizaciones de la Sociedad Civil que Promueven la Democracia?' *Revista Mexicana de Ciencias Políticas y Sociales*, N° 170, October–December.

Chalmers, D. *et al.* (1997) 'Associative Networks: New Structures of Representation for the Popular Sectors?', in Chalmers, D. *et al. The New Politics of Inequality in Latin America*, Oxford: Oxford University Press.

Chase, R. S., Hill, E. B. and Kennedy, P. (1996) 'Pivotal States and U.S. Strategy', *Foreign Affairs*, 75 (1).

Chazan, N., Mortimer, R., Ravenhill, J., Rothchild, D. (1992) *Politics and Society in Contemporary Africa*, Boulder, Colorado: Lynne Reinner.

CIVICUS (1998) 'Social Capital and the Civil Society Movement', *Civicus World*, January–February.

Clark, J. (1990) *Democratizing Development. The Role of Voluntary Organizations*, West Hartford, Conn.: Kumarian Press.

Colas, A. (1997) 'The Promises of International Civil Society', *Global Society* 11 (3).

Collier, D. (ed.) (1979) *The New Authoritarianism in Latin America*, Princeton: Princeton University Press.

Collier, D. and Levitsky, S. (1997) 'Democracy with Adjectives Conceptual Innovation in Comparative Research' *World Politics*, 49 (3) .

Collier, D., and Mahoney, J. (1996) 'Insights and Pitfalls. Selection Bias in Qualitative Research', *World Politics* 49 (1).

Collier, R. B. (1993) 'Combining Alternative Perspectives. Internal Trajectories versus External Influences as Explanations of Latin American Politics in the 1940s', *Comparative Politics* 26 (1).

Cook, M. L. (1997) 'Regional Integration and Transnational Politics: Popular Sector Strategies in the NAFTA Era', in D. Chalmers *et al.*, *The New Politics of Inequality in Latin America*, Oxford: Oxford University Press.

Corrin, C. (1993) 'People and Politics', in White, S., Batt, J., and Lewis, P. (eds), *Developments in Eastern European Politics*, Basingstoke: Macmillan.

Council of the European Union (1995a) 'Common Position of 20 November 1995 on Nigeria', document 95/515/CFSP.

Council of the European Union (1995b) 'Common Position of 4 December 1995 on Nigeria', document 95/544/CFSP.

Cranenburgh, O. Van (1995) 'Development Cooperation and Human Rights: Linkage Policies in the Netherlands', in Baehr, P. *et al.* (eds), *Human Rights in Developing Countries Yearbook 1995*, Oslo and The Hague: Kluwer and Nordic Human Rights Publications.

—— (1996) 'Tanzania's 1995 Multi-party Elections: the Emerging Party System', in *Party Politics*, 2 (4) .

Crawford, G. (1997) 'Human Rights and Democracy in EU Development Co-operation: Towards Fair and Equal Treatment', Centre for Development Studies, University of Leeds (mimeo).

Cremona, M. (1996) 'The New Associations: Substantive Issues of the Europe Agreements with the Central and Eastern European States' in Konstadinidis, G., *The Legal Regulation of the EC's External Relations after the Completion of the Internal Market*.

Dahl, R.A. (1971) *Polyarchy: participation and opposition*, New Haven: Yale University Press.

De Feyter, K. *et al.* (1995) *'Ontwikkelingssamenwerking als Instrument ter Bevordering van Mensenrechten en Democratisering*, Vlaamse Interuniversitaire Raad.

Desfor Edles, L. (1995) 'Rethinking Democratic Transition: A Culturalist Critique and the Spanish Case', *Theory and Society* 24 (3).

Di Palma, G. (1990) *To Craft Democracies. An Essay on Democratic Transitions*, Berkeley: University of California Press.

—— (1991) 'Why Democracy Can Work in Eastern Europe', *Journal of Democracy*, 2 (1).

Diamond, L. *et al.* (1990) *Political Culture and Democracy in Developing Countries*, Boulder, Colorado: Lynne Reinner.

Diamond, L. (1992) 'Economic Development and Democracy Reconsidered', in Diamond, L. and Marks, G. (eds), *Reexamining Democracy. Essays in Honour of Seymour Martin Lipset*, Newbury Park: Sage.

—— (1993) 'The Globalization of Democracy', in Slater, R. O., Schutz, B. M. and Dorr, S. R. (eds), *Global Transformation and the Third World*, Boulder, Colorado: Lynne Reinner.

—— (1994) 'Rethinking Civil Society: Towards Democratic Consolidation', *Journal of Democracy* 5 (3).

—— (1996a) 'Three Paradoxes of Democracy', in Diamond, L. and Plattner, M. (eds), *The Global Resurgence of Democracy* (2nd Ed.), Baltimore: Johns Hopkins University Press.

—— (1996b) 'Toward Democratic Consolidation', in Diamond, L. and Plattner, M. (eds), *The Global Resurgence of Democracy* (2nd Ed.), Baltimore: Johns Hopkins University Press.

—— (1996c) 'Is the Third Wave Over?', *Journal of Democracy* 7 (3).

—— (1997) 'Promoting Democracy in the 1990s: Actors, Instruments, and Issues', in Hadenius, A. (ed.), *Democracy's Victory and Crisis*. Cambridge: Cambridge University Press.

Drake, P. (1994) *International Factors in Democratization*, Instituto Juan March de Estudios e Investigaciones; Madrid.

Dryzek, J. S. (1996) 'Political Inclusion and the Dynamics of Democratization', *American Political Science Review*, 90(1).

EBRD (1990) *Agreement Establishing the EBRD*, London.

EBRD (1992) *Political Aspects of the Mandate of the EBRD*, London.

Eckstein, H. (1966) *Division and Cohesion. A Study of Norway*, Princeton: Princeton University Press.

ECOWAS (1990) 'Decision A/DEC.2/8/90', Banjul, 7 August.

ECOWAS (1993) 'Agreement Between the IGNU, the NPFL and the ULIMO', Cotonou, 25 July.

ECOWAS (1994) 'Akosombo Agreement', Akosombo, 12 September.

ECOWAS (1995) 'Abuja Accord', Abuja, 19 August.

Edwards, M. and Hulme, D. (1995a) 'Introduction and Overview', in Edwards, M. and Hulme, D. (eds), *Non-governmental Organisations – Performance and Accountability. Beyond the Magic Bullet*, London: Earthscan.

—— (1995b) 'Beyond the Magic Bullet? Lessons and Conclusions', in Edwards, M. and Hulme, D. (eds), *Non-governmental Organisations – Performance and Accountability. Beyond the Magic Bullet*, London: Earthscan.

—— (1996) 'Too Close for Comfort? The Impact of Official Aid on Nongovernmental Organisations', *World Development* 24 (6).

Ekiert, G. and Kubik, J. (1997a) 'Contentious Politics in New Democracies: Hungary, Poland, Slovakia and Former East Germany Since 1989', Working Papers Series No. 41, Program on Central and Eastern Europe, *Center for European Studies*, Harvard University.

Ekiert, G. and Kubik, J. (1997b) '(Post)Totalitarian Legacies, Civil Society, and Democracy in Post-Communist Poland, 1989-1993', Institute for European Studies Working Paper No. 97.4, *Slavic and East European Studies*, Cornell University.

Ekokko, A. E. and Vogt, M. A. (eds) (1990) *Nigerian Defence Policy – Issues and Problems*, Lagos: Malthouse Press.

Escobar, A. and Alvarez, A. (eds) (1992) *The Making of Social Movements in Latin America: Identity, Strategy and Democracy*, Boulder, Colorado: Westview.

EU-Slovakia Joint Parliamentary Committee, *Declarations and Recommendations*, constituent meeting, Bratislava, 22–24 November 1995.

European Commission (1990) *Association Agreements with the Countries of Central and Eastern Europe: a General Outline*, Brussels, 27 August.

—— (1993) *Towards a Closer Association with the Countries of Central and Eastern Europe, Background Report*, Brussels, 17 February.

—— (1995a) *The Europe Agreements with Poland, Hungary, Romania, Bulgaria and the Czech and Slovak Republics, Background Report*, Brussels, September.

—— (1995b) *The European Union and Latin America: The Present Situation and Prospects for Closer Partnernship, 1996-2000*, Brussels: European Commission.

—— (1996) 'An Overview of EU/Nigeria Cooperation – Information Note, June 1996', presented at a workshop on 'The Nigerian Democratization Process and the European Union' organized by the Centre d'Etude d'Afrique Noire, Bordeaux, 12–14 September.

—— (1997). *Democracia y Derechos Humanos en América Latina. Construir una Cultura de Justicia y Paz*, Brussels, European Commission, DG I.

Fine, R. (1997) 'Civil Society Theory, Enlightenment and Critique', *Democratization* 4 (1).

Foley, M. W. and Edwards, B. (1996) 'The Paradox of Civil Society', *Journal of Democracy*, 7(3).

FOSIS (Fondo de Solidaridad e Inversión Social) (1994) *Estúdio de Proyectos de FOSIS según Ejecutores y Temáticas: Periodo 1990 a Agosto 1993* Santiago, Chile: Departamento de Planificación, Fondo de Solidaridad e Inversión Social.

Foweraker, J. (1995) *Theorizing Social Movements*, London: Pluto Press.

Fowler, A. (1991) 'The role of NGOs in Changing State-Society Relationships: Perspectives from East and Southern Africa', *Development Policy Review* 9 (1).

—— (1993) 'Non-Governmental Organizations as Agents of Democratization: an African Prespective', in *Journal of International Development* 5 (3).

—— (1997) *Striking a Balance. A Guide to Enhancing the Effectiveness of Non-Governmental Organisations in International Development*, London: Earthscan.

Fowler, A. and Bierkart, K. (1996) 'Do Private Agencies Really Make a Difference?' in Sogge, D. (ed.), *Compassion and Calculation. The Business of Private Foreign Aid*, London: Pluto Press.

Franck, T. M. (1992) 'The Emerging Right to Democratic Governance', *American Journal of International Law* 86 (4).

Frentzel-Zagorska, J. (1990) 'Civil Society in Poland and Hungary', *Soviet Studies*, 42 (4).

Freres, C. (1993) 'El apoyo europeo a la democracia en América Latina: análisis de los casos de Alemania, Suecia y el Reino Unido en el Cono Sur' *SINTESIS* (Madrid) N° 21.

—— (1998) 'Vision general de la cooperacion civil de la Union European con America Latina', C Freres (ed.) *La Cooperacion de las Sociedades Civiles de la Union Europea con America Latina*, Madrid: AIETI.

Friedman, J. (ed.) (1996) *The Rational Choice Controversy. Economic Models of Politics Reconsidered*, New Haven: Yale University Press.

Funes, M.J. (1995) *La Ilusión Solidaria: Las Organizaciones Altruistas como Actores Sociales en los Regimenes Democráticos*, Madrid: Universidad Nacional de Educacion y Distancia.

170

Garba, J. (1987) *Diplomatic Soldiering: The Conduct of Nigerian Foreign Policy, 1975-1979*, Ibadan: Spectrum books .

Garretón, M. A. (1989) 'Popular Mobilization and the Military Regime in Chile: the Complexities of the Invisible Transition', in S. Eckstein (ed.) *Power and Popular Protest: Latin American Social Movements*, Berkeley, Los Angeles and London: University of California Press.

Garton Ash, T. (1990) *The Magic Lantern: The Revolution of '89 Witnessed in Warsaw, Budapest, Berlin, and Prague*, New York: Random House.

Gbanabome, B. (1992) 'The Guinea Connection', *West Africa*, 26 October–1 November.

Geisler, G. (1993) 'Fair? What Has Fairness Got to Do With It? Vagaries of Elections Observations and Democratic Standards', in *Journal of Modern African Studies* 31, 4.

Geremek, B. (1992) 'Problems of Postcommunism: Civil Society Then & Now', *Journal of Democracy*, 3 (2).

Giddens, A. (1990) *The Consequences of Modernity*, Cambridge: Polity Press.

Gonick, L. S., and Rosh, R. M. (1988) 'The Structural Constraints of the World Economy on National Political Development', *Comparative Political Studies* 21.

Gonzalez, C., *et al.* (1995) 'Participación de la Sociedad Civil en la Definición de Políticas Públicas' *Pobreza Urbana y Desarrollo*, Año 4, Nº 10 (agosto).

Gordenker, L. and Wiess, T. (eds) (1996) *NGOs, the UN and Global Governance*, Boulder, Colorado: Lynne Reinner.

Green, A.T. and Skalnik Leff, C. (1997) 'The Quality of Democracy: Mass Elite Linkages in the Czech Republic', *Democratization*, 4 (4).

Green, D. P. and Shapiro, I. (1994) *Pathologies of Rational Choice Theory. A Critique of Applications in Political Science*, New Haven: Yale University Press.

Grugel, J. (1991) 'Transitions from Authoritarian Rule: Lessons from Latin America', *Political Studies* 39 (2).

—— (1995) *Politics and Development in the Caribbean Basin*, Basingstoke: Macmillan.

—— (1996) 'Supporting Democratisation: A European View. European Political Parties and Latin America', *The European Review of Latin America and the Caribbean Studies* 60.

—— (1998) 'State and Business in Neo-Liberal Democracies in Latin America', *Global Society* 12 (2) May.

—— (1999) 'European NGOs in Latin America: Civil Society, Citizenship and Democratization', *Journal of Interamerican Studies and World Affairs* (forthcoming) .

Hadenius, A. (1992) *Democracy and Development*, Cambridge: Cambridge University Press.

Haggard, S. and Kaufman, R. (1992) *Political Economy of Democratic Transitions*, Princeton, NJ: Princeton University Press.

Hall, J. (1995) 'In Search of Civil Society', in Hall, J. (ed.), *Civil Society, Theory, History and Comparison*, Cambridge: Polity Press.

Hartlyn, J. (1994) 'Democracias en la Actual América del Sur: Convergencias y Diversidades', *SINTESIS* (Madrid), No. 22.

Hartmann, C. (1997) Demokratisierung und das internationale System. Anmerkungen zu einigen Querverbindungen zwischen IB-Forschung und Komparatistik, *Zeitschrift für Internationale Beziehungen* 4 (2).

Havel, V. (1988) 'Anti-Political Politics', in Keane, J. (ed.), *Civil Society and the State*, London: Verso.

—— (1991) *Open Letters*, London: Faber and Faber.

—— (1997) *The Art of the Impossible: Politics as Morality in Practice*, New York: Alfred A. Knopf.

Havel, V., Klaus, V. and Pithart, P. (1996) 'Rival Visions', *Journal of Democracy*, 7(1).

Haynes, J. (1997) *Democracy and Civil Society in the Third World Politics and New Political Movements*, Cambridge: Polity Press.

Healey, J. and Robinson, M. (1992) *Democracy, Governance and Economic Policy: Sub-Saharan Africa in Comparative Perspective*, London: ODI.

Held, D. (1996) *Models of Democracy* (2nd Edition) Cambridge: Polity Press .

Heller, A. (1988) 'On Formal Democracy', in Keane, J. (ed.), *Civil Society and the State. New European Perspectives*, London: Verso.

Helliwell, J. F. (1994) 'Empirical Linkages between Democracy and Economic Growth', *British Journal of Political Science* 24.

Higley, J. and Burton, M. G. (1989) 'The Elite Variable in Democratic Transitions and Breakdowns', *American Sociological Review* 54 (1).

Higley, J. and Gunther, R. (eds) (1992) *Elites and Democratic Consolidation in Latin America and Southern Europe*, Cambridge: Cambridge University Press.

—— (1998) 'Elite Settlements and the Taming of Politics', *Government and Opposition* 33 (1).

Hintjens, H. (1996) 'Comparing Local Development Organisations in the Context of Structural Adjustment: Grassroots Organisations in Burkina Faso and Senegal', in Hampsher-Monk, I. and Stanyer, J. (eds), *Contemporary Political Studies* 1996.

Hirst, P. and Thompson, G. (1996) *Globalization in Question. The International Economy and the Possibilities of Governance*, Cambridge: Cambridge University Press.

Huber, E. (1993) 'The Future of Democracy in the Caribbean', in Dominguez, J., Pastor, R. and Delisle Worrell, R. (eds), *Democracy in the Caribbean Political, Economic and Social Perspectives*, Baltimore: Johns Hopkins University Press.

Huber, E. (1995) 'Assessments of State Strength', in Smith, P. (ed), *Latin America in Comparative Perspective*, Boulder, Colorado: Westview Press.

Huber, E., Rueschemeyer, D. and Stephens, J. D. (1993) 'The Impact of Economic Development on Democracy', *Journal of Economic Perspectives* 7 (3).

Hulme, D. and Edwards, M. (1997a) 'NGOs, States and Donors: An Overview', in Hulme, D. and Edwards, M. (eds) *NGOs, States and Donors Too Close for Comfort?* Basingstoke: Macmillan.

—— (eds) (1997b) *NGOS, States and Donors. Too Close for Comfort?*, Basingstoke: Macmillan.

Human Rights Watch/Africa (1997) *Nigeria: Transition ou Parodie? Le Retour du Nigeria vers un Régime Civil: Un Processus Sans Fin*, 9 (6) October.

Huntington, S. P. (1991) *The Third Wave. Democratization in the Late Twentieth Century*, Norman: University of Oaklahoma Press.

Hyde-Price, A. G. V. (1994) 'Democratization in Eastern Europe. The External Dimension', in Pridham, G. and Vanhanen, T. (eds), *Democratization in Eastern Europe*, London: Routledge.

172

Hyden, G. (1994) 'Political Representation and the Future of Uganda', in *From Chaos to Order: the Politics of Constitution Making in Uganda*, London.

Ihonvbere, J. O. (1991) 'Nigeria as Africa's Great Power: Constraints and Prospects for the 1990s', *International Journal*, 46, summer.

Issac, J. C. (1996) 'The Meanings of 1989', *Social Research*, 63 (2).

Jackson Preece, J. (1998) 'National Minorities and the International System', *Politics* February.

Jelin, E. (1996) 'Citizenship revisited: solidarity, responsibility and rights', in Jelin, E. and Hersberg, E. (eds) *Constructing Democracy Human Rights, Citizenship and Society in Latin America*, Boulder, Colorado: Westview Press.

Jelin, E. and Hersberg, E. (1996) 'Intoduction: Human Rights and the Construction of Democracy', in Jelin, E. and Hersberg, E. (eds) *Constructing Democracy Human Rights, Citizenship and Society in Latin America*, Boulder, Colorado: Westview Press.

Jones, B. (1992) 'The FEHC Agricultural Programme in Southern Ethiopia', in Edwards, M. and Hulme, D. (eds), *Making a Difference: NGO Performance and Accountability in the Post-Cold War World*, London: Earthscan.

Jorgensen, K. E. (1992) 'The End of Anti-Politics in Central Europe', in Lewis, P. G. (ed.), *Democracy and Civil Society in Eastern Europe*, New York: St. Martin's Press.

Kaase, M. (1994) 'Political Culture and Political Consolidation', in Blommenstein, H. J. and Steunenberg, B. (eds), *Governments and Markets. Establishing a Democratic Constitutional Order and a Market Economy in Former Socialist Countries*, Dordrecht/Boston/London: Kluwer Academic Publishers.

Kaldor, M. and Vejvoda, I. (1997) 'Democratisation in Central and East European countries', *International Affairs*, January.

Karl, T. (1990) 'Dilemmas of Democratization in Latin America', *Comparative Politics* 23 (1).

Karl, T. L. and Schmitter, P. C. (1991) 'Modes of Transition in Latin America, Southern and Eastern Europe', *International Social Science Journal* (128).

Keck, M. E., and Sikkink, K. (1998) *Activists Beyond Borders. Advocacy Networks in International Politics*, Ithaca, N.Y.: Cornell University Press.

Kennedy, P. and Russett, B. (1995) 'Reforming the U.N.', *Foreign Affairs*, 74 (5).

King, G., Keohane, R. O. and Verba, S. (1994) *Designing Social Inquiry. Scientific Inference in Qualitative Research*, Princeton: Princeton University Press.

Kitschelt, H. (1992) 'Political Regime Change: Structure and Process-Driven Explanations', *American Political Science Review* 86 (4).

—— (1993) 'Comparative Historical Research and Rational Choice Theory: The Case of Transitions to Democracy', *Theory and Society* 22.

Klaveren, A. Van (1994) 'El apoyo a la democracia en América Latina. ¿Hacía un nuevo regimen internacional', Madrid: SINTESIS.

Kopecky, P. (1995) 'Developing Party Organizations in East-Central Europe: What Type of Party is Likely to Emerge?', *Party Politics*, 1 (4).

Kößler, R., and Melber, H. (1993) *Chancen Internationaler Zivilgesellschaft*, Suhrkamp; Frankfurt am Main.

Kufuor, K. O. (1993) 'The Legality of the Intervention in the Liberian Civil War by the Economic Community of West African States', *African Journal of International and Comparative Law* 5(3).

173

Kuron, J. (1990) 'Overcoming Totalitarianism', *Journal of Democracy*, 1(1).

Kurtán, S. (1993) 'Sozialpartnerschaft in Ungarn?', in Tálos, E. (ed), *Sozialpartnerschaft, Kontinuität und Wandel eines Modells*, Wien: VG Verlag für Gesellschaftskritik.

Leftwich, A. (1996) 'Two Cheers for Democracy?', *Political Quarterly* 67 (4).

Lerner, D. (1958) *The Passing of Traditional Society. Modernizing the Middle East*, New York: Free Press.

Lijphart, A. (1977) *Democracy in Plural Societies: a Comparative Exploration*, New Haven: Yale University Press.

Linz, J. (1997) 'Some Thoughts on the Victory and Future of Democracy', in Hadenius, A. (ed), *Democracy's Victory and Crisis*, Cambridge: Cambridge University Press.

Linz, J. J. and Stepan, A. (1996) (eds) *Problems of Democratic Transition and Consolidation Southern Europe, South America and Post-Communist Europe*, Baltimore: Johns Hopkins University Press.

Lipset, S. M. (1960) *Political Man*, London: Heinemann.

Lipset, S. M., Kyoung-Ryung, S. and Torres, J. C. (1993) 'A Comparative Analysis of the Social Requisites of Democracy', *International Social Science Journal* (136).

Little, W. (1997) 'Democratization in Latin America, 1980-1995', in Potter, D., Goldblatt, D., Kiloh, M. and Lewis, P. (eds), *Democratization*, Cambridge: Open University/Polity Press.

Lomax, B. (1997) 'The Strange Death of Civil Society in Post-Communist Hungary', *Journal of Communist Studies and Transition Politics*, 13 (1).

Londregan, J. B. and Poole, K. T. (1996) 'Does High Income Promote Democracy?', *World Politics* 49 (1).

MacDonald, L. (1997) *Supporting Civil Society: The Political Role of Non-Governmental Organizations in Central America*, Basingstoke: Macmillan.

MacFarlane, S. N. and Weiss, T. G. (1994) 'The United Nations, Regional Organizations and Human Security: Building Theory in Central America', *Third World Quarterly* 15 (2).

Mainwaring, S. (1992) 'Transitions to Democracy and Democratic Consolidation: Theoretical and Comparative Issues', in Mainwaring, S., O'Donnell, G., and Valenzuela, J. S. (eds) *Issues in Democratic Consolidation. The New South American Democracies in Comparative Perspective*, Notre Dame, Indiana: University of Notre Dame Press.

Malova, D. (1997) *Slovensko po roku 1989: Stat, Politika a Spolocnost*, Bratislava: Comenius University.

Maravall, J. M. (1994) 'The Myth of the Authoritarian Advantage', *Journal of Democracy* 5 (4).

Maresceau, M. (1996) 'A Legal Analysis of the Community's Association Agreements with Central and Eastern European Countries' in Konstadinidis, S. (ed), *The Legal Regulation of the EC's External Relations after the Completion of the Internal Market*.

Marsh, D. (1991) 'Privatisation under Mrs Thatcher', *Public Adminstration* 69.

Marshall, T. H. (1973) *Class, Citizenship and Social Development*, Westport, Conneticutt: Greenwood Press.

Maxwell, S. (1996) 'Apples, Pears and Poverty Reduction: an Assessment of British Bilateral Aid', *IDS Bulletin* 27 (1).

McGrew, A. (1997) (ed.) *The Transformation of Democracy*, Cambridge: Open University/Polity Press.

Mendez, R. P. (1995) 'Paying for Peace and Development', *Foreign Policy*, 100.

Merkel, W. (1994) 'Struktur oder Akteur, System oder Handlung: Gibt es einen Königsweg in der sozialwissenschaftlichen Transformationsforschung?' in Merkel, W. (ed.), *Systemwechsel 1: Theorien, Ansätze und Konzepte der Transitionsforschung*, Opladen: Leske abd Budrich.

Michnik, A. (1996) 'The Devil of Our Times', in Matynia, E. (ed.), *Grappling with Democracy: Deliberations on Post-Communist Democracies*, Prague: Sociologicke nakladatelstvi.

Mindua, A. D. (1995) 'Intervention Armée de la CEDEAO au Liberia: Illégalité ou Avancée Juridique?', *African Journal of International and Comparative Law*, vol. 7, no. 1–2.

Ministerio de Planificación y Cooperación (1992) *MIDEPLAN Participación de la Comunidad en el Desarollo Social: Logros y Proyecciones* Santiago, Chile: Ministerio de Planificación y Cooperación.

Ministry of Foreign Affairs (The Netherlands) (1990) *A World of Difference*, The Hague: SDU.

—— (1993) *A World in Dispute*, The Hague: SDU.

—— (1996) *Memorie van Toelichting*.

Miszlivetz, F. (1997) 'Participation and Transition: Can the Civil Society Project Survive in Hungary?', *Journal of Communist Studies and Transition Politics*, 13 (1).

Monroe, K. R. (ed.) (1991) *The Economic Approach to Politics. A Critical Reassessment of the Theory of Rational Action*, New York: HarperCollins.

Moore, B. (1966) *The Social Origins of Dictatorship and Democracy: Lord and Peasant in the Making of the Modern World*, Boston: Beacon Press.

MORI Chile (1998) *Informe de Prensa. Encuesta Latinobarómetro* 1997, Santiago, Chile (mimeo).

Morlino, L. (1995) 'Democratic Consolidation: Definition and Models', in Pridham, G. (ed.), *Transitions to Democracy. Comparative Perspectives from Southern Europe, Latin America and Eastern Europe*, Dartmouth: Aldershot.

Munck, G. (1991) 'Social Movements and Democracy in Latin América. Theoretical Debates and Comparative Perspectives', paper delivered at XVI International Congress, Latin Américan Studies Association, Washington, DC (mimeo).

N'Diaye, T. M. (1996) 'Legal Questions Raised by the Peace-keeping Operations in Chad and Liberia', in Vogt, M. A. and Aminu, L. S. (eds), *Peace Keeping as a Security Strategy in Africa – Chad and Liberia as Case Studies*, Enugu: Fourth Dimension Publishing Co.

National Democratic Institute (NDI), Washington (1992), *Report*, 5 May.

Ndegwa, S. (1996) *The Two Faces of Civil Society NGOs and Politics in Africa*, West Hartford, Connecticut: Kumarian Press.

Nelson, D. N. (1996) 'Civil Society Endangered', *Social Research*, 63 (2).

Nelson, J. (1979) *Access to Power. Politics and the Urban Poor in Developing Nations*. Princeton, N. J: Princeton University Press.

Niklasson, T. (1994) 'The Soviet Union and Eastern Europe, 1988–9: Interactions Between Domestic Change and Foreign Policy', in Pridham, G. and Vanhanen, T. (eds.), *Democratization in Eastern Europe*, London: Routledge.

North, D. C. (1989) 'A Transaction Cost Approach to the Historical Development of Polities and Economies', *Journal of Institutional and Theoretical Economics* 44.

Nwajiaku, K. (1994) 'The National Conferences in Benin and Togo Revisited', *Journal of Modern African Studies*, 32 (3).

Nwokedi, E. (1985) 'Sub-Regional Security and Nigerian Foreign Policy', *African Affairs*, 84 (235).

O'Donnell, G. (1994) 'Delegative Democracy', *Journal of Democracy* 5 (2).

O'Donnell, G. and Schmitter, P. (1986) *Transitions from Authoritarian Rule: Tentative Conclusions About Uncertain Democracies*, Baltimore: Johns Hopkins University Press.

O'Donnell, G., Schmitter, P. C. and Whitehead, L. (eds) (1986) *Transitions from Authoritarian Rule. Prospects for Democracy*, Baltimore: Johns Hopkins University Press.

Odinkalu, C. A. (1996) 'The Management of the Transition by the Military', paper presented at a workshop on 'The Nigerian Democratization Process and the European Union' organized by the Centre d'Etude d'Afrique Noire, Bordeaux, 12–14 September.

OECD (1996a), Development Assistance Committee/DAC *Shaping the 21st Century: The Contribution of Development Co-operation*, Paris, May.

OECD (1996b) *Development Cooperation* 1995 Report, Paris, OECD .

Offe, C. (1997) 'Micro-aspects of Democratic Theory: What Makes for the Deliberative Competence of Citizens?' in Hadenius, A. (ed.), *Democracy's Victory and Crisis*. Cambridge: Cambridge University Press.

Official Journal of the EC (1991) *Proceedings of the EP*, 9 to 13 September.

Ofodile, A. C. (1994) 'The Legality of ECOWAS Intervention in Liberia', *Columbia Journal of Transnational Law*, vol. 32, no. 2.

Ofori, R. (1991) 'What Price Peace?', *West Africa*, February 4–10.

Oxhorn, P. (1991) 'The Popular Sector Response to an Authoritarian Regime: Shanty Town Organizations since the Military Coup', *Latin American Perspectives* 18, Winter.

—— (1994) 'Understanding Political Change after Authoritarian Rule: the Popular Sectors and Chile's new Democratic Regime', *Journal of Latin American Studies* 26 (3).

—— (1995) 'From Controlled Inclusion to Coerced Marginalization: the Struggle for Civil Society in Latin America', in Hall, J. (ed.), *Civil Society, Theory, History and Comparison*, Cambridge: Polity Press.

Parry Williams, J. (1992) 'Scaling-up via Legal Reform in Uganda', in Edwards, M. and Hulme, D. (eds), *Making a Difference: NGOs and Development in the Post Cold War World*, London: Earthscan.

Pearce, J. (1997a) ' Between Cooptation and Irrelevance? Latin American NGOs in the 1990s', in Hulme, D. and Edwards, M. (eds), *NGOs, States and Donors Too Close for Comfort?* Basingstoke: Macmillan.

—— (1997b) 'Civil Society, the Market and Democracy in Latin America', *Democratization* 4 (2).

Pereira A. (1993) 'Economic Underdevelopment, Democracy and Civil Society: The North-East Brazilian case', *Third World Quarterly* 14 (2) .

Petras, J. (1997) 'La Izquierda Devuelve el Golpe' *Ajoblanco* (Madrid) Especial Latinoamérica, N° 4 Spring.

Pinder, J. (1997) 'The European Community and Democracy in Central and Eastern Europe', in Pridham, G., Herring, E. and Sanford, G. (eds), *Building Democracy? The International Dimension of Democratisation in Eastern Europe*, London: Leicester University Press.

Pinkney, R. (1994) *Democracy in the Third World*, Buckingham and Philadelphia: Open University Press.

Pithart, P. (1993) 'Intellectuals in Politics: Double Dissent in the Past, Double Disappointment Today', *Social Research*, 60 (4).

Potter, D. (1997) 'Explaining Democratization', in D. Potter, D. Goldblatt, M. Kiloh and P. Lewis (eds), *Democratization*, Cambridge: Open University/Polity Press.

Pridham, G. (1984) 'Comparative Perspectives on the New Mediterranean Democracies: A Model of Regime Transition?', *West European Politics* 7 (2).

—— (1991a) 'International Influences and Democratic Transition: Problems of Theory and Practice in Linkage Politics', in Pridham, G. (ed.), *Encouraging Democracy The International Context of Regime Transition in Southern Europe*, London: University of Leicester Press.

—— (ed.) (1991b) *Encouraging Democracy: the International Context of Regime Transition in Southern Europe*, Leicester: Leicester University Press.

—— (1995) 'The International Context of Democratic Consolidation: Southern Europe in Comparative Perspective' in Gunther, R. Diamandouros, N. and Puhle, H. J. (eds), *The Politics of Democratic Consolidation*, Baltimore: Johns Hopkins University Press.

—— (1996) 'Transnational Party Links and Transition to Democracy: Eastern Europe in Comparative Perspective' in Lewis, P. (ed.), *Party Structure and Organization in East-Central Europe*, Cheltenham: Edward Elgar.

Pridham, G. and Vanhanen, T. (eds) (1994) *Democratization in Eastern Europe. Domestic and International Perspectives*, London: Routledge.

Pridham, G., Herring, E. and Sanford, G. (1994) *Building Democracy: The International Dimension of Democratization in Eastern Europe*, London: Routledge.

Princen, T. and Finger, M. (eds) (1994) *Environmental NGOs in World Politics*, London: Routledge.

Prikic, F. (1997) 'Le Nigeria, Puissance Régionale, et sa Politique vis-à-vis des Pays Francophones Voisins, du Liberia et de la Sierra Leone', paper presented at the Centre des Hautes Études sur l'Afrique et l'Asie modernes (CHEAM), Paris, 17 December.

—— (1998) 'Le Ghana et la Gestion de la Crise Libérienne', in Toulabor, C. (ed.), *Ressources Politiques et Légitimité au Ghana: le Cas J. J. Rawlings*, Paris: Karthala, (forthcoming).

PRISMA (1994) *La Cooperacion No-Gubernamental European hacia Centroamerica: La Experiencia de los Ochenta y las Tendencias en los Noventa*, San Salvador: PRISMA.

Przeworski, A. (1986) 'Some Problems in the Study of the Transition to Democracy', in O'Donnell, G., Schmitter, P. C. and Whitehead, L. (eds), *Transition from Authoritarian Rule. Prospects for Democracy*, Baltimore: Johns Hopkins University Press.

—— (1991) *Democracy and the Market. Political and Economic Reforms in Eastern Europe and Latin America*, Cambridge: Cambridge University Press.

Przeworski, A. *et al.* (1995) *Sustainable Democracy*, Cambridge: Cambridge University Press.

Przeworski, A. and Limongi, F. (1993) 'Political Regimes and Economic Growth', *Journal of Economic Perspectives* 7 (3).

—— (1997) 'Modernization: Theories and Facts', *World Politics* 49 (2).

Putnam, R. (1993) *Making Democracy Work. Civic Traditions in Modern Italy*. Princeton: Princeton University Press.

Quigley, K. F. F. (1997) *For Democracy's Sake: Foundations and Democracy Assistance in Central Europe*, Washington: Woodrow Wilson Center Press.

Remmer, K. L. (1991) 'New Wine or Old Bottlenecks? The Study of Latin American Democracy', *Comparative Politics* 23 (4).

Republic of Liberia (1991) 'Final Report on the Proceedings of the All-Liberia National Conference, March 15th – April 20th'.

Rhodes, R. (1994) 'The "Hollowing out" of the State: the Changing Nature of the Public Service in Britain', *Political Quarterly* 65.

Risse-Kappen, T. (1994) 'Ideas Do Not Flow Freely. Transnational Coalitions, Domestic Structures, and the End of the Cold War', *International Organization* 48 (2).

Risse, T., Ropp, S. C. and Sikkink, K. (eds). (1999) *The Power of Principles. International Human Rights Norms and Domestic Practice*, Cambridge: Cambridge University Press.

Ritchie-Vance, M. (1996). 'El Capital Social, la Sostenibilidad y la Democracia en Acción', *Desarrollo de Base*, Vol. 21 (1).

—— (1992), *El Arte de Asociarse: las ONG y la Sociedad Civil en Colombia*, Arlington, Virginia: Inter-American Foundation.

Robinson, M. (1993) 'Governance, Democracy and Conditionality: NGOs and the New Policy Agenda', in Clayton, A. (ed.), *Governance, Democracy and the Conditionality: What Role for NGOs?* Oxford: INTRAC.

—— (1995) 'Political Conditionality: Strategic Implications for NGOs', in Stokke, O. (ed.), *Aid and Political Conditionality*, London: Frank Cass.

—— (1996) 'The Role of Aid Donors in Strengthening Civil Society' (mimeo).

Robinson, P. T. (1994) 'Democratization: Understanding the Relationship between Regime Change and the Culture of Politics', *African Studies Review* 37 (1).

Rose, R. (1994) 'Post-communism and the Problem of Trust', *Journal of Democracy*, 5 (3).

Rosenau, J. (1990) *Turbulence on World Politics: A Theory of Continuity and Change*, Princeton: Princeton University Press.

Rueschmeyer, D, Stephens, E. and Stephens, J. (1992) *Capitalist Development and Democracy*, Cambridge: Polity Press.

Ruhl, J. M. (1996) 'Unlikely Candidates for Democracy: The Role of Structural Context in Democratic Consolidation', *Studies in Comparative International Development* 31 (1).

Rustow, D. (1970) 'Transition to Democracy towards a Dynamic Model' *Comparative Politics* 3 April.

Salmon, L. M. (1993) 'The Global Associational Revolution: the Rise of the Third Sector on the World Scene' *Occasional Papers* No 15, Institute for Policy Studies, Johns Hopkins University; Baltimore.

Sand, K. Van de (1996) 'Towards more Donor Coordination? OECD Prepares for 21st Century' *D+C Development Cooperation* Frankfurt, 5 Sept–Oct.

Sandbrook, (1985) *The Politics of Africa's Economic Stagnation*, Cambridge: Cambridge University Press.

Schmitter, P. (1994) 'The Proto-Science of Consolidology: Can it Improve the Outcome of Contemporary Efforts at Democratization?', *Politikon* 21 (2).

—— (1995a) 'Transitology: the Science or the Art of Democratization?', in Tulchin, J. and Romero, B. (eds), *The Consolidation of Democracy in Latin America*, Boulder, Colorado: Woodrow Wilson Centre Current Studies on Latin America, Lynne Reinner.

—— (1995b), 'The International Context of Contemporary Democratization' in Pridham, G. (ed.), *Transitions to Democracy: Comparative Perspectives from Southern Europe, Latin America and Eastern Europe*, Dartmouth: Aldershot.

Schmitter, P. and Karl, T. (1991) 'What Democracy is . . . and is Not', *Journal of Democracy* 2 (3) Summer (also in Diamond, L. and Plattner, M. (eds), *The Global Resurgence of Democracy* (2nd Ed 1996), Baltimore: Johns Hopkins University Press).

Schmitz, H. P. (1998) *Puzzling Causes and Effects: Structure and Agency in the Study of Democratization*, Konstanz: unpublished manuscript.

—— (1999) 'Transnational Human Rights Activism and Political Change in Kenya and Uganda' in Risse, T., Ropp, S. C. and Sikkink, K. (eds), *The Power of Principles. International Human Rights Norms and Domestic Practice*, Cambridge: Cambridge University Press.

Schubert, G., Tetzlaff, R. and Vennewald, W. (eds) (1994) *Demokratisierung und politischer Wandel: Theorie und Anwendung des Konzepts der strategischen und konfliktfähigen Gruppen (SKOG)*, Münster: Lit-Verlag.

Schuman Institute for Developing Democracy in Central and Eastern Europe (1995) *Statute*, article 1/1, September.

Segal, G. (1991) 'International Relations and Democratic Transition', in Pridham, G. (ed.), *Encouraging Democracy. The International Context of Regime Transition in Southern Europe*, New York/London: Leicester University Press.

Seligman, A. (1992) *The Idea of Civil Society*, Princeton: Princeton University Press.

Sell, K. (1997a) *Globalization, Institutional Schizophrenia, and the Question of Legitimacy: Proposal for a New Analytical Model of Democratization*, Berlin: unpublished manuscript.

—— (1997b) 'The Role of Intermediary Institutions in the Consolidation of Democracy: The Example of the Hungarian Council for Interest Reconciliation' in Los-Nowak, T. and Armstrong, D. (eds), *Emerging Conceptions of Democracy in Transition Europe*, Wroclaw: University of Wroclaw and International Centre at Tübingen.

Serbin, A. (1997) 'Globalization, Democratic Deficit and Civil Society in the Greater Caribbean Integration Process', paper presented to LASA Conference; Gadalajara, Mexico.

Sesay, A. (1995) 'Humanitarian Intervention in Liberia: Implications for State and Sub-Regional Security and International Society', paper presented at the workshop on Humanitarian Intervention and International Society, Department of International Relations, London School of Economics, 13 May.

Shaw, M. (1994) 'Civil Society and Global Politics: Beyond a Social Movement Approach', *Millennium: Journal of International Studies* 23 (3).

Shin, D. C. (1994), 'On the Third Wave of Democratization. A Synthesis and Evaluation of the Recent Theory and Research', *World Politics* 47 (1).

Sikkink, K. (1993) 'Human Rights, Principle Issue-networks and Sovereignty in Latin America', *International Organization* 43 (3).

—— (1995) 'Nongovernmental Organizations, Democracy and Human Rights in Latin America', in Farer, T. (ed.), *Beyond Sovereignty. Collectively Defending Democracy in the Americas*. Baltimore: Johns Hopkins University Press.

—— (1996) 'The Emergence, Evolution and Effectiveness of the Latin American Human Rights Network', in Jelin, E. and Hershberg, E. (eds) *Constructing Democracy Human Rights, Citizenship and Society in Latin America*, Boulder, Colorado: Westview.

Smilie, I. (1992) 'Changing Partners: Northern NGOs, Northern Governments', in Smilie, I. and Helmich, H. (eds), *Non-Governmental Organizations and Governments: Stakeholders for Development* Paris: OECD.

—— (1995) *The Alms Bazaar Altruism under Fire – Non-Profit Organisations and International Development*, London: Intermediary Technocolgy Publications.

Smith, P. H. (1991) 'Crisis and Democracy in Latin America', *World Politics* 43 (4) .

Smith, W C.; Acuña C. H., and Gamarra, E. A. (eds) (1994) *Latin American Political Economy in the Age of Neo-liberal Reform: Theoretical and Comparative Perspectives for the 1990s*, Coral Gables: University of Miami, North-South Center.

Smolar, A. (1996) 'From Opposition to Atomization', *Journal of Democracy*, 7(1).

Sokolewicz, W. (1995), 'The Relevance of Western Models for Constitution-building in Poland' in Hesse, J. J. and Johnson, N. (eds), *Constitutional Policy and Change in Europe*, Oxford: Oxford University Press.

Tanaka, M. (1996) 'La Participación política de los Sectores Populares en América Latina: Algunas Conclusiones Comparativas sobre la Consolidación Democrática', *Debates en Sociología* (Lima), N° 20–21.

Tarrow, S. (1996) 'Fishnets, Internets, and Catnets: Globalization and Transnational Collective Action'. Madrid: Instituto Juan March de Estudios e Investigaciónes, Centro de Estudios Avanzados en Ciencias Sociales, Estudio/Working Paper 1996/78.

Taylor, L. (1995) 'Strangers in Democracy: Problems of Social Movements in the Process of Democratic Consolidation', in Lovenduski, J. and Stanyer, J. (eds), *Contemporary Political Studies 1995* Belfast: Political Studies Association.

—— (1996) 'Civilising Civil Society: Dissociating Popular Participation from Politics Itself', in Hampsher-Monk, I. and Stanyer, J. (eds), *Contemporary Political Studies 1996* Belfast: Political Studies Association.

—— (1998) *Citizenship, Participation and Democracy: Changing Dynamics in Chile and Argentina,* Basingstoke: Macmillan.

Tilly, C. (1995) 'Democracy is a Lake', in Reid Andrews, G. and Chapman, H. (eds), *The Social Construction of Democracy, 1870-1990*, Basingstoke: Macmillan.

Tischer, (1984) *The Spirit of Solidarity*, London: Harper and Row.

Tovias, A. (1984) 'The International Context of Democratic Transition', *West European Politics* 7 (2).

Tsingos, B. (1996) 'Underwriting Democracy: the European Community and Greece', in Whitehead, L. (1996) (ed.), *The International Dimensions of Democratisation: Europe and the Americas*, Oxford: Oxford University Press.

Tsoukalis, L. (1981) *The European Community and its Mediterranean Enlargement*, London: George Allen and Unwin.

Urban, J. (1996) 'The Future of Central Europe's Civil Society' in Matynia, E. (ed.), *Grappling with Democracy: Deliberations on Post-Communist Democracies*, Prague: Sociologicke nakladatelstvi.

Valdés, T and Weinstein, M. (1993) *Mujeres que Sueñan: Las organizaciones de Pobladores en Chile 1973-1989*, Santiago, Chile: FLACSO.

Valenzuela, J. S. (1992) 'Democratic Consolidation in Post-Transitional Settings: Notion Process and Facilitating Conditions', in Mainwaring, S., O'Donnell, G. and Valenzuela, J. S. (eds), *Issues in Democratic Consolidation The New South Américan Democracies in Comparative Perspective*, Notre Dame Indiana: University of Notre Dame Press.

Valenzuela, M. E. (1995) 'The Evolving Roles of Women under Military Rule', in Drake, P. and Jaksæ, I. (eds), *The Struggle for Democracy in Chile*, Lincoln and London: University of Nebraska Press.

Vanhanen, T. (1990) *The Process of Democratization. A Comparative Study of 147 States, 1980–88*, New York/London: Crane Russak.

Vilas, C. (1992) 'The Hour of Civil Society', *NACLA Report of the Americas*.

—— (1994) 'Democratización y Gobernabilidad en un Escenario Posrevolucionario: Centroamérica', *Foro Internacional* (México, DF), 34 (1) (January–March).

Vogt, M. (1991) 'Nigeria's Participation in the ECOWAS Monitoring Group – ECO-MOG', *Nigerian Journal of International Affairs*, 17 (1).

Waylen, G. (1994) 'Women and Democratization: Conceptualizing Gender Relations in Transition Politics', *World Politics* 46 (3) .

Weffort, F. (1995) 'What is a "New Democracy"?', *International Social Science Journal* (136).

Weiner, M. (1987) 'Empirical Democratic Theory and the Transition from Authoritarianism to Democracy', *Political Science & Politics* 20 (4).

Whitehead, L. (1986) 'International Aspects of Democratization', in O'Donnell, G., Schmitter, P. C. and Whitehead, L. (eds), *Transitions from Authoritarian Rule. Prospects for Democracy*, Baltimore: Johns Hopkins University Press.

—— (1990) 'The Imposition of Democracy', in Lowenthal, A. (ed.), *Exporting Democracy: The United States and Latin America Themes and Issues*, Baltimore: Johns Hopkins University.

—— (1991) 'Democracy by Convergence and Southern Europe: A Comparative Politics Perspective', in Pridham, G. (ed.), *Encouraging Democracy. The International Context of Regime Transition in Southern Europe*, New York/London: St. Martin's Press/Leicester University Press.

—— (1996) (ed.) *The International Dimensions of Democratisation: Europe and the Americas*, Oxford: Oxford University Press.

—— (1997) 'Bowling in the Bronx: The Uncivil Interstices between Civil and Political Society', *Democratization*, 4 (1).

Wiesenthal, H. (1995) *Preemtive Institutionenbildung: Korporative Akteure und institutionelle Innovationen im Transformationsprozeß Postsozialistischer Staaten*, Berlin: Wissenschaftszentrum.

—— (1996) *Globalisierung. Soziologische und Politikwissenschaftliche Koordinaten eines Unbekannten Terrains*, Berlin: Max-Planck-Gesellschaft.

Wojcicki, K. (1991) 'The Reconstruction of Society', *Telos*, 18 (47).

World Bank (1981) *Accelerated Development in Sub-Sahara Africa: an Agenda for Action*, Washington: World Bank.

—— (1989) *From Crisis to Sustainable Growth*, Washington: World Bank.

—— (1991) *World Development Report 1991. The Challenge of Development*, Oxford: Oxford University Press.

Yoroms, G. J. (1993) 'ECOMOG and West African Regional Security: A Nigerian Perspective', *Issue*, 21 (1–2).

Zartman, I. W. (1995) 'Posing the Problem of State Collapse' in Zartman, I. W. (ed.), *Collapsed State – The Disintegration and Restoration of Legitimate Authority*, Boulder: Lynne Reinner.

INDEX

For Product Safety Concerns and Information please contact our EU
representative GPSR@taylorandfrancis.com
Taylor & Francis Verlag GmbH, Kaufingerstraße 24, 80331 München, Germany

www.ingramcontent.com/pod-product-compliance
Lightning Source LLC
Chambersburg PA
CBHW070422270326
41926CB00014B/2898